Capital Markets in Southeast Europe

"The role and structure of capital markets in south-eastern European countries is an important topic not often discussed due to the lack of historical data and the bank centricity of local financial markets. The topic is tackled head on by this book as the author successfully gives a comprehensive overview of the current state and of the historical development of capital markets in select SEE countries. Using rigorous scientific methods market efficiency is examined and results offer factual discernment into the state of the markets. The writing forms an interesting and formidable base for discussion on the capital markets part in capital allocation and furthering of economic growth. Having witnessed the development of said markets firsthand I find the historical overview detailed and compelling and the conclusions and recommendations offered by the author both prescient as well as insightful."

—Andrija Hren, *Chief Investment Officer, Erste Plavi Pension Fund Management Company, Zagreb*

"As one of the small but strange breed of direct investors in this region over the past 16 years, I urge all practitioners to read this book. It tackles head on the key issues that have hindered inward investment and made those of us passionate about the region struggle so hard to convince investors to commit to the emerging growth story here. I encourage readers to focus on the conclusions, with especial attention on the author's views on transparency, minority rights and on inter-regional integration which I feel has much merit. Finally, for those new to the region, the country-by-country analysis, from historical overview (so critical in understanding these markets) to contemporary setting and finally legal framework, is essential homework. Congratulations Ante, this is a fabulous piece of work."

—Anthony Stalker, *Partner, CEECAT Capital—A leading private equity and private credit investor focused on Emerging Europe*

Ante Dodig

Capital Markets in Southeast Europe

Origins and Efficiency in a Cross-Country Analysis of Transition Economies

palgrave
macmillan

Ante Dodig
International Finance Corporation
Washington DC, USA

ISBN 978-3-031-07209-3 ISBN 978-3-031-07210-9 (eBook)
https://doi.org/10.1007/978-3-031-07210-9

This Palgrave Macmillan imprint is published by the registered company Springer Nature Switzerland AG
The registered company address is: Gewerbestrasse 11, 6330 Cham, Switzerland

Epigraph

In growing uncertainty from innovation with financial products, claims that a smaller capital market economy cannot be competitive versus market "Goliaths," and that large or advanced market failures are necessarily hereditary to developing markets should be thoroughly questioned. In one example where large and advanced capital electronic markets exhibit overextended moves in volatile environment, a nascent, smaller capital market may be naturally hedged and thus serve as a global example of a better-struck balance.

Foreword

It is always a challenge to write a science-based book about pioneering and frequently failing attempts to establish an industry, as capital markets have been in southeast Europe and in many other emerging market economies. In this book you will quickly learn that the author's refreshing honesty and inspiring knowledge, and insights are picked from own professional experience and complementary academic work. This comprehensive text arrives at the right time as the global economic scene transitions to new challenges with increasing divergence in wealth. My background in academia, finance industry, and policy making guides me to find this book demonstrating reliable value in clear explanation and distinction between real trends and fads, and in search for deeper evidence based insight in frontier industry evolvement. As such, it advances new ideas in fragile economic landscape. I have co-mentored Mr. Dodig in completing his Ph.D. dissertation on capital markets development and thereto personally have witnessed his motivation and solid approach to research.

This is a very much needed work on capital markets with a cross-country analysis on selected transition economies. The author successfully weaves empirical evidence on interconnectedness between macroeconomic indicators and capital markets performance while revealing often contemplated divergences between the more and less developed global counterparts.

The well-researched statistical review is observed under the weak form Fama's theorem with results substantiating evidence of markets inefficiency. The study examines vertically and presents horizontally an immersion of full economic cycle and peak volatility performances under the 2007/2008 financial crisis and the Covid-19 crisis impact that is still yielding uncertainty in realms of the looming stagflation and prospects of interest rates hikes. The story provides lessons of experience and dispels pre-conceived transmissible traits in capital market role. This book valuably illuminates the potentials in effective capital market functioning, creating innovation, and serving as an impetus for increasing economic output.

Akin to much of Central Europe, to Eastern Europe, and to the Baltics, capital markets emerged in the early 1990s as by-products, for the purpose of transferring ownership from state-owned to private hands. The local institutional, legislative, and regulatory framework development lagged. As a result, capital, though initially amassing, concentrating, and attracting foreign portfolio investments, was not adequately protected and guided. Thus the quick growth in size and turnover suddenly elapsed through initial systemic volatility downturn, with long-term negative memory. In Southeast Europe capital markets have not yet served the full purpose of effectively providing protection for minority ownership rights, for instilling best practice corporate governance, and for providing for a sustainable liquidity basis.

When facing the outlook, many initial steps are still to be resolved and these include the strengthening transparency of corporate governance and better harmonizing legislative, judicial, and regulatory environment. Routes to improvement may ponder upon continuation in regional integration to align with the real sector integration, to reach better liquidity, greater operating efficiencies, set-up of central counterparty and the broader safety net, and more scalable exposure to the international scene. Lastly, for greater progress an essential policy support is required for a greater local institutional participation and reform.

This book offers an insightful perspective and supports a distinct and objective emphasis on the paradigm in market search for efficiency globally. The book is very valuable for understanding the development and outlook for capital markets in cross-vetting under variable background constraints. This work constructs an exemplary, fundamental, and intriguing basis to increase awareness of all around cointegration between social, economic, capital markets, and policy environment. As such, it is a valuable read to academics, investors, regulators, and enquiring general public.

Dejan Soskic, Ph.D.
Professor of Economics and Finance
Faculty of Economics
University of Belgrade
Belgrade, Serbia

Disclaimer

This writing and author's views are independent and are for information and discussion purposes only. Unless otherwise expressly indicated, this writing does not consider the investment objectives or financial situation of any person or company. Recipients should obtain advice based on their own individual circumstances from their own tax, financial, legal, and other advisors before making an investment decision, and only make such decisions based on the investor's own objectives, experience and resources. The information contained in this book is based on generally available information and, although obtained from sources believed to be reliable, its accuracy and completeness cannot be assured, and such information may be incomplete or condensed. Any analysis or information generated is for illustrative purposes only.

The provision of information does not constitute investment advice and the author is not making a recommendation as to the suitability of any of the products or transactions mentioned. The author will have no liability to the reader, user, or third party for quality, accuracy, timeliness, and continued availability for any data or calculations shown in this book.

Contents

About the Author

Ante Dodig was born in Mostar in 1987. He lived and completed his education in Bosnia and Herzegovina, Switzerland, the United States, and Serbia while in parallel professionally working globally in frontier and developing markets across Europe, Asia, and Africa. His personal and professional background epitomizes cultural and economic intersection between advanced and developing environment assembling in growing globalization and greatest modern financial and economic health crisis. Ante Dodig is an Investment Officer at International Finance Corporation with over a decade of global experience in developing markets through leading groundbreaking institutional financial investing in emerging economies. He has a PhD in Business Management from School of Economics and Business at University of Sarajevo and is an Assistant Professor teaching Investments, Investment Banking, and Capital Markets courses at Union University in Belgrade.

Abbreviations

ADF	Augmented Dickey-Fuller test
AIC	Akaike Information Criterion
ALM	Asset and Liability Management
ARDL	Autoregressive Distributed Lag Model
ARIMA	Autoregressive Integrated Moving Average
ATP	Autonomous Trade Preference
ATVP	Agencija za Trg Vrednostnih Papirjev
B&H	Bosnia and Herzegovina
BAM	Bosnia and Herzegovina Convertible Mark
BATS	Better Alternative Trading System
BATX	Bosnian Traded Index—Top up to six issuers with four on the SASE and two on the BLSE ranked by market capitalization. Stock weighting is capped at twenty-five percent
BELEX15	Blue-Chip Index of Belgrade Stock Exchange—*composed of up to fifteen largest and most liquid stocks. Stock weighting is capped at ten percent.*
BIRS	Berzanski Indeks Republike Srpske—*share index of up to twelve largest companies listed on Banja Luka Stock Exchange. Stock weighting is capped at twenty percent*
BIS	Bank for International Settlements
BLSE	Banja Luka Stock Exchange
BOPNFA	Balance of Payment Net Financial Account
BSE	Belgrade Stock Exchange
BSI	National Bank of Slovenia
CAGR	Compound Annual Growth Rate
CAPM	Capital Asset Pricing Model

CBB&H	National Bank of Bosnia and Herzegovina
CBOE	Chicago Board Options Exchange
CCP	Central Clearing Counterparty
CDCC	Central Depository and Clearing Company in Croatia
CE	Cointegrating vector
CEBS	Committee of European Banking Supervisors
CEE	Central and Eastern Europe
CIS	Commonwealth of Independent States—*Organization of former Soviet republics excluding the Baltic countries*
COICOP	Classification of Individual Consumption by Purpose
COVID-19	*Coronavirus disease (COVID-19) is an infectious disease caused by the SARS-CoV-2 virus. It was a globally widespread pandemic causing economic shutdowns*
CPI	Consumer Price Index
CROBEX	Croatia Zagreb Stock Exchange Index—*Zagreb Stock Exchange capitalization weighted index of up to twenty-five listed companies. Stock weighting is capped at fifteen percent*
CROSEC	Croatian Securities Exchange Commission
DFE	Dynamic Fixed Effects
EAD	Exposure at Default
EBA	European Banking Authority
EBRD	European Bank for Reconstruction and Development
ECB	European Central Bank
ECOICOP	European Classification of Individual Consumption by Purpose
ECT	Error Correction Term
EIOPA	European Insurance and Occupational Pensions Authority
EME	Emerging Market Economy—*Classification criteria is not globally universal, and this study considers all Southeast European countries as frontier capital markets and emerging economies despite recognizing World Bank classification of high-income countries as developed economies (in our sample the case of Slovenia and Croatia) and World Economic Forum classifying Slovenia as an advanced economy*
EMIR	European Market Infrastructure Regulation
ESA	European System of National and Regional Accounts
ESMA	The European Securities and Markets Authority
ETF	Exchange-Traded Fund
EU	European Union
EURIBOR	Euro Interbank Offer Rate
FB&H	Federation of Bosnia and Herzegovina—*Entity in Bosnia and Herzegovina*
FDI	Foreign Direct Investments
FDIC	United States Federal Deposit Insurance Corporation

FED	Federal Reserve System
FEVD	Forecast Error Variance Decomposition
FI	Financial Institution
FX	Local Currency Exchange Rate with US$.
GDP	Gross Domestic Product
GDPPC	Gross Domestic Product Per Capita
GEM	Global Entrepreneurship Monitor
GLS	Generalized Least Squares
GMM	Generalized Method of Moments
GNI	Gross National Income
GSIB	Global Systemically Important Banks
H#	Hypothesis Number
HANFA	Croatian Financial Services Supervisory Agency
HBOR	Croatian Bank for Reconstruction and Development
HICP	Harmonized Index Consumer Price
HNB	National Bank of Croatia
HRK	Croatian Kuna
IAS	International Accounting Standard
IASB	International Accounting Standards Board
ICAAP	Internal Capital Adequacy Assessment Process
ICPFs	Insurance Corporations and Pension Funds
IFI	International Financial Institution
IFRS	International Financial Reporting Standard
IMF	International Monetary Fund
IPI	Industrial Production Index
IRB	Internal Rating Based
IRF	Impulse Response Function
ISDA	International Swaps and Derivatives Association
KDD	Central Securities Clearing Corporation in Slovenia
LCR	Liquidity Coverage Ratio
LEI	Legal Entity Identifier
LGD	Loss Given Default
LIBOR	London Interbank Offer Rate
LLC	Levin, Lin, and Chu test
M	World Bank Group broad money supply indicator—*includes the sum of currency and deposits in the central bank (M0), plus transferable deposits and electronic currency (M1), plus time and savings deposits, foreign currency transferable deposits, certificates of deposit, and securities repurchase agreements (M2), plus traveler checks, foreign currency time deposits, commercial paper, and shares of mutual funds or market funds held by residents (M3)*
MAIC	Modified Akaike Information Criteria

MBI10	Macedonia Stock Exchange Price Index—*consists of up to ten companies weighted by market capitalization*
MDB	Multilateral Development Bank
MENA	Middle East and North Africa
MG	Mean Group
MiFID	Markets in Financial Instruments Directive
MiFIR	Markets in Financial Instruments Regulation
MMIR	Money Market Interest Rate
MREL	Minimum Regulatory Eligible Liabilities
MSE	Macedonian Stock Exchange
MTF	Multilateral Trading Facility
NA	Not Available
NBFI	Non-Bank Financial Institution
NBRM	National Bank of Republic of Macedonia
NBS	National Bank of Serbia
ND	Non-Deliverable
NSFR	Net Stable Funding Ratio
OECD	Organization for Economic Co-operation and Development
OLS	Ordinary Least Squares
OTF	Organized Trading Facility
PD	Probability of Default
PMG	Pooled Mean Group
PP	Phillips Perron test
PwC	PricewaterhouseCoopers
RORAC	Return on Risk-Adjusted Capital
RS	Republika Srpska—Entity in Bosnia and Herzegovina
RSD	Republic of Serbia Dinar
RWA	Risk-Weighted Asset
SAA	Stabilization and Association Agreement
SASE	Sarajevo Stock Exchange
SASX-10	Sarajevo Stock Exchange Index Ten—*top up to ten issuers on the Exchange ranked by market capitalization and frequency of trading Stock weighting is capped at twenty percent*
SBIC	Schwarz Bayesian Information Criterion
SBITOP	Slovenian Blue-Chip Index—*Composed of most liquid shares at Ljubljana Stock Exchange. Stock weighting is capped at thirty percent*
SDR	Special Drawing Rights
SEE	Southeast Europe
SMA	Security Market Agency in Slovenia
SMI	Stock Exchange Market Index
SOE	Sovereign Owned Entities
TLAC	Total Loss Absorbing Capacity

UL	Unrealized Losses
US$	United States Dollar
VaR	Value at Risk
VAR	Vector Autoregressive
VECM	Vector Error Correction Model
VIF	Variance Inflation Factor
VIN	Varazdin Index
WB	Western Balkans

List of Figures

List of Tables

CHAPTER 1

Capital Markets Efficiency in Global and Local Realms

1.1 Research Topic—Efficiency Case and Capital Markets Nexus from Global to Regional and to Local Interplay

In the global economic environment in the past few decades, the frontier and emerging markets continued to post the strongest economic growth rates, led by long-standing locomotive, the People's Republic of China (China). Emerging market economies (EMEs) account for more than seventy-five percent of global growth in output and consumption, which is almost double the share from just two decades ago (International Monetary Fund, 2017). In parallel the integration of developing markets into the global economy continued and the global capital markets' proportional share of gross domestic product (GDP) continued to increase at a faster pace. The sheer growth reflects alike in global sovereign balance of payments positions wherein the growing indebtedness and the increasing income inequality pave risks for the future harmonized development prospects. Developed markets have added tailwind to spillover effects through pursuing long-standing monetary quantitative easing programs that supplemented global capital liquidity and helped kick-start their own growth. As a result, we have witnessed global listed equity stock market capitalization reach record heights in 2016, outpacing the 2007/ 8 pre-financial and economic crisis peaks (2007/ 8 crisis), and recovering from halving in value during 2008. In a similar trend,

A. Dodig, *Capital Markets in Southeast Europe*,
https://doi.org/10.1007/978-3-031-07210-9_1

the value of public debt securities has almost doubled over the past ten years. With the onset of the COVID-19 pandemic and economic crisis in 2019 (COVID or COVID-19 crisis) the increase in money supply has shifted to an even higher magnitude. In the aftermath, the supply chain disruptions and a growing demand have caused a record-setting inflation levels globally and monetary policies have turned to a raising rates environment in order to try and curb the inflation levels. Simultaneously, the trade barriers have evolved into conflicts with the war in Ukraine dividing the global politics and economics into multipolar setting and a growing sentiment of uncertainty and the likelihood of recession.

The income inequality is widening more in frontier and emerging markets, which also tend to struggle for longer to recover from the crises' impact. Despite global productivity rise and the ongoing economic growth, the disparity is widening and brings concern that calls for a closer review of the current global economic, financial, and capital markets' structure. It is without a question that the sheer price growth (e.g. through capital market size or through undeniable continuous growth in real estate prices) does not resemble entire relevance nor warrant the fair and most productive distribution. Disproportions are exemplary in emerging economies capital markets size at under fifteen percent of the global total, yet the GDP size is at more than half of the global total, and the population forms more than eighty percent of the global total. Today's economic environment is one where it is expected that globally two-thirds of the new generation will be relatively poorer than their parents. One solution on the table is offered by prominent economist, Thomas Pikkety, who calls for an increase in progressive income and inheritance taxation of the wealthiest.

Global debt to GDP ratio has increased to peak values, led by a rise in governments' debt and non-financial corporate debt, whereas household debt remains below the 2007/ 8 crisis level. Nevertheless, the long-run sovereigns' financial position, as measured in net worth, is relatively weaker. Countries with stronger balance sheets fare more resilient amidst recessions. For example, the negative net worth of government financial position may lead, particularly in the recession period, to pressurized efforts to privatize and sell assets to reduce financial liabilities. The prolonged low-interest rate environment over the past decade has impacted industries variously, from life insurance companies facing a more difficult environment to meet their obligations, to the overvaluing of the excessively growing developing market currencies. The economic cycle moved from the 2007/ 8 crisis first to recovery and then to the growth cycle. In the three years preceding 2021, however, the initial slowdown was more recently fast sped by the COVID-19 pandemic induced shutdowns that then have caused the recession and have opened questions of long-run impact on the developing markets.

Developing markets, vis-à-vis advanced markets, face considerable gaps in (a) per capita income, (b) institutional frameworks' capacities, (c) economic openness and safeguarding trade integration, (d) containing vulnerabilities amidst high levels of current account deficits, high external borrowing, and growing overall public debt, and (e) lesser transparency and more uncertain rule of law, *inter alia multa*. Years 2018 and 2019 marked unprecedent movements of protectionism amongst the global economic superpowers in the form of trade barriers and of commercial sanctions. Investors in global markets showed nervousness about potential capital controls possibly leading to a liquidity crisis, then a credit crisis, and ultimately a financial downturn. The imminent impact is reflected in quick global contagion and investors' speculative attacks on the smaller frontier and emerging capital markets. COVID-19 crisis further pressed the precedent reduction of aggregate economic growth toward a recession and into puzzling long-run implications on economic development. This book reveals and studies capital efficiency by implications of the historical dynamic relationship between macroeconomic indicators and capital market returns in the sample of selected countries. It also deals with the interlink between the short-run and long-run relationships. Finally, it explains the significance of the distinct structure and development stage of the environment relevant for economic, financial, and capital markets.

The broad term "financial markets" refers to the environment that aggregates buyers and sellers who create liquidity in ultimately addressing diverse living needs. Financial markets channel liquidity in enhanced fundraising, cost improvements, risk offsetting, risk transferring, and information sharing and transparency, amongst others. Capital markets are a constituent of financial markets, which are both complementary and overlapping with the banking industry, non-bank financial industry (insurance, leasing, microfinance, etc.), private equity industry, financials derivatives market, etc. Capital markets foster more direct and continuous liquidity and access to information through custom solutions addressing diverse demands, and through the effective overcoming of high-cost barriers. In their continued evolvement capital markets exemplify inherent financial innovations catering to the needs of growing global demand.

Globalization promotes economic integration and an increase in financial markets growth by means of increasing efficiency in policy coordination, information flow, and ultimately increasing trade and investments. As financial innovation opens new access paths, financial literacy lags and causes misconception and uncertainty paramount to slower development of legislation and regulatory tracking. It is no wonder thus that in the capital markets the business volume of the regulated exchange trade continues to grow at a rate outpacing that of the over-the-counter (OTC) trade. The reason is that the trade at regulated exchanges exemplifies higher transparency and standardization, while the OTC trade is less regulated and is opaquer. Financial derivatives and securitized products are often drivers of capital markets growth and profitability both in the OTC trade and on the regulated organized exchange. However, in the Southeast Europe (SEE) these products are seldom used and are not traded on a regulated organized exchange. The scope of financial derivatives reach has infinite possibilities to address variable global distresses. Once thought of as "exotic" financial derivatives and securitization products today represent mainstream financial instruments with an outstanding market estimated at more than ten times the total world GDP (Maverick, 2016). The big shift in the landscape is still widely inadequately understood and market sentiment on these products quickly moves in a pendulum fashion, from criticism to praise. The criticism is epitomized by names such as "financial weapon of mass destruction" (Buffet, 2012) for the ability to enhance risk through over-leverage, speculation, contagion, and avoidance of capital controls, taxes, and regulation. The praise, on the other hand, pertains to their capacity to unbundle, redistribute and reduce risk, enable increased capital flows, and increase opportunities for portfolio diversification (Lien & Zhang, 2008).

A wide range of opinions exists amongst the society at large. For one example, during his tenure as chairman of the United States of America (USA) Federal Reserve, the country's central bank, Paul Volcker expressed the opinion that automatic teller machines were the only useful financial invention in the previous twenty years (Wall Street Journal, 2009). On the contrary, Kenneth Arrow, a Nobel laureate in economics, in his 1962 research on the endogenous-growth theory, notably remarked that the well-being of an economy is tied to its ability to innovate. Robert Solow, also a Nobel laureate in economics, in his 1956 research calculated that about four-fifths of the growth in output per worker in the United States was attributable to technological progress. Innovation does introduce new risk, which is nevertheless a desirable attribute and a fundamental trait of development that is beyond marginal utility decrease or conversion. The most important and the predominant use of financial derivatives and structured products is as a risk management tool. Yet, financial derivates also serve to develop markets, discover prices, and ultimately increase access to finance for a wide set of users, from large financial institutions (FIs) on OTC markets to private individuals and exchange-traded markets.

This research focuses on the aspects of capital markets development and the relationship of capital markets' performance with macroeconomic indicators in the selected intertwined economies in SEE, specifically those of the Republic of Croatia (Croatia), the Republic of Serbia (Serbia), Bosnia and Herzegovina (B&H), the Republic of Slovenia (Slovenia), and the Republic of North Macedonia (North Macedonia). The five countries selected for the research represent the largest economies of the seven independent countries formerly united in a single country, Yugoslavia. The selected countries share numerous traits: (a) ethnic, cultural, and language similarities, (b) legacy and new joint infrastructure, (c) commercial brands recognition, (d) the common path toward a single market and membership in the European Union (EU), and (e) relatively sizeable but relevantly unimportant capital markets, amongst many others. Slovenia and Croatia joined the EU in 2004 and in 2013, respectively. Bosnia and Herzegovina, North Macedonia, and Serbia share clear aspirations and joint efforts in acceding to the EU. Ultimately, all the researched markets are amongst each other's top ten international trade partners. The selected SEE markets fail to show significant economic growth and progress in catching up with the advanced markets. The SEE capital markets differ from global trends in their significance for the overall financial system and the economy. In SEE, financial markets are largely centric on the banking system, whose assets form the overwhelming majority of the overall financial markets' assets. Financial derivatives are very seldom used, they are not available for use on a regulated exchange and are very often insufficiently understood.

This research presents the bottom-up perspective in testing the relationship between macroeconomic indicators and capital markets' performance. The surrounding market structure, legal, regulatory, policy, and infrastructure framework of the relevant capital markets lag the more investor-attractive advanced capital markets. The study provides a parallel bottom-up deep investigative insight into the current bottlenecks, trends, and prospects of individual and holistic SEE capital markets. Although historical literature provides prominent evidence of the relationship between macroeconomic fundamentals and advanced capital markets, research of developing markets, let alone frequently frontier SEE markets, remains scarce and with widely differing implications of results. SEE capital markets illustrate short-lived existence, meager impact on economic performance, and limited data availability, which spurs statistical approach inconsistencies and deters significant research to date. Moreover, the frontier markets' research has produced multiple studies with no clear results.

Empirical research focusing on macroeconomic indicators' impact on financial markets stems from the financial growth to economic growth nexus under improved savings, liquidity, productivity, and profitability fostering growth in economic output. In the past, attention was paid to studying the relationship with the pioneering role of the banking sector, while more recently the attention has switched to the presently dominant capital markets. First empirical research on capital markets looked at the level of development as approximated through market size and/or turnover. More recently, attention has shifted to the relationship between economic performance to capital markets' price growth and/or financial returns. In such research type the temporal dynamism in relationships is least tested, though there is a consensus in the available research on the existence of short-run relationships (Fama, 1981; Lazarov et al., 2016; Levine & Zervos, 1998; Naceur et al., 2007), yet with more conflicting results for the long-run studies (Barbic & Condic-Jurkic, 2011; Lee & Wang, 2015; Megaravalli & Sampagnaro, 2018). As empirical researching expands to new regions, as new statistical methods and techniques are introduced, and as different study periods are captured, the variability in results increases thereby enriching knowledge. In one example, Nasseh and Strauss (2000) utilized the vector error correction model (VECM) and variance decomposition test. They obtained results that depict a significant and strong relationship between interest rates and Consumer Price Index (CPI) as explanatory variables. Such results show the negative correlating predictability power of thirty-seven to eighty-two percent, respectively, with listed stocks' prices. Nasseh and Strauss empirically tested quarterly study data on Western European stock markets from 1962 to 1995. VECM was utilized on the country-level data with a lengthy sample, which removes otherwise frequent indicators' small data bias, collinearity existence, and results' non-reliability at large. In another example, Errunza and Hogan (1998) utilized a similar methodology in the VAR test from 1959 to 1993 listing stocks' returns and macroeconomic indicators' data. Their aim was to depict enhanced stocks' returns by incorporating lagged money supply growth rates for cases of Germany and France, but not for cases of the United Kingdom, Belgium, or Switzerland. Thus, it seems that the relationship between capital markets and macroeconomic indicators is not perfectly clear-cut and illustrates periodical patterns and occasional behavioral trends. The existence of the relationship between macroeconomic indicators and capital markets' performance tends to be adjusted for and relatively weakens in the very long run. Otherwise, capital markets are rather more predictable than efficient and subsequent capital markets' prices do not represent random departures from previous prices.

The exchange-traded capital market in the selected SEE countries has sizeable capitalization at an estimated aggregate value of United States dollars (US$) fifty billion. However, the capitalization is concentrated among a small number of large companies. The selected exchange-traded capital markets manifest shallow liquidity and capital flow, with an aggregate estimated daily turnover of US$ 6.5 million. Capital markets in the selected SEE countries are inefficient due to a lack of liquidity to support continued demand and supply. Barbic and Condic-Jurkic (2011) research on the relationship between macroeconomic indicators and listed stock markets in the selected Central and Eastern European (CEE) countries showed that the exchange-traded markets in Croatia and Slovenia did not incorporate complete and timely information in the listed prices. Thus, those markets proved inefficient. The study included natural logarithms on variables data from periods from 1998 to 2010 utilizing Johansen cointegrating and Granger causality statistical testing. This study adds to the former research by including new countries and by expanding the time coverage for a longer post-crisis period including economic recovery and growth cycles. Besides, it utilizes panel cross-country testing to resolve possible multi-collinearity. It also grasps single country data heterogeneity and resolves possible small data size constraints. Olgic Drazenovic and Kusanovic (2016) researched the impact on the level of development of capital markets to prove a positive determinant causality impact on the size of capital markets in CEE countries (Croatia, Slovenia, the Czech Republic, Hungary, Poland, and Slovakia). Their study used the scope of institutional investors' involvement (of pension funds, investment funds, and insurance companies), scope of reforms (European Bank for Reconstruction and Development—EBRD, and Infrastructure Index and Heritage Foundation Index, amongst others), and macroeconomic indicators' performance (GDP growth, inflation, and savings rate). The study period covered annual data from 1995 to 2010 in the unbalanced panel regression testing methodology. Results implied the shallow statistical significance at the five percent level given the very limited data constraint and short-lived nature of the studied markets. They revealed the statistical significance of the impact of privatization reform, investment funds' depth, life insurance premiums' size, and inflation on capital markets' depth. The mentioned regional studies have tested for the existence of the direct relationship between macroeconomic indicators and capital markets' depth. This study adds to the former research by implementing the most coherent statistical testing methodologies and by giving an insight into capital market patterns in the never clear time-varying performance of the underlying business environment.

The main aim of the research is to investigate the dynamics and presence of the relationship between the selected macroeconomic indicators and SEE-regulated exchange-traded markets' performance. This study encompasses the latest SEE capital markets' developments in an approximated full-economic cycle time coverage. This includes lengthier and most recent ex post 2007/ 8 crisis and post-period research on the effect of the structural reforms and later waves of privatizations that occurred in the process of transitioning from planning to capital market economies beyond its initial first decade of operation. The reason is that the initial years following capital market establishment are usually excluded from research due to the de facto frequent failures to execute transactions. The relevant market occurrences in the selected SEE countries include Zagreb Stock Exchange (ZSE) 2015 acquisition of Ljubljana Stock Exchange (LJSE). As of 2014, Zagreb, Sofia, and Skopje stock exchanges have jointly used the SEE Link platform for live investment listing and data information access. The use of the platform was later expanded to include all the stock exchanges in markets under research. The selected coverage period extends from the end of 2005 through the end of 2016 as data for target capital markets' exchange-traded indices are captured. The observed indices were founded as follows: (a) Croatian Zagreb Stock Exchange Index (CROBEX) in September 1997, (b) Slovenian Blue Chip Index (SBITOP) in April 2006, (c) Macedonian Stock Exchange Price

Index (MBI10) in December 2004, (d) Belgrade Stock Exchange Blue Chip Index (BELEX15) in September 2005, (e) Berzanski Indeks Republike Srpske (BIRS) in May 2004, (f) Sarajevo Stock Exchange Index 10 (SASX-10) in February 2006, and (g) Bosnian and Herzegovinian Traded Index (BATX) in December 2009.

The study discusses the efficient capital markets theorem (Fama & Malkiel, 1970), the underlying assumption of which is that listed stocks' prices instantaneously, always, and fully incorporate and reflect accurate resources allocation under informational transparency and rational behavior. In the perspective of an efficient market theorem, values of macroeconomic indicators ought to inherently be a priori captured by listed stocks' prices and thus there should not exist a causal impact relationship. Many studies have confirmed cases where macroeconomic activity affects prices of exchange-traded securities, yet conflicting results and mean reversion of long-run relationships call for repetitions of studies to capture more holistic markets, longer periods, new techniques and methodologies, etc. (Barbic & Condic-Jurkic, 2011; Dumas et al., 2003; Fama, 1981, 1990; Karamustafa & Kucukalle, 2003; Megaravalli & Sampagnaro, 2018).

What is distinctive for the selected SEE markets and furthermore for the focus of this research is in-depth profiling of individual country capital markets assessed in the context of the available information on the current market structure, trends, and prospects. In addition, the study investigates the potential of and barriers to the use of financial derivatives and structured financial products. In the current market, the OTC products, as the only existent market products, are used only sporadically. More importantly, financial derivatives are not used in the regulated exchange-traded markets. Historically, the predominant providers and users of these products are commercial banks in what are the already bank-centric financial markets.

This study researches the current state of development and the surrounding framework of capital markets in selected SEE countries, Croatia, Serbia, B&H, North Macedonia, and Slovenia. The research models and analyzes the existence and implications of the relationship between macroeconomic indicators and capital markets' performance as measured through stock exchange indices (SMIs). The selected macroeconomic indicators include: (a) gross domestic product per capita (GDPPC), (b) industrial production index (IPI), (c) balance of payments' net financial account (BOPNFA), (d) local currency exchange rate with

US$[1] (FX), (e) money market interest rate (MMIR), and (f) harmonized index consumer price (HICP) as tracked by Eurostat (2018) or in proxy by consumer price indices by local standards to indicate inflation. For the cases of B&H, North Macedonia, and Serbia, this study is the first statistical testing of the capital market efficiency in this structure, while altogether, including Croatia and Slovenia, it represents the broadest covering study of its kind. It demonstrates the first-time use of the simultaneous panel pooled mean group (PMG) estimation technique, panel vector auto regression (VAR), Granger, and Johansen methods statistical tests utilizing time-series and cross-country analyses on bi-variate and multi-variate relationship existence, causality, and statistical predictive power. The empirical results are limited by the small sample and to resolve this the panel analysis is employed to apply multiplicity and capture country-level economic heterogeneity. In practice, the results are relevant for enhancing knowledge of the systemic structure and importance of capital markets in these economies. This two-pillar review presents an in-depth platform for studying capital market structures as a means to assess the dynamic relationship between macroeconomic indicators and capital market performance (Fig. 1.1).

1.2 Theoretical Concept—Weak Form of Efficient Capital Markets Theorem

The study discusses the **efficient capital markets theorem** developed by Eugene Fama and Burton Malkiel (Fama & Malkiel, 1970). The underlying presumptions of the theorem are that prices always reflect the available information in full transparency and under investors' rational behavior. In all forms of capital markets' efficiency, the impact of macroeconomic indicators ought to be fully a priori incorporated in listed stock prices. The efficiency forms are as follows:

[1] US$ currency is selected as counter-currency due to the greater variability power versus otherwise most prevalent SEE markets' foreign currency, Euro. Bosnia and Herzegovina's local currency, Convertible Mark (BAM), has a fixed exchange rate regime to the Euro. Slovenia was de facto using Euro over almost the entire research period. Other selected SEE countries exhibit very high Euroization level and the extent of managed float to the Euro.

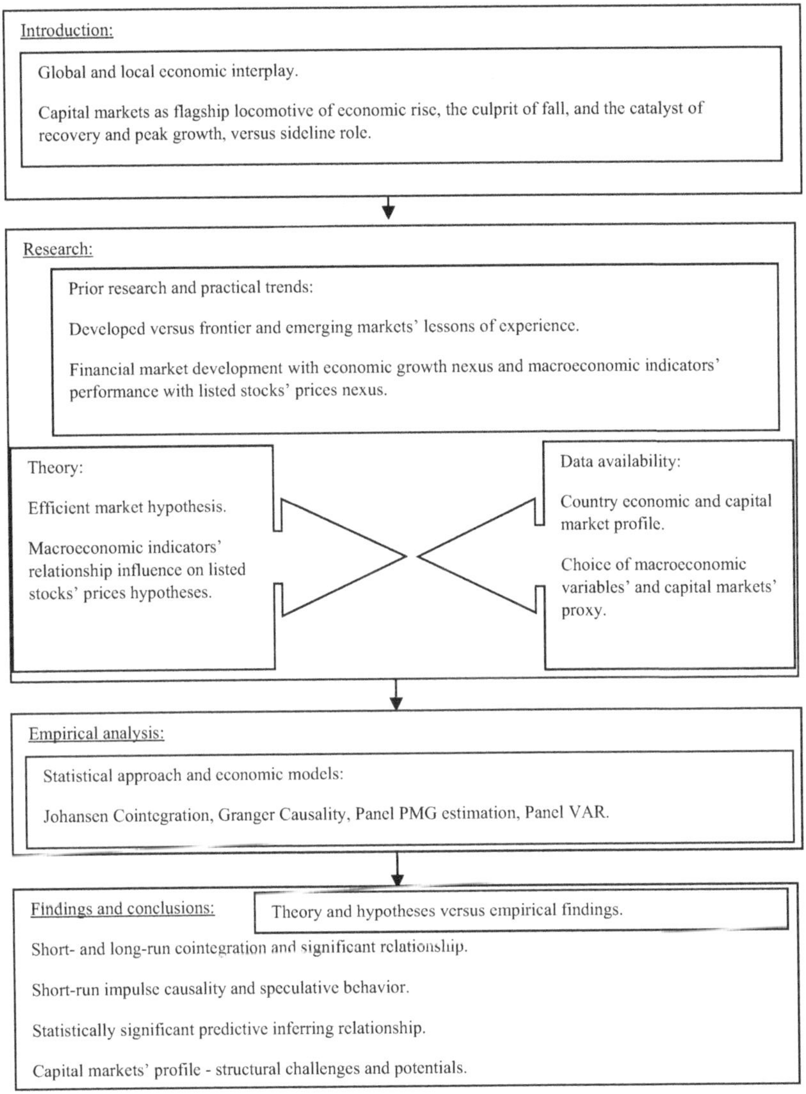

Fig. 1.1 Study paradigm structure

1. Weak form, in which listed stocks' prices capture all the data of past prices and publicly available information in an environment where future stocks' prices ought to be independent of historical stocks' prices. Therefore, technical analysis is worthless for investors seeking additional gains;
2. Semi-strong or event form, where listed stocks' prices adjust rapidly to the release of new publicly available information. Therefore, technical and fundamental analysis is worthless for investors; and
3. Strong or private-information form, where investors' insider information is a priori fully captured in listed stocks' prices. As the hypothesis of strong capital market efficiency is a precondition for transaction and information costs to be inexistent, the theorem clearly deals with an effective approximation of a perfectly efficient capital market, which is not studied here.

This research relates to the weak form of the efficient capital markets theorem by testing for the explanatory relationship inference from historical time-series and cross-country interaction between the selected macroeconomic indicators and prices in capital markets. It analyzes the sample and time-specific patterns in the relationships as it recognizes the limitations of not testing a very long-run series behavior and not controlling for all factors of the external risk influence. It does not test for the event form of capital markets efficiency for practical reasons (e.g. due to the inexistence of liquid free float daily data, lengthy data set, and frequent corporate actions in the sample which could be analyzed). In the weak form of the efficient capital market hypothesis, listed stocks' prices in efficient markets should not be predictable from prior stocks' prices and macroeconomic indicators as the factors should be independent. In the general market equilibrium, the expected prices are constant over time as prices follow a "random walk" in restrictive precondition of fair market competition and homogeneity in behavior.

In practice, it is recognized that capital markets' prices variation through time is common and that it is in plausible ways related to overall market conditions incorporating sample-specific business environment. In recognizing practical market anomalies, exemplary contemporary plausible SEE market-specific conditions are reviewed. The structure of the specific business environment is investigated to shed light on the surrounding conditions under which the statistical tests are conducted, and the results obtained. Future researchers are invited to endogenize testing on further business environment factors such as the scope of corporate governance quality, foreign investors' involvement and prevalence, domestic institutional investors' involvement and prevalence, judiciary effectiveness, etc. Empirical tests employed in this study primarily enrich knowledge of the behavior of capital markets in emerging SEE countries in relation to the selected macroeconomic indicators in the study period. In this assumption the study does not test the realism of theory assumptions and its constraints; rather, it tests the acceptability of its implications. In addition, it seeks to enrich the knowledge component in the unique and most comprehensive to date research on the history, trends, structure, and overarching capital markets environment in the selected SEE countries. The summary of the presented literature research is not an exhaustive compilation of findings on the set relationship. It is focused on a subset of findings with the most robust studies in relevance to grasped time, markets, indicators, and methodological and practical view advances. Due to the contemporary immaterial turnover and contributory significance of listed stocks' markets to the relevant SEE economies, for practical reasons the study does not test for the seldom researched concept of the efficient capital market theorem by means of the existence of listed stocks' prices influence on macroeconomic indicators. Similarly, due to market structure with non-prevalence of such products, market efficiency is not tested by a standalone test of options' or bonds' prices. The principal theoretical economic background in this research rests on reviewing the weak form of capital market efficiency in set preconditions of the inherent business environment.

References

Barbic, T., & Condic-Jurkic, I. (2011). Relationship between macroeconomic fundamentals and stock market indices in select CEE countries. *Ekonomski Pregled, 62*(3–4), 113–133.

Buffet, W. (2012). *2012 Berkshire Hathaway annual report*. Annual Report.

Dumas, B., Harvey, C., & Ruiz, P. (2003). Are correlations of stock returns justified by subsequent changes in national outputs? *Journal of International Money and Finance*, 777–811.

Errunza, V., & Hogan, K. (1998). Macroeconomic determinants of European stock market volatility. *European Financial Management, 4*(3), 361–377.

Eurostat. (2018). Eurostat databased. Retrieved November 3, 2018, from https://ec.europa.eu/eurostat/data/database

Fama, E. F. (1981). Stock returns, real activity, inflation and money. *The American Economic Review, 71*(4), 545–565.

Fama, E. F. (1990). Stock returns, expected returns, and real activity. *The Journal of Finance, 45*(4), 1089–1108.

Fama, E., & Malkiel, B. (1970). Efficient capital markets: A review of theory and empirical work. *The American Finance Association—The Journal of Finance, 25*(2), 383–417.

International Monetary Fund. (2017). *Global financial stability report: Is growth at risk?* World Economic and Financials Surveys.

Karamustafa, O., & Kucukalle, Y. (2003). *Long run relationships between stock market returns and macroeconomic performance.* Finance, University Library of Munich.

Lazarov, D., Miteva-Kacarski, E., & Nikoloski, K. (2016). An empirical analysis of stock market development and economic growth: The case of Macedonia. *South East European Journal of Economics and Business, 11*(2), 71–81.

Lee, Y.-M., & Wang, K.-M. (2015). Dynamic heterogenous panel analysis of the correlation between stock prices and exchange rates. *Economic Research-Ekonomska Istraživanja, 28*(1), 749–772.

Levine, R., & Zervos, S. (1998). Stock markets, banks, and growth. *American Economic Review, 88*(3), 537–558.

Lien, D., & Zhang, M. (2008). A survey of emerging derivatives markets. *Emerging Markets Finance and Trade, 44*(2), 39–69.

Maverick, J. (2016). *Investopedia.* Retrieved January 1, 2016, from http://www.investopedia.com/ask/answers/052715/how-big-derivatives-market.asp

Megaravalli, A. V., & Sampagnaro, G. (2018). Macroeconomic indicators and their impact on stock markets in ASIAN 3: A pooled mean group approach. *Cogent Economics and Finance, 6*(1), 1–14.

Naceur, S. B., Ghazouani, S., & Omran, M. (2007). The determinants of stock market development in the Middle-Eastern and North African region. *Managerial Finance, 33*(7), 477–489.

Nasseh, A., & Strauss, J. (2000). Stock prices and domestic and international macroeconomic activity: A cointegration approach. *The Quarterly Review of Economics and Finance, 40*(2), 229–249.

Olgic Drazenovic, B., & Kusanovic, T. (2016). Determinants of capital market in the new member EU countries. *Economic Research—Ekonomska Istrazivanja, 29*(1), 758–769.

The Wall Street Journal. (2009, December 8). Retrieved December 8, 2017, from http://blogs.wsj.com/marketbeat/2009/12/08/volcker-praises-the-atm-blasts-finance-execs-experts/

CHAPTER 2

Financial Innovation Spiral

2.1 Global Evidence—Financial Markets and Economic Transition Nexus

The relationship between financial markets and aggregate economic performance has long caught attention of various academics, investors, and policy makers, amongst many others. In 1969, Goldsmith (1969) conducted a path-breaking study in assessing whether finance influences economic output growth. Examining data on thirty-five countries in the study period from 1860 to 1963 Goldsmith observed a positive correlation between the proportional size of financial intermediary sector and GDP indicator of aggregate economic growth. While pioneering and knowledge enriching, Goldsmith's research did not account for an extensive capital market data sample as capital markets had at that time existed only for a short period. Besides, the study did not grasp a global sample, thus not controlling for international factors influencing growth. Lastly, the study did not gauge deeper on selecting the most relevant indicators. King and Levine (1993) added on Goldsmith's research in a study on the significant regression correlations for seventy-seven countries. They captured the time period from 1960 to 1989 to prove a positive relationship between financial market depth indicator, measured as broad money supply indicator (M3) liquid liabilites to GDP ratio, and stronger economic output growth. Samargandi, Fidrmuc, and Ghosh (2014) also utilized M3 indicator to GDP ratio under a panel PMG model empirical

A. Dodig, *Capital Markets in Southeast Europe*,
https://doi.org/10.1007/978-3-031-07210-9_2

testing. They showed short-run statistical non-significance but a long-run statistical significance of financial development on economic growth in a global sample of middle-income countries for the study period from 1998 to 2008. La Porta, Lopez, and Schleifer (2000) studied twenty years data on ninety-two countries, in the period from 1975 to 1995, to show that a comparatively greater concentration of government-owned banks in the banking sector is associated with a lower aggregate economic output growth. **Together with other similar researches, the initial empirical statistical studies focused primarily on the banking sector's sole contribution through financial market to the aggregate economic performance.**

Levine and Zervos (1998) studied sample data for forty-two countries in the period from 1976 to 1999 to assess capital markets' independent contribution to aggregate economic output growth. They utilized VAR and ordinary least squares (OLS) estimation methodology in statistically testing the explanatory parameters input. The selected capital market indicators included capitalization to GDP size ratio, capital market turnover values, and capital market turnover to capitalization and to GDP ratios. In their research they proved statistically significant positive relationship with economic growth, yet they failed to use lagged dependent variables and they did not control for country fixed-effects staticity or simultaneity bias. Levine and Beck (2002) repeated the study in 2002 but used a five-year moving average data to improve the potential business cycle data bias. Importantly, they used panel estimator to eliminate country-specific biases, while controlling for many other growth determinants. In confirmation, the results again proved the positive relationship between indicators of capital markets' development and aggregate economic output growth. This study seeks to add new value to former researches through conducting statistical tests on the existence of the relationship and impact of the specific set of macroeconomic indicators on capital markets' prices in the unique SEE emerging markets' environment. The econometric analysis is strengthened with the addition of simultaneous multiple time-series and cross-country analyses and bi-variate and multi-variate models. Previous studies have to a large extent proven a complementary favorable impact of both banks and capital markets on economic performance, particularly through increased investments as both industries contribute to lower liquidity risk and to lower informational asymmetries, amongst others (James, 1987). Levine (1997) studied the static percentage of GDP ratio parameters to highlight a breakdown for low-, middle-, and high-income countries' financial development. These parameters include relative central banks' assets size, commercial banks' assets size, non-banks' assets size, stock markets' capitalization, and stock markets' trading volume. In this breakdown Levine (1997) shows the increasing predominance of the latter factors (stock markets' capitalization and trading versus banks' assets) in higher income countries.

Economists' views and results of diverse empirical research differ on the relationship between financial system and aggregate economic output growth, though overall a positive relationship sentiment prevails. In addition, it is advocated that both capital markets and banking industry individually spur the aggregate economic output growth. Beck, Levine, and Loayza (2000) conducted several studies on this topic, covering seventy-four countries in the period from 1960 to 1995. They reached the conclusion that components of financial intermediary development are positively associated with the aggregate economic output growth. Yet, cross-country variations exist due to differences in accounting and legal systems. Namely, they utilized the generalized method of moments (GMM) estimator in a panel form to test for weak instruments regressors' statistical significance. With the second method (e.g. the panel cross-sectional instrumental variable estimator) the researchers dealt with bias issues due to simultaneity, omitted variables, and unobserved country-specific effects. The chosen regressors were the size of financial intermediation, the size of involvement by central banks, and the size of private credit to GDP ratios. The indicators' values showed large variance in the study data set, which involves underdeveloped, emerging, and advanced markets alike. Two years later, in 2002, Beck and Levine separately researched the individual impact of banks and capital markets on industrial growth. They found that both industries independently and positively spur growth; however, it is difficult to identify the specific association of substitutes, complements, or conduciveness factor with the aggregate economic output growth (2002). Beck and Levine conducted cross-industry and cross-country panel two-stage least squares regression estimates utilizing data on forty-two countries and thirty-six industries in the study period from 1980 to 1990. Their research results showed the developed financial markets to be more capital markets' centric versus banks' centric, to have fewer regulatory restrictions on bank activities, and to have less governments' ownership of banks. With two-stage least square econometric technique as an extension of OLS estimator the researchers resolved the omitted variable and unknown error biases; nonetheless, heterogeneity bias failed to be successfully resolved. In response the innovations in panel PMG estimation technique by fixing long-run coefficients for cross-groups' homogenic characteristics help resolve the heterogeneity bias. In the research shown in this book the selected markets share a similar economic structure and the study models the relationship between macroeconomic indicators performance and capital markets' prices by employing panel PMG technique. With this technique a dual benefit is reached through resolving country bias issues in fixing panel long-run coefficients, and through allowing variability in the short-run coefficients per individual country.

The relationship between macroeconomic indicators and capital markets' prices may be observed in diverse perspectives. Changes in capital markets' prices and in various macroeconomic indicators may be observed for a short-run relationship through the arbitrage pricing theory model of first differences, assuming a stationary trend, or through discounted cash flows and a cointegration approach for longer-term horizon relationship. Fama proved a positive relationship between industrial production, capital expenditure, gross national product (GNP), and expected future aggregate economic output on stocks' returns (Fama, 1990). Dumas, Harvey, and Ruiz (2003) confirmed a positive relationship with GDP growth rates on stocks' returns. Chen, Ross, and Roll (1986) confirmed a positive relationship with money supply, inflation, interest rate, and exchange rate macroeconomic indicators to capital markets' returns. These two tests identified a statistically significant positive impact of macroeconomic factors on stocks' returns. In a multi-factor arbitrage pricing model, the two research tested further for whether factor loadings explain the cross-section of returns. The disadvantage of the used model is the possibility of spurious relationships due to the loss of data information under the data stationarity transformation processes. In improving the methodological robustness, this study seeks to use level series data on stocks' prices with the aim to maintain high-level information that would otherwise be lost through processes of data differencing and transforming. In general, the standard results of the studies using the mean reversion test rest on the hypothesis of investors' rational behavior and do not dwell further on the adequate sensibility of the assumption in practical business conditions. **Attention of more recent studies shifted to the explanation of anomalies through volatility tests** (e.g. in the form of seasonality or disproportionate frequency in stocks' returns to capture the micro-structure explanation for the observed deviations) (Ariel, 1990). In his research, Ariel observed the study period from 1963 to 1982 with data from New York Stock Exchange (NYSE) and American Stock Exchange (AMEX). In the generalized autoregressive conditional heteroskedasticity (GARCH) model which tested the conditional volatility of data on second-level residuals, the results revealed that a third of aggregate annual returns occurred in the last monthly trading days.

Flannery and Protopapadakis (2002) confirmed that macroeconomic factors influence aggregate stocks' returns and turnover volume through future cash flows or discount rates which are a priori set as input determinants in valuation methodologies. Flannery and Protopapadakis employed autoregressive integrated moving average (ARIMA) model in proving a statistically significant negative relationship between consumer price index (CPI), producer price index (PPI), and broad money supply (M1) macroeconomic indicators and stocks' return and turnover levels. ARIMA model specifically requires more than fifty observations, ideally more than one hundred observations, and is well compatible with the second-level time-varying versus fixed-coefficients statistical testing. Flannery and Protopapadakis then utilized GARCH model in testing daily returns and conditional volatility relationships with seventeen macroeconomic announcements in the study period from 1980 to 1996 to show that M1 macroeconomic indicator is the single one affecting both return and conditional volatility. In this non-linear research, the second-level relationship is observed for developed capital markets and an event study proved the efficient market hypothesis to be significantly statistically incorrect. The statistical testing results revealed the markets to be inefficient. The SEE data are limited by non-extensive data sample, which is a necessary precondition for the robust use of this testing method. Yet, as ARIMA is more useful for the autoregression test of single variables, its parsimony hints that PMG is more useful for the nature of this research since it utilizes the impact of other multi-variate and unrestricted environment factors while dispersing the bias tendency embedded in a small-size dataset.

Results of the empirical research in developing markets are even more diverse and inconclusive and thus call for more frequent studies. Two independent studies on CEE and Commonwealth of Independent States (CIS) transition economies show different conclusions. First, Koivu (2002) used data from twenty-five countries for the period from 1993 to 2000 to conclude that in one financial development proxy, banking sector's interest rate margin indicator, there is an apparent negative statistically significant relationship with aggregate economic output growth. In other words, a more efficient, lower risk, a more developed, and more cost-effective banking sector improves financial market and spurs economic growth. However, in using another financial development indicator, credit volume, her research results indicated that, apparently, growth in bank credit does not speed up economic growth. She based her opinion on the unsustainability in the credit growth and on soft constraints of the sample observed in the transition economies. Koivu utilized the fixed-effects panel model to empirically test the finance to economic growth nexus. The estimation technique method utilized in research shown in this book, panel PMG, uses time-variant relationship dynamics not employed in fixed-effects model to deal with time-invariant input in endogenous regressors. Cojocaru, Falaris, Hoffman, and Miller (2015) acknowledged that specific buffers in CEE and CIS transition economies, such as a soft controlled budget or lower banking sector competition, weaken the impact of financial system development on economic growth. Nevertheless, their research encompassed a longer period, from 1990 to 2008, and the results pointed to a statistically significant positive relationship between financial sector development and economic growth. Financial sector development was measured as private credit to GDP and liquid liabilities to GDP ratios, and economic growth was measured as GDPPC, in fifteen CEE countries and ten CIS countries. Furthermore, their results imply that financial system efficiency and competitiveness are more important factors to contribute to economic growth than is the sheer size of a market. In comparison to Koivu, the later research employed GMM estimation technique to fix for time-invariant country fixed-effects bias. The research revealed in this book utilizes panel PMG estimation technique to treat GMM illustrated biases in the case of small samples and the non-reliability in not being able to handle simultaneous stationarity and non-stationarity in data. Besides, GMM cannot account for error correction in panel data. Fink, Haiss, and Vuksic (2005) found that financial intermediation domestic credit and bonds' indicators contributed to economic growth, but, simultaneously, that the private credit and the stock exchange markets' indicators did not have statistically significant effect on the economic growth. These studies conducted panel cross-country regression on the dependent variable of economic output per capita and included data on twenty-seven countries, nine of which were the EU accession countries (including Slovenia amongst the countries selected for this research), in the period from 1996 to 2000. They included regressors of capital stock per capita, change of labor participation rate, educational attainment, and financial development indicators. Fink, Haiss, and Vuksic utilized pooled panel data regression with common intercept technique. On the other hand, panel PMG estimation technique provides more reliability in case of small study sample biases. It should be noted that Fink, Haiss, Vukcic results on no significance in the relationship between stock exchanges markets' capitalization and GDPPC growth correspond to those in the SEE research by Lazarov et al. (2016). Capital market liquidity is a pragmatic indicator of market activity but due to limitation in the immateriality of turnover amount as a constituent of the aggregate economic activity, the indicator's importance is less relevant. Future research ought to maintain a closer focus on the liquidity parameter in the case of improvements.

Observing the relationship between macroeconomic indicators and capital markets' prices in the EMEs, Karamustafa and Kucukalle (2003) researched the cointegrated relationship of macroeconomic indicators of money supply, FX, trade balance, and IPI with listed stocks in Turkey. While stocks' prices were the leading indicators for macroeconomic proxy money supply, the reciprocal was not true for any of the selected macroeconomic indicators. Karamustafa and Kucukalle utilized Engle-Granger test and Johansen and Juselius maximum likelihood procedure on monthly data from 1990 to 2001. In Sri Lanka post-war research for the period from 1980 to 2012, Nijam, Ismail, and Mustafa utilized OLS estimation technique to study the relationship between macroeconomic indicators and the Sri Lankan listed stocks' market performance. The research findings proved a statistically significant positive relationship between GDP, FX, and interest rates' indicators and the stocks' returns, but a negative relationship between inflation rate and the stocks' returns, and a statistically non-significant relationship for the balance of payments indicator (Nijam et al., 2015). In comparison the study shown in this book utilizes a panel analysis to eliminate further single country data sample biases.

In a similar setting, Hasseeb's (2015) research in Europe, Middle East, and North Africa (EMENA) revealed a strong long-run positive relationship between foreign direct investments (FDI) and stock exchange markets' capitalization size. Hasseeb studied annual data from 1995 to 2014 in fifteen Middle East and North Africa (MENA) listed stocks' markets. They proved the presence of dichotomous factor in sample data as oil industry dependent countries showed a statistically significant positive relation between the inflation indicator and the stocks' prices, versus the opposite relationship in non-oil dependent economies. Naceur et al. (2007) studied twelve MENA region countries to uncover macroeconomic indicators determinants of listed stocks' market development. They researched the impact of multiple macroeconomic indicators on listed stocks' market capitalization to GDP ratio in the study period of up to twenty years, starting from 1979, and in various observations at a country level. The researchers utilized unbalanced panel fixed effects, random effects, and OLS regression to show statistical significance of national savings rate, credit to GDP ratio level, listed stocks' market turnover to GDP ratio, and inflation. Study revealed in this book adds to these prior researches of utilizing fixed effects, random effects, and least squares testing by improving statistical robustness as it includes panel PMG testing that resolves the static and stationarity inconsistencies. Panel PMG improves reliability by increasing the degrees of freedom between groups and by improving relationship association in allowing intercepts, short-run coefficients, and cointegrating terms to differ across cross-sections. In addition, it analyzes a more approximate full economic cycle data set, thus reducing single economic cycle bias, and it includes better comparable single country economies in the shared structure and integration profiles. Other research have pointed to a strong link in that in a financial stress situation the strength of national net reserves indicates a positive impact on net inward investments flow (Alberola, Erce, & Serena, 2014). Alberola, Erce, and Serena studied data in sixty-three countries in the period from 1991 to 2010 utilizing dynamic panel cross-country and cross-sectional regression. The research performed fixed-effects linear testing and dichotomous quadratic data testing to test event and static events; yet the latter comes at loss of significance in inferring determinant predictability due to data transformations.

The efficient capital market theme was very recently explored in Megaravalli and Sampagnaro's (2018) research, where they examined the long- and short-run relationship between listed stocks' markets performance and macroeconomic variables of foreign exchange rate and inflation indicators. They studied performance in two developing economies giants, India and China, and in an advanced market representative, Japan. The two researchers utilized monthly time-series data from 2008 to 2016 performing the unit root test, cointegration test, Granger test, VECM, and PMG estimation to reveal relationship dynamics. The results showed statistically significant cointegration in all relationships, a bi-directional causality with foreign exchange rate, and unidirectional causality with inflation indicator. Moreover, the PMG test showed that foreign exchange rate indicator has a statistically significant positive long-run relationship with listed stocks' prices. VECM tests showed statistically significant positive causality of foreign exchange rate on the stocks' prices. Taken together, the above results show an opportunity for lower volatility by portfolio diversification. In the study on SEE countries that is revealed in this book an enhancement captures new and broader set of macroeconomic variables and new markets that are more intra-integrated with similarities in structure for expected more holistic and inducive results from common factors. It also utilizes panel VAR research to investigate exogenous variables' shock impact on forecast error variance in relationships.

Pilinkus (2010) researched monthly data for three Baltic states from January 2000 to December 2008 to model the impact of ten macroeconomic indicators on listed stocks' indices in Lithuania, Latvia, and Estonia. Utilizing Granger causality, Johansen sample and multiple cointegration, and panel VAR methods in testing, the results showed that macroeconomic indicators yielded roughly forty percent explanatory power of fluctuations in the indices' value. Individually, almost all comparable indicators were statistically significant in the long run; yet, in the short run GDP indicator proved non-significant for all indices. In the short run, HICP and short-term interest rates' indicators proved statistically significant solely for the Latvian stocks' market index. Lee and Wang (2015) performed the dynamic heterogenous panel analysis on twenty-nine countries utilizing quarterly data to find a statistically significant relationship between foreign exchange rate indicator and listed stocks' prices. Their research confirmed the appropriate choice of panel PMG model to address cross-sectional and heterogenous data while implying importance of time dynamism in results. In the Lee and Wang research, the results of the impact of foreign exchange rate indicator in the short-run relationship proved negative thus confirming the portfolio movements theory of pulling away from investments in a falling currency. Yet, the long-run relationship exhibited positive impact and return to equilibrium, which confirmed the traditional economic approach of falling currency supporting exports and performance of the relevant underlying company. Other researches have tested efficient capital market theorem by many other approaches including: (a) testing for existence of causal influence of stocks' prices on macroeconomic indices, e.g. study in Germany utilizing Granger causality test (Plihal, 2016), (b) utilizing other parameters such as ratio of listed stocks' exchange shown liquidity to capitalization, ratio of listed stocks' exchange shown liquidity to GDP, ratio of transaction cost to transaction value, options' prices, bonds' prices, etc. (Philips & Clifford, 1980; Roll et al., 2008).

In the study revealed in this book the added value rests in extending the number of observations to capture further capital markets' advancements in the post-financial crisis period in the SEE market and by performing the first relationship nexus study in the cases of Serbia, B&H, and North Macedonia. Furthermore, it is the first study to perform the complementary time-series regression and cross-country analysis in the selected countries by utilizing panel PMG test and panel VAR as the most appropriate approaches under homogenous but shallow markets. Under the SEE markets' data limitation it is also important to preserve information rather than to allow loss of information through data transformations. By using panel PMG the study seeks a more robust significance in dynamic relationship between macroeconomic indicators and capital markets' prices. Baltagi and Griffin (1997) showed that pooled estimators have desirable properties and typically outperform their heterogeneous counterparts. Similar other studies utilizing PMG include Ferrucci (2003), who studied determinants of emerging market economies' (EMEs') sovereign bonds' spreads; Megaravalli and Sampagnaro (2018), who investigated the impact of foreign exchange rate and inflation indicators on stocks in India, Japan, and China, and many others. This research investigates capital markets interconnectivity beyond the headline figures so far used in testing the nexus relationships in SEE countries. It deals with the quantitative and qualitative aspects of capital markets in SEE countries. Quantitative assessment manifests aspects of macroeconomic indicators' statistical significance of the impact and relationship association with capital markets' prices. In addition, the quantitative figures show capital markets' very low volumes in turnover, the origins and destinations of capital flows, and the degree of the integration of regional and global capital markets. In the evolving process the study qualitatively and quantitively highlights new market players, new market products, as well as legal, regulatory, and infrastructure advancements.

2.2 Operating Context

2.2.1 *Financial System and Financial Markets*

"Finance is the stomach of the country, from which all other organs take their tone." William Gladstone, a former British Prime Minister, in the parliamentary year 1858 deliberately delivered this now globally recognized phrase on the importance of financial markets. This book shows that financial markets are the lifeblood and the nerve center of the economic environment. Financial markets play a critical role in promoting economic growth by increasing accumulation of capital and production of goods and services. Through financial markets, resources are more efficiently allocated in financial planning and decision making. (a) Capital markets, (b) commodities' markets, (c) foreign exchange markets, (d) money markets, (e) financial derivatives' markets, (f) financial services' markets, (g) depository markets, and (h) non-depository markets jointly and severally form continually evolving types of financial markets. Within them, (a) banks, (b) non-banks' financial institutions (NBFIs), (c) companies, (d) individuals, (e) legislators, and (f) regulators altogether play an active and an interconnected role. In other words, finance is part of everyone's life no matter the career or personal life stage, the sector or industry one is in, or the business specifics. In today's environment a crucial aspect of aggregate economic growth is whether an economy has access to a well-functioning financial system, whereas the exact composition of the financial system is of secondary importance (Crane et al., 1995; Levine, 2005). Similar to the above, the inclusion of new financial instruments (e.g. structured products, asset-backed securities, swaps, futures, forwards, options, etc.) builds depth and breadth to sustaining resilience and growth in a financial system. Innovative financial markets and financial instruments lead the developmental progress in the global output. Innovation using comparative advantages in simultaneously available and complementary multiple financial market forms upholds sustainability in economic growth, whereas a lack of any new feature removes the function of a spare wheel in a financial system sphere.

Non-exhaustive functions of financial markets provide new value to:

1) Liquidity and inclusiveness for savers and borrowers,
2) Risk management and diversification,
3) Time preference and portfolio management,

4) Providing payment and settlement mechanism,
5) Disseminating information.

The importance of a financial system is further vital in an environment of an increasing global demand under an ever further-reaching globalization and economic integration levels. Underdeveloped financial system and/or inadequate financial management (e.g. in subpar risk, liquidity, screening, and/or portfolio management) lay ground to higher volatility build-up that may exacerbate economic inequality and poverty. The volatility spill-over risks and the relatively weaker efficiency of financial market are prominently central for developing countries, which are a depth base of poorer economic living standards and are ones with more exacerbated inequality. The recent global financial crisis has proven that even the richest countries, which might have previously been thought of as examples of a well-functioning financial, legal, and regulatory system, face damaging financial instability resulting in economic retrenchment. However, the crises also show that the more developed countries recover faster. Hence, it is critical to embrace the role of the evolvement of a sound financial system as the vital facilitator for economic growth. To that end, an efficient financial system is superior at favoring better asset allocation and spurring competitiveness and growth. Nonetheless, it is necessary to realize that the financial system is only one of the formative factors and not a replacement for the umbrella of dynamic and diverse socio-economic prospects.

This research contributes to creation and sharing of knowledge on the state of the dynamic relationship of capital markets with macroeconomic indicators in the selected SEE countries, the relationships' tradeoffs and synergies. The research topic is approached by highlighting the diverse facets of financial system designs. The prevalent types of financial markets and their characteristics are reviewed in an effort to remove the esoteric cognizance of financial markets. The book also includes an inherent overview of the development level of individual countries' capital markets. It also presents (a) the legal and regulatory scope, (b) financial infrastructure, (c) trade liberalization, (d) corporate governance, and (e) institutional capacities. All these are part of integration, harmonization, and/or obstacles for the inclusive capital markets and economic growth. SEE countries' accounting standards are largely harmonized with the best international practices. Therefore, the book deals only with the global accounting environment scene without an in-detail analysis at an individual SEE country level. It should also be noted that the research does not track frequently identified subpar judicial effectiveness, presence of systemic corruption, and behavioral traits that may act as important components in the operating environment.

Multi-faceted financial market types continue to evolve and increase in scale and under intertwined roles. The common classification by the market level class is that of the primary financial market, which is where new products issues occur, and the secondary financial market, where trading occurs. **The classification by security type is typically the following:**

1) Commodities and foreign exchange markets facilitate spot and forward trading.
2) Money markets provide short-term (under one year in maturity) debt financing and investments.
3) Financial derivatives markets provide instruments for management of financial risk. Financial derivatives are derived and traded based on an underlying security.
4) Capital markets deal with debt and equity securities with maturity longer than one year.
5) Financial services' markets provide for various arrangements such as underwriting, brokerage, dealing, etc.
6) Depository markets consist of accepting deposits to on-channel and participate in other markets.
7) Non-depository markets consist of financial intermediating in selling insurance, providing leasing, investment and asset management, etc.

The distinction between the two principally present financial system models, the intermediary based and the direct capital market based, is the extent of financial intermediation moving funds from net savers to net borrowers (see Fig. 2.1). In the direct market, funds flow directly from savers to borrowers through the purchase of securities and direct claims on the borrower. In the banking sector, or through other financial intermediaries, funds flow indirectly from savers to borrowers.

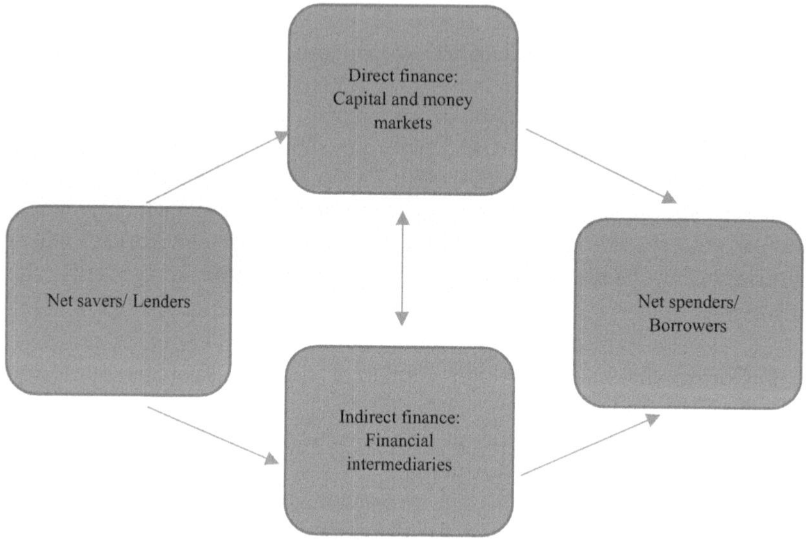

Fig. 2.1 Financial system illustration (*Source* Author)

2.2.2 *Banking Sector*

Banking sector is the pioneer driver of a financial system formation. Banks are an underpinning foundation of modern economies through the sector's long history, high level of regulation, proven survival through financial crises, and ultimately through the recognized brand of trust amongst customers. In the essential form, banks perform the task of holding assets for others. These assets are then further invested as a leveraged product. For this reason, clients pay banks for intermediating service. Banks enjoy protection through (a) customers' brand recognition, (b) confidence in deposit savings, (c) payrolls or pension processing legacy strong market position, and/or (d) creating and funding investment plans. **With historical track record, dominant market position, and developed internal systems and skills, banks have developed expertise to distinguish between good and bad borrowers while providing more certainty in the wealth growth accumulation.** Financing through banks is an effective solution to information asymmetries, moral hazard, and adverse selection between lenders and borrowers. The banking sector is here analyzed in a separate chapter due to its significance for financial systems in SEE countries, where the banking sector prevails and represents a large majority of all financial assets in each of the individual financial markets (Fig. 2.2).

Banking sector continually evolves beyond its principal role in managing deposit accounts for businesses and individuals and granting public loans through deposits use. Banks obtain resources through a multitude of instruments involving bonds, deposits, and commitments, amongst others. In their role of intermediary agent banks facilitate the flow of and access to capital through a diverse set of tools involving loans and mortgages, amongst others, in an exchange for interest and fees. Banks hold a systemic role in a modern financial market and resemble the greatest direct exposure to the poorer. Therefore, banks' principal goal is to protect clients' interests through lower risk threshold. However, banks always run a risk of insolvency due to the possibility of a withdrawal of deposits causing the loss of its liabilities base, which is necessary to sustain banks' assets. Other forms of insurance exist in the form of safety nets through insurance on a portion of deposits, in guarantees on certain debt, or in the form of systemic banks bailouts by governments, amongst others (Table 2.1).

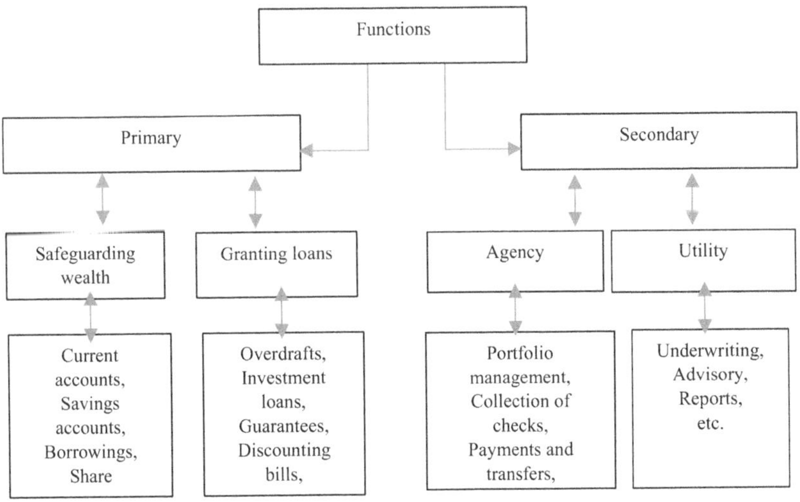

Fig. 2.2 Simplified bank role (*Source* Author)

Table 2.1 Banks' business models and geographical strategies (year-end 2018 or latest available data)

Model	Description	Percent of global systemically important banks (GSIB) assets		
Universal	Balance of household and business services	56		
Corporate	Lending to businesses	12		
Investment	Capital market services, advisory, mergers, and secondary market sales and trading	3		
Transaction	Corporate transaction services, including payments, and institutional services, including settlement, clearing, and custody	1		
Consumer	Natural persons/retail entities' banking including lending (mortgages, credit cards, other unsecured credit), savings, and payment services	23		
Wealth	Asset management, private banking, and insurance	4		
Percent share in GSIBs' assets:		Geographic reach:		
		Global	Regional	Local
		52	18	31

Note Global market size for total exposures, level three assets, payments, and OTC derivatives are calculated using the GSIB indicator metrics. "Total exposure" is a proxy for banks' total asset exposures, which includes total consolidated assets, derivatives exposures, and certain off-balance-sheet exposures. This is the same as the denominator used for the Basel three ratio. Emerging markets' US$ project finance includes syndicated loans only. GSIBs' apparently low share of international loans reflects the nearly pure domestic focus of the local category banks. Global banking loans and assets are calculated using a sample of more than three thousand five hundred banks
Source International Monetary Fund (2017).

The most common types of banking include private banking, commercial natural persons/retail entities and legal entities/business banking, wholesale or industrial banking, and home banking. Private banking is dedicated to financial advisory and asset management to meet high net worth individuals' or family groups' clients' investment, wealth, financial, and tax planning targets. Commercial banking is aimed at small savers and investors for the natural persons/retail entities, entrepreneurship, and corporate segments. Typical natural persons/retail entities' products include checking and savings accounts, credit cards, cash loans, mortgage loans, etc. Business products also include checking and savings accounts, lines of working or capital credit, guarantees,

2.2.3 Capital Markets

Capital markets can broadly be classified into two types. The type of market where equity and debt securities are issued in a private or public placement for the first time is the primary capital market. The other market, where these securities are traded through organized exchange or over the counter in search of liquidity is the secondary capital market. Financing through capital markets is an effective solution for overcoming a high fixed-costs barrier and addressing non-consensus on how companies are to be managed. It is also an effective platform to respond to growing securitizations markets, and to growing technological and decentralization advances. Capital markets form an investment avenue to mobilize savings in continuous need of new funding. **Constituents of capital markets include (a) capital providers (e.g. funds, banks, insurance companies, corporations, individuals, etc.), (b) market regulators, (c) centralized exchanges and clearing houses, (d) financial registrars and central financial depositaries, (e) intermediaries (e.g. brokers and dealers, underwriters, custodians, accounting companies, etc.), and others.**

Providers of capital are frequently non-bank entities. Non-bank sector is the complementary and alternative form of intermediation in a financial system environment. The loose distinction from the banking sector is the non-requirement of a full banking license, a non-deposit taking role, and non-regulation by any banking regulatory agency. In specific, the NBFIs enhance unbundling, targeting, and specializing to address the growing customized client needs. Depending on the nature of activities, **frequent classifications of NBFIs fall into categories of finance companies** (e.g. (a) developmental finance institutions, (b) leasing companies, (c) microfinance institutions, (d) consumer lending companies, (e) real estate financiers, etc.), securities companies (e.g. brokers and dealers), and investment fund and asset managers (e.g. (a) pension funds, (b) private equity funds, (c) hedge funds, (d) venture capital funds, (e) insurance companies, (f) crowdfunding, etc.). The importance of NBFIs in an economy is growing and is closely correlated to the evolvement of capital markets, a market-based finance in which non-bank financing posts the strongest growth.

Banking sector and capital markets complement each other and are thoroughly interconnected in a mutually beneficial relationship despite numerous thoughts on a "banks versus capital markets" distinction that one evolves at the expense of the other. In one example capital markets' securitizations provide banks with a platform to achieve a lower cost capital stemming from a more direct and liquid form of intermediation. In addition, banks benefit from income that stems from service-based fees in capital markets' advisory business. The additional income then adds more capital for bank stability and lending multiplication capacity. Furthermore, banks' lending attests bankable borrowers' creditworthiness that may then attract more trustworthiness and capital market's solicited third-party investments. In an indirect relationship banks' comparative advantage in credit analysis that comes through exclusivity to information provides a signal to capital market investors on a potential value of companies. Higher-quality lenders provide more informative awareness and signaling on an exchange-traded firm valuation prospects (Billet et al., 1995; Dahiya et al., 2003). Investors' perception of pre-existence of bank lending corresponds to better information and thus likely less severe under-pricing in issuances, to likely lower costs of fundraising as manifested by lower yield spreads, and likely to lower underwriting fees (Drucker & Puri, 2005). The benefits of the two-way relationship include (a) reduction of costs, (b) improving returns, (c) enabling more efficient instruments of risk management, (d) improved screening of borrowers, (e) the capacity to manage financial capital with fewer resources, and (f) increased competitiveness (Bossone & Lee, 2004; Bossone & Promisel, 2012). Capital market developments prompt banks to activities which exploit complementariness and thus near the level playing field with that of non-bank services competition (Bossone, Mahajan, & Zahir, 2003). The interconnectivity provides for a "checks and balances" kind of support between the two segments. The interconnectivity is two sided and needs skilful navigation and management to avoid conflict of interest amidst "steering in the rocky and highly volatile roads." In case of universal banks' broad operations multifaceted interconnectivity may lead to *pari passu* treatment conflict of interest in simultaneous operations akin to (a) issuance of securities to cover own financing needs, (b) assisting other institutions to obtain financing, (c) financing other institutions, (d) providing means of payment, (e) safekeeping securities and cash accounts, (f) brokering and assets managing, etc. In a more direct example, investment banks may be on both the buy and sell side of merger and acquisition transactions. Thus, to avoid conflicted interest one may seek to prohibit the exchange of information between the activities at the origin of issuances and those in the acquisition of such issuances for managing own equity, or proprietary trading thereof.

Despite the gradual retrenchment of advanced economies' GSIBs from operations in the emerging markets, the financial globalization has continued to post growth, with foreign investments of US$ 132 trillion at the end of 2016, versus US$ 103 trillion at the end of 2007.[2] Next to the sheer growth in size, the structural representation has changed. Specifically, foreign investors owned a quarter of equities worldwide at the end of 2016, versus seventeen percent at the end of 2000. Besides, they owned thirty-one percent of bonds at the end of 2016, versus eighteen percent at the end of 2000. Emerging market countries are becoming more connected to global finance. At the end of 2016 emerging markets held sixteen percent of total foreign investments versus eight percent at the end of 2006. Capital markets are the leading stage of connectivity and their forefront growth stems in parallel with advances in information technology and carefully harmonized regulation by governments. Excessive deregulation can have a destabilizing effect on economies given easy access for speculative capital in betting on only partial information about investment opportunities. The 2007/8 crisis showed the resulting negative effects of speculative investments. The period after the 2007/8 crisis is marked by the emergence of a more risk-sensitive, rational, and resilient version of global integration. In this setting, global current and capital account imbalances decreased from 2.5 percent of GDP at the end of 2007 to 1.7 percent at the end of 2016. FDI, as a more committed and longer-term partnership, formed a larger share of gross capital flows at sixty-nine percent share at the end of 2016 versus thirty-six percent share at the end of 2007. Moreover, banks had stronger capital and liquidity cushions (Mckinsey & Company, 2017). As of 2019 COVID-19 induced health and then economic crisis has caused increasing fiscal deficits, then covered by increasing debt burden. However, in the re-occurring of the trend, this time the banking sector and international multilateralism and investments proved more resilient. The increased risks can be seen in peaking equity valuations, structural and supply bottlenecks burning inflation, turn of monetary policy cycle in the United States, an ever more volatile macroeconomic and foreign exchange environment, and greater speculative downside contamination risk due to deeper global integration.

[2] Sourced on March 27, 2018, from Mckinsey Global Institute report "The New Dynamics of Financial Globalization."

2.2.4 *Financial Derivatives' Markets*

The sheer size of financial derivatives' markets and frequent new all-time highs raise eyebrows globally. Headline figures do not speak plentifully about (a) counterparties, (b) collateral, (c) offsetting positions, (d) capacity to execute, or (e) whether trades are centrally cleared, amongst many important underlying sides of the markets. In an effective structural, legal, regulatory, and judicial environment, financial derivatives should be the most liquid financial instruments. Yet, in practice and statute, court rulings in the United Kingdom in the 1990s or in Milan in 2013 proved the financial derivatives contracts unenforceable because of a lack of commercial purpose and unequal counterparties positions when entering the contracts, amongst others (McLannahan, 2018). This book presents research on global trends in financial derivatives use and the local SEE capacities to catch up. It assesses SEE markets' specificities with a structural review of financial derivatives characteristics and practicality for inclusion in the local financial environment and thereafter in the wider regional and global sphere.

In the contemporary global financial market trend, an increasing share of revenue comes from financial derivatives business, and within the industry predominantly from use of hedging-related products. The fixed-income, currencies, and commodities revenues are on an increasing trend, while investment banking revenues are more volatile due to frequent conduct and litigation charges and a shift in favor of boutique services, *inter alia*. The market structural shift appears in a technology-driven migration to a significant off-take by principal trading firms across electronically trading asset classes. Centralizing OTC execution, mandated by regulatory authorities in relation to markets in financial instruments regulation (MiFIR), moves more revenues to organized exchanges. Increasing internationalization of emerging markets' currencies and diversifying away from US$ as the predominant reserve currency adds more importance to hedging foreign exchange risk. In the rise of emerging markets there has been a surge in commodity futures and options trading, led by the geographical market in Asia. In the current environment the progress in the economic cycle from low interest rate environment to higher interest rates creates more attention to interest rate derivatives contracts. The sustainable growth in financial derivatives' markets rests on dominant OTC market by which businesses seek to address needs in increasing operating efficiencies and enhancing counterparty risk mitigation.

Financial derivatives offer various types of risk protection while simultaneously allowing innovative and custom structures on virtually all types of investment assets. The OTC segment accounts for close to ninety percent of the total financial derivatives market in terms of the outstanding notional value of contracts, while the remainder is traded on the regulated organized exchanges. The market volume is about equally split between bilateral trading and multilateral trading, which involves organized marketplaces such as brokers and dealers and electronic platforms. About a third of the notional value of contracts is cleared through central counterparties who consolidate and manage risks for an effective fulfillment of contracts. Bilateral contracts may contain partial risk mitigation through bilateral collateralization, while it is estimated that about a third of contracts' exposures are not secured at all. In financial derivatives' markets the predominant contracts, with more than half the market size, are in swaps, followed by futures and forwards, options, credit derivatives, etc. The predominant underlying assets with more than half the market size are interest rates products, followed by foreign exchange currencies products, credit derivatives' products, commodities' products, etc. The composition did not change drastically in the past other than that the dominating representation by swap derivatives and underlying interest rate assets are decreasing marginally. North America is the dominating geographical market for financial derivatives use and GSIBs are the dominating market users with most holdings and trading.

The building blocks of derivatives markets include amongst others:

1) **Market composition** for product structure that includes economic rationale for hedging, a liquid cash market, market determinable prices, and financial system stability.
2) **Legal and regulatory framework** tackling legal clarity including standards and enforceability, level playing integration and tax field to avoid moral hazard, transparency and disclosures on capital, and accounting and reporting standards.
3) **Infrastructural requirements** on central clearing counterparty (CCP), international swaps and derivatives association (ISDA) master agreement and close-out and netting matters in contracts, certified investors with codes of conduct, strong safety nets, and prudent capital and margin requirements by brokers and dealers and clearing houses.

Most financial derivatives markets developed subsequently to cash markets for already well-established underlying products. Questions pertaining to the effective structure of a financial derivatives' market include ones on whether a financial derivatives' exchange should be part of an existing capital markets' exchange or a separate one and whether it should be a membership or a non-profit exchange. The primary and fundamental element in developing financial derivatives' markets is in knowledge creation and sharing for universal broad awareness of products characteristics. Financial derivatives provide for a more effective risk allocation with minimal upfront investment. Primarily, financial derivatives enable price-discovery capacity. In addition, financial derivatives can be tailored to specific needs, thus allowing flexibility and more incentive on innovation. On the flip side, financial derivatives are (a) complex to understand, (b) they allow a tracking error margin against the underlying asset, and (c) they call for frequent capital reserves, margin posting, and short-term tax accounting complexities.

Financial markets frequently function in a beehive trend in times of prosperity, but when tide turns and panic begins to spread, independence and shielding factor exacerbate volatility in the market. Such trend then highlights an example of investors' irrational behavior. Additional evidence of such behavior is in put-to-call options market ratios, otherwise known as "fear gauge" and a contrarian indicator. Put-to-call ratios reach peak levels in imminent pre-crisis periods as pessimistic sentiment prevails and peak economy liquidity acts as an additional tail wind to downhill spiraling markets' performance (The Economic Times, 2016). Global capital and economic volatility spillovers create a substantial peril to developing markets due to lower scale of comparable market tools and lower level of efficiencies to readily counter downside shocks, or, equivalently, to recognize opportunity for upside shocks transmission. Financial derivatives' markets have supported capital inflows into emerging markets economies while, on the other hand, they also exacerbated volatility and later accelerated capital outflow in negative economic impact trends. With evidence from the 2007/8 crisis, Cetorelli and Goldberg's (2011) report showed an imminence in the occurrence of an emerging market slowdown. Capital placements in emerging markets decreased from over US$ one trillion to under US$ three hundred billion in just over two years, from year-end 2007 to year-end 2009. Cetorelli and Goldberg considered one hundred thirteen countries, ninety-four of which were emerging markets, to test with OLS estimation and fixed data effects method the impacts on banks' balance sheets and cross-border transactions in relation to endogenized US$ stress events. Financial derivatives characteristics may provide an opportunity to discover risk information and to manage risk exposures effectively, which can benefit emerging markets in their growth and integration into global capital market.

The state of financial derivatives' use manifests that in the decade preceding 2010, the financial derivatives markets in emerging economies expanded four times, to a daily turnover of over six percent of GDP, in contrast to thirty-six percent in advanced economies. In parallel, a growing share of transactions is done cross-border and offshore for EME currencies. In comparison, the selected SEE countries' financial derivatives trade is immaterial for OTC markets, while it is entirely inexistent for regulated exchange-traded markets. Triennial survey[3] demonstrates correlation in the growth of GDPPC and the growth of financial derivatives' markets volume in emerging economies. Besides, the same survey shows that foreign exchange derivatives' turnover in emerging economies, versus advanced economies, is predominantly with commercial and investment banks' counterparties, versus other NBFIs such as pension and hedge funds. An increase of institutional investors in emerging economies, including pension funds, hedge funds, and insurance companies, is outpacing the issuance of local assets. It creates a supply to demand imbalance but also an opportunity gap for financial derivatives to address (Halilbegovic & Mekic, 2017). Currency and capital movement policy controls curb turnover in financial derivatives. Frequently control policies are implemented with the intention to minimize speculation and exchange rate misalignment. As legislation and regulation updates frequently fall

[3] The BIS Triennial Central Bank Survey enhances the semiannual survey by collecting data from a much broader sample of derivatives dealers—as many as 53 jurisdictions participate in the survey. Like the semiannual survey, the Triennial Survey captures notional amounts outstanding and gross market values. In addition, it captures turnover in OTC interest rate and foreign exchange derivatives markets. The semiannual survey is conducted under the auspices of the Committee on the Global Financial System and provides information about the size and structure of the largest OTC derivatives markets. It captures notional amounts outstanding, gross market values, gross credit exposures, and Herfindahl concentration measures. Central Banks and other authorities from the following 13 jurisdictions currently participate in the survey: Australia, Belgium, Canada, France, Germany, Italy, Japan, the Netherlands, Spain, Sweden, Switzerland, the United Kingdom, and the United States.

behind market innovation, in this example controls often only suppress onshore markets into offshore non-deliverable markets. It in turn causes trading activity to fragment as spot and residents' trading activities are prone to direct control (Tsuyuguchi & Wooldridge, 2008). Typically, restrictions are imposed on cross-border deliverability of a currency via a requirement for central banks' approval for foreign exchange transactions. The role of central banks heavily influences the level and volatility of an emerging markets' currency, the internationalization of that local currency, and the participation of foreign investors (Canales-Kriljenko, 2004). Participation of foreign investors is closely linked to the development stage of emerging countries' capital markets as multi-currency FDIs and portfolio investors are heavily deterred by currency volatility and a lack of hedging opportunities (Ramaswamy & Scott, 2005). The trait of an underdeveloped foreign exchange market and capital market altogether is often first demonstrated by low foreign investors' participation in local bonds products. Such hesitance owes to absence of a liquid market to hedge currency risk as an underdeveloped money market makes it difficult to execute foreign exchange swaps and short-term funding. Therefore, such environment exhibits cash market growth limits. Underdeveloped cash market then reveals non-existence of a prerequisite to further financial derivatives' market development.

Global turnover in foreign exchange markets is about thirty times greater than trade in goods and services. This ratio indicates that turnover in internationalized currencies is generated by trade in financial assets versus exclusively in physical assets. The constructive development of financial derivatives' markets needs to be supported by sound macroeconomic fundamentals, which enable growth in use, as well as updated financial policies and regulations for sustainable implementation (Lien & Zhang, 2008). Implicit policies in the contemporary geopolitical economic scene are frequently directed through financial markets' tools and in strategic prelude through foreign exchange currency value. Examples of such are discussions on establishment of the EU competitor to SWIFT system (Munchau, 2018), considerations to establishment of central banks digital currencies in response to the rise of blockchain technology reliability and opaque competition in Bitcoin or Libra, and in historic accussations of Japan's or China's prolonged currency manipulation strength to artificially support current account positions and export economies. Lee and Wang (2015) studied quarterly data on twenty-nine countries from 2000 to 2011, in a mix of emerging and advanced markets, by empirically testing with the PMG estimation the significance of relationship between foreign exchange rates and listed stocks' prices. According to their results, the two parameters have a long-run cointegrating relationship, short-run negative correlation, and long-run, post error correction adjustment, positive relationship. These results prove dynamic features in the foreign exchange markets' capacities.

2.2.5 *Infrastructure Setting and Institutional Capacity*

Infrastructure setting theme is very broad and diverse to be able to provide a holistic assessment within the limits of the presentation in this book. This review assesses a narrower scope on the following themes: (a) available exchanges' custodian and depository capacities, (b) clearing and settlement providers, (c) clearing and settlement electronic versus manual execution, (d) CCP presence, (e) settlement cycle days required, (f) existence of international custodians, (g) existence of master ISDA, (h) nature of trading system in electronic versus manual type, (i) number of trading days, (j) close-out and netting matters in contracts, (k) foreign investors' participation, (l) participation of certified investors with codes of conduct, (m) capital safety nets availability, (n) and capital margin requirements by brokers and dealers. CCPs are FIs acting as clearing houses between counterparties to contracts in one or more financial markets. CCPs are buyers to every seller and sellers to every buyer, thereby ensuring the future performance of open contracts. The observed countries do not contain a qualified CCP and market stakeholders face higher hurdles in assessing counterparties' credit risks. ISDA is an organization of OTC market participants, wherein ISDA master agreement terms are a form of standardized derivatives contract mandated for single and multiple jurisdiction dealings. ISDA terms include items such as (a) netting, (b) set-off, (c) force majeure, (d) grace period, (e) close-outs, (f) credit annex, (g) jurisdiction, etc., with high-level requirements for participants in the standardized terms. Advanced economies comprise a diverse set of private and public exchanges, custodians, brokers and dealers, and overall qualified counterparties enabling an increase in competition, economies of scale, and greater market access to public.

The role of infrastructure is a founding element and often a lengthy prerequisite to develop an organized exchange, in particular a regulated organized exchange. In combination with the general absence of strong market liquidity in the selected SEE countries' capital markets, the exchange-traded markets lack infrastructure capacities. In such an environment progress is often identified through mutually beneficial partnerships and joint ventures between the existing stock exchanges (Crane et al., 1995). Partnerships form an apparent trend in the selected SEE markets as is seen in the 2014 establishment of SEE link infrastructure for real-time trading of securities between Skopje, Sofia, Zagreb, Banja Luka, Sarajevo, and Belgrade Stock Exchanges' listings. It is also apparent in data exchange agreements between the individual SEE stock exchanges with the Vienna Stock Exchange. Vienna Stock Exchange also produces separate indices for the SEE markets, which creates market visibility for the inter-regional international investors. More recently, in 2015, the Zagreb Stock Exchange acquisition of Ljubljana Stock Exchange is another example of integration. As data information between investors is more readily accessible and as trading processes are moving to closer harmonization, the next step forward may appear in integrating cross-memberships on the stock exchanges. In this trend competition increases through search for more cost-effective, leaner, and broader service then altogether increasing the underlying markets liquidity base. To resolve hurdles, it is important to develop better understanding of financial derivatives and securitized instruments concepts in both theory and then in best-use practical examples. Experiences from the 2007/8 crisis, the Euro financial crisis, and the COVID-19 crisis are a fundamental source of knowledge sharing for learnings-based sustainable application of innovative financial products in emerging smaller economies.

None of the selected SEE capital markets exhibits a qualified CCP capacity due to the inherent illiquidity and shallow sub-elements equity base, which is necessary to meet European Market Infrastructure Regulation (EMIR) standards for close-out netting in capital calls. For this reason, in this book a **consideration is given to potential establishment of a regional CCP** that might fill the capacity for the whole regional market on its already evolving integration path. Creation of CCP enables larger international investments and broader investors' diversification, an improved liquidity in higher trading volumes and listings, and lower counterparty collateral postings toward net versus gross open positions. Overall, the efficient CCP strengthens capital market resilience and provides an opportunity for strong medium- and long-term economic gains. In consideration of the high financial costs of starting a CCP, the case of regional CCP is a more economically viable start-up option due to lower minimum capital and upfront costs per country.[4] Global regulation provides a tailwind to the process as the like of MiFID II clearly concentrates an increasing trading volume through organized exchanges; yet headwind risk exists in the legal space and in regulatory governance differences. Despite the increasing convergence to the harmonized EU legislative rules, risks are poised in difficulties to have local brokers' regional partnerships with a CCP and in implementation of regional coverage funds. While individual SEE capital markets have established guarantee and investor protection funds, in scope these are limited to cover fractional daily cash settlement trades. Besides, they do not encompass a qualified CCP role with multiple lines of defense securing market resilience from default failure. These include (a) stronger variable and initial margins, (b) stronger CCP reserves, (c) stronger than available investor and guarantee funds coverage amounts, and, finally, (d) a formidable CCP capital base. Overall, the SEE markets share traits of fragmentation which undermines a sustainable growth.

2.2.6 *Legal, Regulatory, and Accounting Environment*

Capital market changes are rapid and are driven by a rise in international interconnectivity and by advancements in informational technology. The evolution in legal standards tends to follow ex-post versus ex-ante disposition of market shifts. Legislation, largely encompassing topics of (a) flow of capital, (b) securities, (c) exchanges, (d) consumer protection, and (e) competition protection is construed at an individual country or union level. Besides, more advanced markets (e.g. market in the United States) frequently pioneer in innovative legislation as other individual countries or unions seek reciprocal position when altering their own legislation. The common view, in the perspective that finance is a set of legal contracts, is that the fundamental differences in financial development stage are pre-set and better explained by differences in the stage of legal system development (La Porta, Lopez-de-Silanes, Shleifer, & Vishny, 2000). It should be noted that in the contemporary market performance, conduct and

[4] EMIR minimum requirement is EUR 7.5 million for capital base, with additional contributions to default fund.

litigation charges materially impact the financial profitability metrics of FIs. The implications of the recent more stringent legal and regulatory standards reflect at first in the increasing costs of capital then hurting returns on equity. Implications can also be seen in businesses' shift to innovation and technology improvements to reach cost-cutting and an increasing access to clients. In a reverse relationship, an excessive growth in derivatives contracts occurred after 1999 when the Glass-Steagall Act[5] in the United States was repealed, which then allowed banks to re-engage as brokerage shops and in proprietary trading. In later years segments of the Dodd-Frank Act[6] comprehensive financial regulatory overhaul has been under scrutiny for reversal. Those segments pertain to the classification of municipal bonds as high-quality liquid assets, a lower threshold for capital retention at custodian banks, liberalization from Volcker rule[7] ban on speculative trading that is applicable for banks with total assets under US$ ten billion, etc. The period following the 2007/8 crisis has fast sped introductions of standards such as **Basel III and IV, IFRS 9, and MiFIR**.

The observed SEE countries are either part of the EU or are on an accession path to join the EU. As the research countries are approaching harmonization of legislation and regulation under the EU *acquis*, in relevance this overview presents the competent EU authorities. European Supervisory Authorities are formed by three independent institutions working closely together, specifically European Securities and Markets Authority (ESMA), European Banking Authority (EBA), and European Insurance and Occupational Pensions Authority (EIOPA). These institutions closely collaborate with the supervisory authorities at the individual country level. ESMA (a) supervises the securities sector, (b) forms a single rulebook for EU financial markets, (c) promotes supervisory convergence, and (d) is the direct supervisor of the Credit Rating Agencies and Trade

[5] The Glass-Steagall Act (1933) effectively separated commercial banking from investment banking and created the Federal Deposit Insurance Corporation (FDIC), amongst other things.

[6] The Dodd-Frank Act (2010) made changes affecting all federal financial regulatory agencies and almost every part of the US financial services industry. It eliminated Office of Thrift Supervision, assigned new responsibilities to existing agencies such as FDIC and created new ones, such as Consumer Financial Protection Bureau (CFPB).

[7] The Volcker Rule (2014) prohibits banks from conducting certain investment activities with their own accounts and limits their dealings with hedge funds and private equity funds, also covered funds.

Repositories in the EU. EBA is a banking regulatory agency on the EU banks promoting single rulebook and conducting stress tests to promote increased transparency and stability. EBA holds the power to overrule regulators at the individual country level within the EU. EIOPA is a financial regulatory institution that supervises the insurance and pension sector. European Central Bank (ECB) administers the monetary policy for the Eurozone. ECB's capital stock is owned by the central banks of all the EU member states. Looking ahead, it remains to be seen where mandatory OTC clearing of the euro-denominated products will occur in the medium to long run following Brexit completion as of early 2021 and given London's precedent locational prevalence in this industry continentally and globally. Early on it could be observed that GSIBs, namely Deutsche Bank and Credit Suisse, principally moved their clearing activities from London to Frankfurt. Besides, further reactions were observed in (a) transfers out of the United Kingdom by Refinitiv foreign exchange swaps platform transferring its US$ three hundred billion a day business to Dublin, (b) Chicago Mercantile Exchange's BrokerTec platform shifting US$ two hundred and fifty billion a day repo trading business to Amsterdam, (c) CBOE setting up derivatives trading in Amsterdam, and (d) London Stock Exchange (LSE) transferring its bond MTS Cash company US$ thirteen billion a day intermediary business to Italy, amongst others. The trend continued after Brexit, as January 2021 results already recorded that Amsterdam location surpassed London for the first time as Europe's largest listed shares trading location. Daily shares trading in Amsterdam increased to Euro 9.2 billion (roughly US$ 7.5 billion) versus Euro 8.6 billion (roughly US$ seven billion) in London. Locationally, London marked a loss of Euro 6.5 billion (roughly US$ 5.3 billion)[8] of daily deals. Accordingly, the shift was prompted by the EU ban on the EU-based institutions to trade in the United Kingdom's exchanges and trading avenues due to non-equivalent cross-border recognition on the supervisory status.

[8] Year-end 2020 exchange rate is used.

2.2.6.1 *Basel Regulations*

Prior to the **historical evolution** through Basel reform, in the period preceding 1988, banking regulation was largely determined at an individual country level. Under the increasing globalization, banks' international expansion created more competition and a need for regulatory coordination. In the initial global expansion, the Japanese banks' model was considered as aggressive by Western advanced economies' banks. Accusations arose about unfair competition as Japanese banks carried relatively lower capital ratios. In resolution, Basel I was introduced globally to define both risk weights for assets and minimum capital requirements. It was agreed in 1988 and was first signed by G11[9] countries to be followed by OECD[10] countries and most of emerging markets. Basel II was adopted in 1998 introducing banks' own risk weightings on assets through internal ratings. In the 2007/8 crisis, banks' capital deficit became apparent, and in 2009 Basel II.5 was introduced to address minimum assets risk weightings, principally aimed at securitized assets and trading transactions. Basel III was agreed in 2010, comprising Pillar One requirements on a stricter capital base, an introduction of capital buffers, an introduction of liquidity coverage ratio (LCR), an introduction of net stable funding ratio (NSFR), and an introduction of leverage ratio (LR). Basel III, as was the case with its predecessors, is to be implemented gradually and in a longer period, varying by the individual country's regulatory level standards.

Basel III Pillar One increased capital requirements, targeting minimum Tier One capital at six percent, minimum total capital at eight percent, and minimum total capital plus conservation buffer at 10.5 percent of risk-weighted assets. Common Tier One capital consists of (a) common shares, (b) shares premium, (c) retained earnings, (d) accumulated other comprehensive income and other discloses reserves, and (e) common shares issued by consolidated subsidiaries of the bank and held by third parties (otherwise restricted minority interest). The deductions

[9] Belgium, Canada, France, Germany, Italy, Japan, the Netherlands, Sweden, Switzerland, the United Kingdom, the United States, and Luxembourg.

[10] An intergovernmental economic organization with 35-member countries, founded in 1961 to stimulate economic progress and world trade. It is a forum of countries describing themselves as committed to democracy and market economy, providing a platform to compare policy experiences, seeking answers to common problems, identifying good practices, and coordinating domestic and international policies of its members.

on Tier One capital are to include (a) goodwill and other intangibles, (b) deferred tax assets, (c) cash-flow hedge reserves, (d) gains on sales related to securitization transactions, (e) defined benefit pension funds' assets and liabilities, and (f) all unrealized gains and losses due to changes in a bank's own credit risk. Additional Tier One capital can form up to 1.5% ratio. Additional Tier One capital is formed from regulatory adjustments and Tier Two capital turning into Tier One capital. Contractual terms of Tier Two capital are to include a clause that allows, at the discretion of the relevant authority, a write-off or conversion to common shares if a bank is judged non-viable. Therefore, Tier Two capital is considered as "gone concern" and can form maximum two percent of total capital percentage ratio. A capital conservation buffer is to comprise additionally up to 2.5% ratio and is composed of capital, profit, or dividend distribution constraints. A capital countercyclical buffer is subject of none to 2.5 additional capital percent ratio with common equity Tier One capital ratio. The additional buffer is applicable on systemically important FIs.

Leverage ratio is to exceed three percent of Tier One capital level to on- and off-balance sheet exposures. Besides, leverage ratio supplements risk-based capital requirements by targeting off-balance sheet items. A credit conversion factor of one hundred percent is to be used for all off-balance sheet items other than for those unconditionally cancellable by banks at any time and for which a ten percent credit conversion factor is applicable.

LCR tracks short-term, up to thirty days, liquid assets sufficiency to cover cash outflows by at least one hundred percent (or ninety percent equivalent applicable until the end of 2018). Liquid assets should ideally be eligible at central banks as equivalent of cash collateral and should contain characteristics of (a) low credit and market risk, (b) ease and certainty in valuation, (c) low correlation with risky assets, and (d) an active and sizable market. Level One liquid assets include cash, central bank reserves, and zero percent risk-weighted marketable securities that are traded and show a proven record of liquidity in stressed conditions. Level Two liquid assets can comprise up to forty percent of total, must contain a minimum fifteen percent haircut and include assets that are twenty percent risk-weighted marketable securities, are traded and show a proven record of liquidity in stressed conditions or are non-FIs corporate and covered bonds credit rated at least AA-equivalent. Net cash outflows are tracked in stress scenarios and as an aggregate of total cash outflows in the following thirty days subtracted for the higher of seventy-five percent of the same cash outflows, or of total cash inflows at the same time. Stressed scenarios are to include significant declines in profitability and solvency, credit downgrade, and a material event calling into question the quality of the institution.

NSFR tracks sufficient access to funding that is necessary to sustain assets placements. The ratio targets (a) available high-quality sources of funds including capital, (b) preferred stocks with maturity longer than one year, (c) liabilities with maturities longer than one year, and (d) "sticky" short-term deposits. Implementing the target funding weighting factor on each component, the available stable funding amount sufficiency is intended to cover the required stable funding amount.[11]

Basel III Pillar Two, supervision, requirements address firm-wide governance and risk management capturing the risk of off-balance sheet exposures, securitization and trading activities, and operating risk. These include (a) increasing capital charges for risk concentrations, (b) sound compensation practices, (c) valuation practices, (d) stress testing using value at risk, (e) capital charges on CCPs at two percent, (f) charges for trading book and securitization stress scenario risk increases, (g) more restrictive netting of offsetting positions, etc.

Basel III Pillar Three, market discipline, requirements adhere to stricter (a) frequency, (b) transparency, (c) accuracy, (d) timeliness, and (e) completeness in disclosures on transactions, exposures, and capital. The focus of Pillar Three is on qualitative supervision by regulators on banks' internal risk controls and capital assessment procedures. Basel III increases capital charges materially and makes certain banking activities much more capital intensive.

The advocates of **further regulatory improvements** often point to Basel III regulations' excessive orientation on the numerator definition of qualifying regulatory capital and increased charges of capital, which is a narrower theme *vis à vis* improved clarity in the definition of the denominator, of assets' risk weights. In support of this view, undeniably, the denominator in the capital adequacy ratio is the larger determining factor for the output capital adequacy ratio limits. Generally, Basel III measures have not changed much compared to Basel II. Basel III is characterized by applying more risk-sensitive requirements. These are: (a) stricter, one hundred percent off-balance sheet items credit conversion

[11] The list of available and required funding classifications is available at: https://www.bis.org/publ/bcbs271.pdf.

factor, (b) application of new liquidity factors with greater assets risk-weights coverage, and (c) the incentive to move to advanced internal rating based (IRB) approach by improving risk management systems. It reduces the required total regulatory capital *vis-à-vis* the standardized approach of applying risk weights based on external credit ratings. While the IRB approach shows an advancement toward more differentiation between safer and riskier credit, a long road lies ahead in diversifying beyond current methods of funding type, exposure type, or broad model definitions.

The regulatory reform following the 2007/8 crisis also ensures that banks' liabilities structure provides sufficient total loss absorbing capacity by means of total loss absorbing capital (TLAC) or minimum regulatory eligible liabilities (MREL) for globally systemically important banks. TLAC and MREL have been enacted in the EU since 2019 and in phases through the end of 2022 for TLAC and the end of 2024 for MREL. The final TLAC requirement is for eighteen percent of risk-weighted assets or 6.75% of total assets. MREL requirements as a proportion of total liabilities and own funds are likely to be similar, while still subject to agreement and legal implementation. Significant innovation would be the introduction of loss absorbing capital subordination contractually, statutorily, and structurally. Indeed, MREL and TLAC are expected to introduce the likes of mandatory subordinate debt bonds with equal low-risk assignment within the EU countries. The regulatory standards are still fine-tuned at the country level within the EU capturing the minimum of Basel III capital to risk-weighted assets (RWAs), or double of Basel III capital base when compared to total liabilities ratio. Primary TLAC and MREL targets are intended for GSIBs though with an ongoing expansion to all banks. Basel IV advancements are expected to be finalized between 2021 and 2025 as they will expectedly capture (a) floor for banks to hold capital requirement per 72.5% of standardized rating approach risk calculation in their internal rating risk-based methodology calculation, (b) increase of leverage ratio equal to fifty percent of risk-adjusted return on capital for GSIBs, and (c) simultaneous reductions in standardized risk weights for low-risk mortgage loans.

2.2.6.2 *International Financial Reporting Standards*

In the 2007/8 crisis, accounting weaknesses showed in the necessity of market value adjustments. Leniency in loan loss provisioning led to an erosion of tangible capital in the banking sector. Examples of inadequacies are excessive mark-to-market or value adjustment and net present value inadequate loan loss provisioning for credit event before impairment. In response, IFRS 9 includes a forward outlook on performance and expected losses. In 2009, International Accounting Standards Board (IASB) issued IFRS 9 to replace International Accounting Standard thirty-nine (IAS 39) with an effective implementation from 2018. IAS 39 and its delayed recognition of credit losses were considered as one of reasons for banks' failures during the 2007/8 crisis (Table 2.4).

IFRS 9 creates a significant departure from IAS 39 in the requirement for loan losses to be based on expected losses, without requirement for a credit loss event to have taken place. **For the purposes of loan loss provisioning, under IFRS 9** loans are assessed through the following stages:

1) **Stage one**—Not subject to observable events directly linked to default. Provisions to reflect losses expected to be incurred in the next one-year time.
2) **Stage two**—Loans' credit quality is adversely affected by observable events but without observable losses. Provisions to reflect expected losses over full loan life.
3) **Stage three**—Loans for which losses have been observed and provisions to capture expected losses for full loan life.

Another key area tackled by IFRS 9 is hedge accounting, whereby one hundred percent provision is required on the net market value of financial derivatives (Table 2.5).

Thus, the key advantages of IFRS 9 are early recognition of credit losses, forward outlook on performance, and greater convergence with regulatory capital approaches. IFRS 9 materially increases provisions versus prior practice. Furthermore, large data are required over the life of a loan, which results in possible subjective modeling of qualitative measures.

The analysis of the accounting framework of each individual country is not included, due to the shorter scope of research. Besides, financial systems of all the countries are almost synchronized in the application of the latest global standards.

Table 2.4 IFRS 9—Compatibility with Basel III

Approach to Credit Measurement	*Mode of Credit Risk Computation*	*Provisions for Treatment of Loss*	*IFRS Usability*
Standardized	Regulatory prescribed risk weights used in computation of risk capital	• Incurred loss provision • If a loss has not occurred, a general provision on a group of exposures is added to Tier Two capital, subject to limit of 1.25 percent of risk-weighted assets (RWA)	Data used for computation of regulatory capital do not support data requirement for accounting calculations
IRB	Bank's own estimates of probability of default (PD) over one-year time horizon. Regulatory prescribed loss given default (LGD), exposure at default (EAD), and maturity	Provision is compared to expected loss (EL): • If EL exceeds provision, excess to be reduced from capital • If provision exceeds EL, excess to be added to Tier Two capital and subject to limit of 0.6 percent of RWA	Data used in the estimates of PD can be used for accounting calculations, but with adjustments
Advanced IRB	Bank's own PD, LGD, EAD, and maturity over one-year time horizon	Provision is compared to EL: • If EL exceeds provision, excess to be reduced from capital • If provision exceeds EL, excess to be added to Tier Two capital and subject to limit of 0.6 percent of RWA	Data used in the estimates of PD, LGD, and EAD can be used for accounting calculations, but with adjustments

Source Author

Table 2.5 IFRS 9—Key differences from Basel III

Factors for adjustment	*Basel*	*IFRS*
Time horizon	One-year PD	One-year PD
Observation period	Five years for natural persons/retail entities' exposure, otherwise seven years	No specific period
Statistical approach	Hybrid of point-in-time to through-the-cycle to get to historical long-run average default rates	Point-in-time
Default	Usually ninety days past due	No specific definition. Usually not beyond ninety days past due
Floor	PD and LGD are subject to floors	None
EL	PD multiplied with LGD and multiplied with EAD	PD multiplied with present value of cash shortfalls

Source Author

2.2.6.3 *Markets in Financial Instruments Directive and Regulation*

EMIR is a body of European legislation, defined and supervised under ESMA. Its task is to regulate OTC derivatives, including requirements for CCPs and trade repositories reporting for trade and risk management standards under the objective of reducing systemic risks. EMIR addresses the requirement for the execution of sufficiently liquid OTC derivatives transactions on the regulated exchange or electronic platform. It also requires initial and variation margin posting for cleared and non-cleared OTC transactions. In this context EMIR addresses the transfer of derivative trading activity from the opaque bilateral OTC market to the better regulated and more transparent exchange trade. MiFID II is a legislation under ESMA, applicable across the EU for the accompanying MiFIR regulation implemented in the EU member countries as of January 2018. MiFIR contains standards and requirements on trading platforms, systems, and processes, with a focus on OTC derivatives. MiFIR regulation encompasses rules and guidelines on execution venues, transaction execution, as well as on pre- and post-trade transparency on an increasing number of financial products. The new framework improves investor protection (e.g. prohibition of sale of binary options to natural persons/retail entities and restrictions on contracts for differences sale to natural persons/retail entities) and improves financial markets' functioning to a more efficient, resilient, and transparent model. While EMIR is concerned with improving market stability and reducing counterparty risk,

MiFID is primarily aimed at improving transparency. **MiFID addresses:**

1) Conduct of business and organizational requirements for investment firms. Strong focus is shifted to extended definitions of investment advice and to documenting relationship with clients. Managing bodies of investment firms are to be held accountable for the firm's strategy; additional criteria are introduced for qualified senior staff; and new instructions are included on inducements and remuneration.
2) Authorization requirements for regulated markets.
3) Regulatory reporting of conducted trade transactions to avoid market abuse. Record keeping of trade transactions for operators in MTF, Organized Trading Facilities (OTF), and Systemic Internalizers. MTF trading venues require lighter membership requirements to regulated exchanges and are usually electronic trading systems controlled by approved market operators who play a neutral role in bringing together multiple trading interests. OTF trading venues do not participate in equity trading and represent a trading system bringing together multiple trading interests through active engagement and with own membership requirements. Systemic Internalizers are counterparties who operate on a non-discretionary basis for a single-party interest. For all non-regulated markets, reporting requirements include time, price, and volume, but not necessarily information on investor's identity.
4) Trade transparency obligation for shares. For trading venues these include pre-trade indication of quotes and depth of trading, post-trade display of traded quotes and volume near-time, publication of public data within fifteen minutes, and a stricter exception regime.

For investment firms these include publication of offers, publication through Approved Publication Arrangement,[12] an obligation to report data to national authorities, and trading obligation to regulated market or OTF.
5) Rules for admission of financials instruments on trading. ESMA retains intervention power for limitations on positions.

In the outlook of MiFID II, provisions regulating the non-discriminatory access to CCPs, trading venues, and benchmarks are designed to increase competition. These provisions together with EMIR are expected to increase centralized trading, in particular the organized trading obligation for derivatives product class. In this context a new trading venue category, OTF, is every multilateral system that is not a regulated market, but in which multiple third-party buying and selling occurs. In addition, the MiFID II directive provides more resilient and transparent rules and guidelines on pre- and post- trade transparency on an increasing number of financial products designed to increase competition and centralized trading. Investment banks and brokerage shops face the necessity to unbundle research from trading services. In the outcome commissions and fees might be lower for end-investors; but the quality of research might also be lowered, and more investment concentration could follow in the direction of optioning on passive investments through indexes, tracking exchange-traded funds (ETFs), and alike.

2.3 Global and the Selected Southeast European Capital Markets Comparison Preview

This section presents the tabular and graphical comparative preview of the structure and performance trends of global and the SEE markets. As evident from the available data presented in Table 2.6 below, the selected SEE markets constitute only a marginal fraction of the global economy, at 0.2 percent of global aggregate GDP. This distinction increases further when comparing the size of the financial market, which is at 0.06 percent of global aggregate, and the size of the regulated stock exchanges' market, which is at 0.08 percent of global aggregate capitalization. Aggregate

[12] Approved Publication Arrangement (APA) is an organization authorized to publish trade reports on behalf of investment firms according to Article (4)(1)(52) MiFID II.

Table 2.6 Preview of financial system and capital markets in SEE countries

*Year-end 2021 or latest available**	*Croatia*	*Serbia*	*B&H*	*Slovenia*	*North Macedonia*	*World (Aggregate SEE as proportional percent)***
GDP (US$ billion)	57.4	46.8	21.5	57.6	13.3	84500 (0.2%)
Regulated stock market capitalization (US$ billion)	41.2	3.1	3.6	50.1	4.5	92000 (0.1%)
Stock market domestic shares turnover ratio percent (value traded/market capitalization)	0.6	0.3	2.1	1.8	3	104
OTC (US$ billion):						
1—OTC markets turnover	1.1	28.1 ***	0.002	37.3	2.1	NA
2—Financial derivatives: a) notional contracts value b) gross market value	NA NA	NA NA	NA NA	NA NA	NA NA	580000 16000

*Sourced from World Bank (2022) and per macroeconomic indicators shown in Appendix A.2.1 and per individual SEE country sources shown in Figs. 3.1–3.5.
**Estimated global data and an aggregate of SEE countries as a share of global.
***Year-end 2016 annual report data from the Republic of Serbia Securities Commission (2017). Large majority of recorded OTC transactions involves Central Bank repo transactions and primary sales transactions.

global financial assets' size is greater than the global economy as measured by GDP. However, financial assets in the selected SEE countries are smaller than the size of respective GDP, with the standalone exception of Croatia.

Importantly, liquidity of capital markets in the selected SEE countries is significantly lower than the respective global averages. OTC markets globally outpace the economic output while data for SEE are largely unavailable due to very seldom occurrence and almost exclusive private non-disclosed nature business practice. The scale of turnover per an average transaction is low and volatility in annual turnover is high. In practice these results may be symptomatic of a high concentration to a small number of large transactions that greatly impact the aggregate annual turnover. Individual selected SEE markets are assessed in detail in the following chapters.

Through proportional share to GDP Fig. 2.3 displays a compilation in aggregate data on bank credit to the private sector, pension funds assets, mutual funds assets, and insurance premiums. It serves as a relative benchmark of an individual country's financial institutions depth. Per apparent Croatia and Slovenia are leaders and principally so due to reformed pension system under the World Bank multi-pillar model moving assets from state budget to private management of funds in market investments. All of the SEE countries are laggards when compared to European averages and in particular when compared to more developed markets. Part Four of the book examines in-detail financial and capital market developments at individual SEE country level.

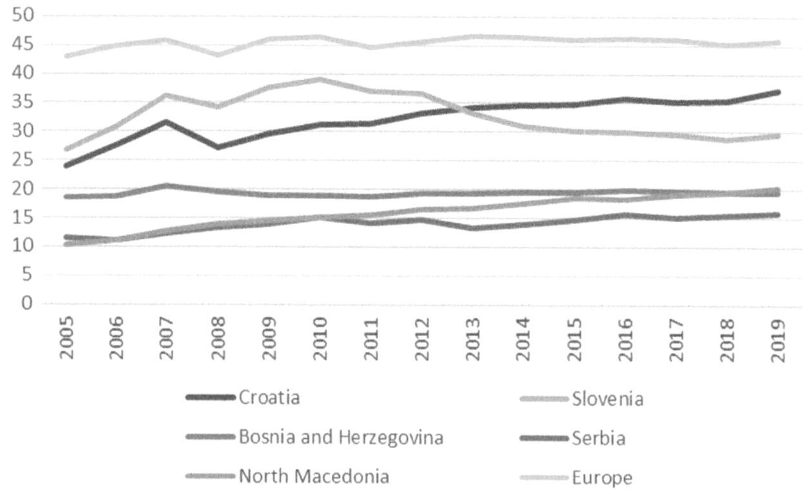

Fig. 2.3 Financial Institution Depth Index (in percent) (*Source* International Monetary Fund [2022])

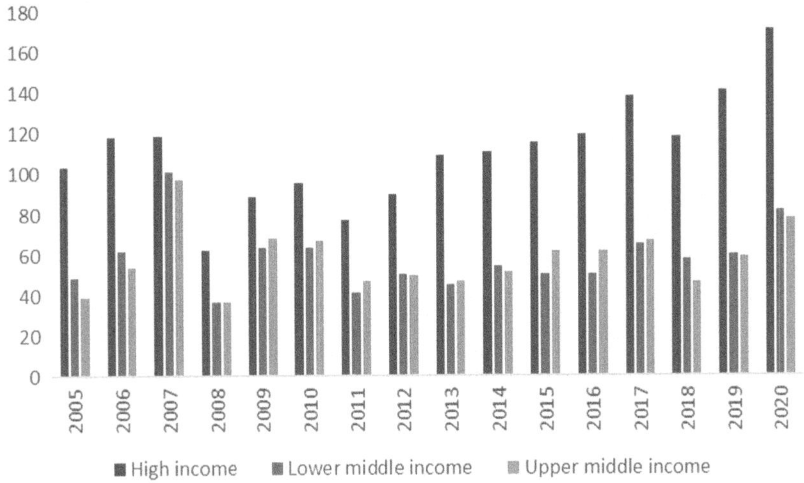

Fig. 2.4 Market capitalization of listed domestic companies (as percent of GDP)—global aggregates (*Source* World Bank [2022])

Figure 2.4 infers that capitalization of stock exchanges in high-income countries[13] has recovered faster from the 2007/8 crisis, while middle-income countries la in the comparative recovery. Besides, it reveals that the ratio of capitalization of regulated stock exchanges to GDP in high-income countries is approximately two times higher than that of both the middle-income groups. Upper and lower middle income countries have similar capitalization levels and interestingly lower middle-income countries capitalization levels recover from crises slumps at similar pace to upper middle-income countries.

Ratio of capitalization of regulated stock exchanges to GDP in the observed SEE countries, presented in Fig. 2.5, shows relatively lower levels than those of global averages for the benchmark income groups of countries. Croatia is an exception as the capitalization level has matched that of the equivalent upper middle-income global income level group average. Meanwhile in 2007 Croatia has graduated to the high-income country group level and when compared to that benchmark group it is a relative laggard, as is Slovenia. In trend comparison the decline of the

[13] World Bank income classification levels are shown in the Appendix A.1—Table A.1.

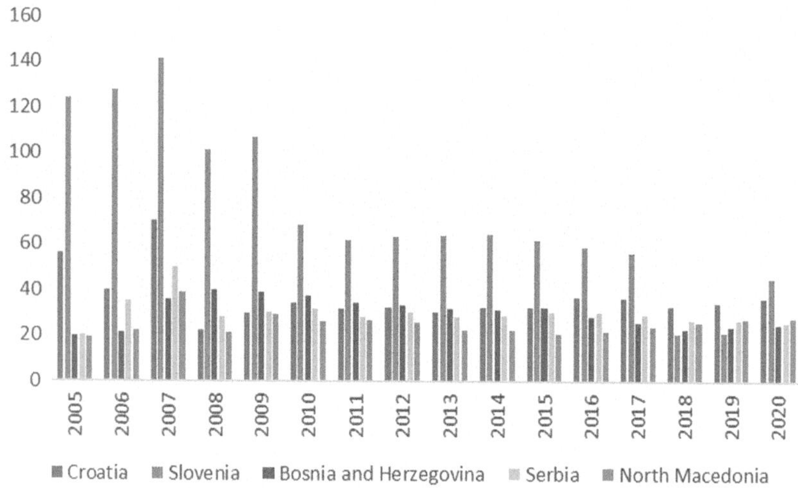

Fig. 2.5 Market capitalization of listed domestic companies (as percent of GDP)—Individual SEE countries (*Source* World Bank [2022], see stock exchanges, and national statistical offices)

capitalization of the selected SEE capital markets during the 2007/8 crisis was steeper and the recovery was slower relative to the benchmark income groups of countries. In the period ex-post 2007/8 crisis the divergence of performance of the regulated stock exchange in Croatia continued through capitalization on ZSE versus the other observed SEE countries. North Macedonia continuously shows the lowest figures, Serbia the steepest fall, and B&H has performed relatively stronger than Slovenia.

The ratio of turnover to capitalization as a liquidity indicator, shown in Figs. 2.6 and 2.7, reveals that recent performance of upper middle-income countries has not only recovered from but has surpassed pre-2007/8 crisis performance. In addition, upper middle-income countries have improved turnover faster than the general performance of high-income countries. By year-end 2020 lower middle-income countries were still to recover from pre-crisis peak performance. For SEE countries the extent of turnover fall in the crisis and the pace of recovery are again subpar compared to own benchmark income group global averages. In addition, the scale of volatility is higher and may be symptomatic of concentrations to single transaction impact on aggregate values.

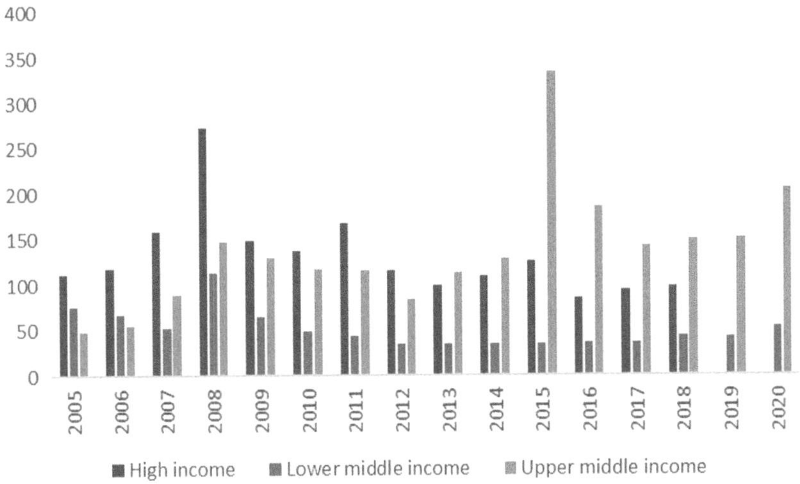

Fig. 2.6 Stocks traded, turnover ratio of domestic shares (as percent of market capitalization)—global aggregates (*Source* World Bank [2022]. 2019 and 2010 data are unavailable for high-income countries)

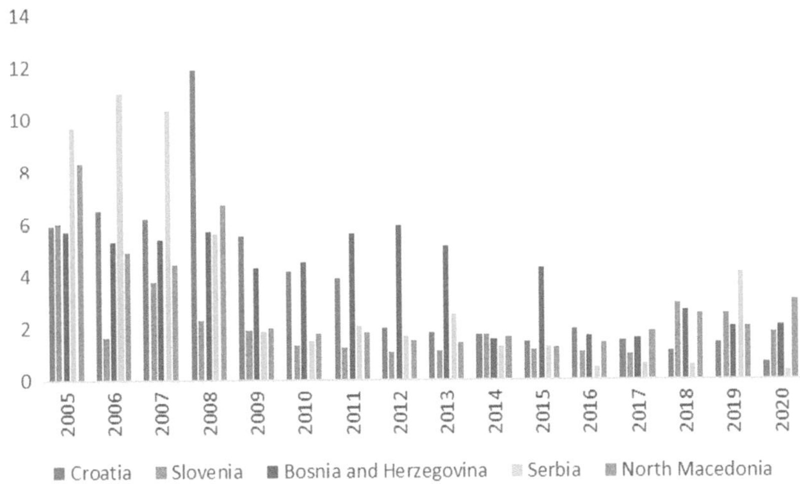

Fig. 2.7 Stocks traded, turnover ratio of domestic shares (as percent of market capitalization)—SEE individual countries (*Source* World Bank [2022], see stock exchanges, and see national statistical offices)

In comparison to global income group benchmarks, the selected individual SEE countries show even weaker performance in measuring turnover than in the ratio of capitalization to GDP. The benchmark averages for global equal income level group are approximately showing a minimum of ten times better market liquidity as measured by annual turnover to capitalization in regulated stock exchanges. Moreover, liquidity in the selected SEE capital markets is still closer to the 2007/8 crisis bottom levels than to pre-2007/8 crisis levels. As a group, SEE countries show similar performance trends in low liquidity throughout the observed period. As the in-depth review of individual countries will reveal, all the studied SEE markets show symptoms of high concentration to equity products and few large and often government-related corporations. Fixed-income products, structured products, and financial derivatives alternatives are sparsely represented in the regulated market and in secondary trade. Likewise, the investor base is shallow with little involvement of natural persons/retail entities' investors, institutional investors, portfolio investors, and foreign investors. As such, the respective capital markets are not diverse, and it is not surprising that the capitalization and liquidity performance are very volatile. The global COVID-19 crisis again showed disparities in the scale of impact between developed and developing markets and the markets in the observed SEE countries. Global GDP contracted by 4.3% in 2020. However, the size of contraction in all the SEE countries, with the exception of Serbia, was larger than that. While MSCI World Index[14] showed a thirty-four percent decline in March 2020, the global stock markets capitalization in year-end 2020 was approximately almost twenty percent above 2019 year-end figures. Similarly, the volume of outstanding derivatives was more than fifty percent higher. At the same time frame, except for Croatia, where figures were slightly higher than in the year-end 2019, the capitalization and turnover of other SEE countries stock exchanges was below 2019 results.

The shown trends do not illustrate low-income countries' aggregates due to data non-availability and lesser significance to the selected SEE markets, which belong to upper middle-income and to high-income groups.

[14] The MSCI World is a market cap weighted stock market index of 1,583 companies throughout the world. It is maintained by MSCI, formerly Morgan Stanley Capital International, and is used as a common benchmark for broad cross-section of global markets.

2.4 Financial Innovation in the Selected Southeast European Countries

The selected SEE countries form a single market with estimated aggregate nominal GDP of US$ 154.9 billion and a population of 19.3 million (Economist Intelligence Unit, 2016). Individually, Croatia, Serbia, B&H, North Macedonia, and Slovenia form, respectively, GDP and population of (a) US$ 48.7 billion and 4.2 million, (b) US$36.5 billion and 7.1 million, (c) US$16 billion and 3.8 million, (d) US$ eleven billion and 2.1 million, and (e) US$ 42.7 billion and 2.1 million. All the observed countries were united under a single country for most of the twentieth century, under the Kingdom of Serbs, Croats, and Slovenes in the earlier period, and under Yugoslavia in the later period. Yugoslavia experienced a violent breakup, with the ex-post independent countries transitioning from socialist to free market systems. In the build-up to the war of the 1990s, Yugoslavia's economy experienced a high increase in its current account deficit, growth of external debt, growing fiscal deficit and, finally, extensive inflation fuelling public discontent and increasing poverty. The economic downturn in Yugoslavia accelerated after the direct spill-over impact of the 1970s fossil fuels' crisis and the ripple effects of the global economic slowdown. From both economic and social perspective, the growing indebtedness and the spill-over impacts show comparable traits with the 2007/8 crisis and the continued market uncertainty. The outlook thus indicates an interlink between economic and political factors in an ever more thorough analysis of environment and perspectives of the sustainable implementation of collaborative risk sharing concepts in fragile surroundings.

Capital markets were nascent in all the selected SEE countries during the **post-socialist to free market transition in the 1990s**. The present scale of the capital market development in each country is still rather shallow, as apparent in low liquidity. However, the scope is wide-ranging and is also determinable by structure, legal, regulatory, institutional, political, real economic sector, and the macroeconomic environment. In the transition period, capital markets initially evolved as one of the strategic by-products in the process of privatizations in the transfer of ownership from former state-owned enterprises (SOE). Simultaneously, institutions and institutional funds first evolved as principally targeted ownership transferring vehicles during the privatization process. In this respect, the pace of evolvement of legal, regulatory, institutional, infrastructure, and corporate governance framework was not synchronized with that of the growth in the size of the capital markets. As a result, a lot of uncertainty arose and is still present in respect of the surrounding framework. Pension funds, insurance companies, and insurance funds marginally continue to increase their presence in the capital markets. This trend accompanies the aging demographics and an increasing plethora of pension and insurance products offer. All the observed capital markets are stigmatized with the public perception of non-transparent and unequal treatment under insider trading and poor corporate governance. That perception is to an extent due to the suspected and rather light regulatory supervision and an inefficient judicial system under a crony capital collaboration. Besides, the public belief highlights a lack of improvements in the techno-managerial skills, which enterprise owners need to understand to utilize the role of efficient regulated capital exchanges and to develop and sustainably integrate their businesses locally and internationally. On the other hand, capital markets are often considered solely as a targeted one-way sell-out exit avenue to foreign investors. In these markets, the investment turnover is shallow and trade mostly occurs in primary market subscriptions for state-owned securities' listings. The subscribers are mostly commercial banks, who already largely dominate the financial system and who then keep these securities through to redemption at maturity.

On a comparative case of the Czech Republic, as a transition economy, Fungacova and Hanousek (2011) proved that the bottom-up regulated stock exchange growth soon manifested massive de-listings. The process financially hurt small investors and brought negative sentiment and lesser liquidity to the Czech capital market that for some time put off the enhanced capital market development. In researching the determinants, Fungacova and Hanousek (2011) observed one thousand six hundred and sixty-four listed non-financial companies in the privatization and post-privatization trading during the study period from 1992 to 2006. Modeling de-listing as zero–one phenomenon, linear probability Heckit multinomial regression was utilized to reveal that lower capitalization scale companies, lower transaction price, and lower government stake owned companies tend to be de-listed sooner. In much of CEE as well as almost entirely in SEE, the respective capital markets have not served their full functional purpose in providing protection for minority ownership rights, in increasing corporate governance standards, and in enabling sustainable liquidity.

The second wave of investments in Croatia appeared jointly with an increasing institutional presence that evolved under the pension system reform which implemented capitalized savings as the compulsory second pension pillar (Drazenovic & Kusanovic, 2016). **Researching the level of capital market development in SEE countries,** Drazenovic and Kusanovic (2016) considered level of institutional investors' involvement, scope of reforms, and macroeconomic indicators' impact to prove statistically significant positive determinant causality on the size of capital markets in the selected six then new EU member countries (Croatia, the Czech Republic, Hungary, Poland, Slovakia, and Slovenia). The research results have implied a few statistically significant determinant variables. The statistically significant factors included impact of privatization reform, size of investment funds, size of life insurance premiums, and inflation indicator on the underlying capital markets' depth. Other factors, which proved non-significant, were size of existing pension funds, EBRD's indicator of large-scale privatization level scope, EBRD's indicator of banking FIs reform level, gross savings' indicator, and nominal GDP growth rate. Drazenovic and Kusanovic used annual data for the years 1995 to 2010 in the panel model utilizing fixed and random effects statistical testing to grasp both qualitative and quantitative time variant and invariant factors.

Lazarov et al. (2016) observed a statistically significant positive relationship between the level of capital markets development and aggregate economic output growth. They investigated ten SEE countries (including countries studied in this book) and four CEE countries in the period from 2002 to 2012 and under the threshold of twenty observations per variable. The level of capital markets' development was tracked by the indicator of listed stocks' market capitalization size. Impact on GDP growth was also studied by using explanatory variables including: (a) indicators for corporate governance (which proved as a statistically non-significant explanatory factor), (b) inflation rate indicator, (c) fixed capital accumulation to GDP ratio indicator, (d) sum of exports and imports to GDP ratio as trade openness indicator, and (e) banks' credit growth rate indicator. Other statistically significant influential factors on GDP growth included fixed capital accumulation and trade openness. Bayraktar (2014) researched the relative development level of fifty-eight developing and forty-six advanced economies' capital markets utilizing panel GMM estimation technique. That study analyzed annual dataset in the study period from 1990 to 2012. The researcher tested for actual capital market development, proxied through listed stocks' market capitalization to GDP ratio, to modeled capital market development capacity. In that testing macroeconomic, financial, and institutional indicators values were regressed onto listed stocks' market capitalization level. Macroeconomic indicators included GDPPC, inflation level, real interest rate, savings to GDP ratio, and FDI to GDP ratio. Financial indicators included stock market turnover to GDP ratio, domestic credit to GDP ratio, and broad money supply (M2) liabilities to GDP ratio. Institutional indicators were rated from worst to best at zero to six and were sourced from PRS group's International Country Risk Guide, which includes Corruption Index, Political Risk, Bureaucracy Quality, and Democratic Accountability[15] (The International Country Risk Guide, 2018). The panel results showed a statistically significant and positive factor relationship with lagged values of GDPPC and with all of the individual financial indicators. Individual countries' results illustrate that amongst the countries studied in this research, the development of Slovenian and North Macedonian listed stocks' market is close to modeled capacity, at close to ninety percent. On the other hand, Croatia and Serbia are already overextended at one hundred and fifty-three percent and two hundred and seventy-nine percent respectively over the modeled capacity.

In study revealed in this book enhancements add to the aforementioned related research by improving the statistical testing reliability through expanding the study sample number of observations for quantitative macroeconomic variables. It utilizes the panel PMG estimation technique to adjust for heterogeneity in the results and allows dynamic, short- and long-run, relationship testing through increased variance and reduced collinearity bias. It focuses on the impact on capital markets' prices rather than on capitalization levels since capitalization is less relevant under historical market illiquidity. It follows this approach due to a priori awareness of SEE markets' imminent shallowness in trading despite relatively large capitalizations, which is shown in profiling investigated markets and trends analysis (Dodig, 2020; Dodig & Bugarcic, 2022). The research shown in this book relates to now more mature capital markets with expected fewer non-typical values and under lesser uncertainty and

[15] PRS group is quant-driven political and country forecasting and risk rating company. Firm's roots are in academia and joint research with the US State Department and the Central Intelligence Agency; yet the firm is now standalone by interfacing its longstanding data series with artificial intelligence to produce truly outstanding, predictive results.

fewer market failing unsettled trades. In developing economies, capital markets' setting is relatively limited by extent of development and existence; yet it is more volatile and at times rapidly changing, which calls for repeated investigations of the relationships for the listed factors.

Currently available market research on the relationship of macroeconomic indicators with capital markets' prices in SEE countries has not been extensive. Barbic and Condic-Jurkic (2011) studied the existence and the spurious nature of relationship between stock markets' indices and selected macroeconomic variables in Croatia, the Czech Republic, Hungary, Poland, and Slovenia. The selected variables were inflation rate, money market rates, money supply, and foreign exchange reserves. Their results from the Johansen bi-variate cointegration procedure pointed to the existence of bi-variate long-run relationship between macroeconomic variables and listed stocks' indices, thus attesting to an apparent market inefficiency in this respect. The Granger causality test, however, showed no short-run causal relationship between the same indicators in Croatia, Hungary, and Poland. Where a causal relationship appeared likely, the transactions costs, delays, and further emerging market uncertainties prevented correction and again highlighted capital markets' inefficiencies.

The extent of SEE research to date faces limitations concerning the short history of capital market development and studies' frequent exclusion of first nascent years in the study data due to non-typical values. This review reveals the available review of complementary economic development factors that Drazenovic and Kusanovic (2016), and Nikoloski, Lazarov, and Miteva-Kacarski (2016) attempted to endogenize in the empirical statistical analysis. Nonetheless, the review is limited given the short history of pension reform, privatization process, and early stage development of institutional investors and policies' reform processes. Eric and Stosic (2012) called on EBRD's assessment of transition changes, World Bank's Doing Business rankings, and World Economic Forum's Index of Competitiveness in their survey, which showed that the financial crisis had left larger and longer post-effects in the fragmented selected SEE countries' markets while exposing deep structural problems. Eric and Stosic (2012) further showed that regulatory improvements are making the greatest progress and that the EU directive on markets in financial instruments (MiFID) is implemented together with the latest changes. Nonetheless, shallow market depth limits regulatory efficiencies to be most effectively used in the market. In an example of the case of MiFID clearing orders, while information is readily available, there isn't a sufficient market demand to operationalize the regulatory regime. Specifically, MiFID impacts multilateral trading facilities (MTF) trading, which is growing in capitalization and turnover. Therefore, efficiency gains may become more apparent for SEE capital markets under integration and inclusion to larger markets. These include non-necessity to "go public," zero or low requirements to list, more efficient trading, quicker and easier execution of orders, better price formation, and easier monitoring. Most importantly it is a gateway to a higher segment of organized exchange, which is a regulated exchange.

This study observes prospects in a common capital market integration and a simultaneous convergence to a greater access to the EU capital market expansion catalysts. For regulated exchanges, an opportunity for progress may appear in integrating stock exchanges to allow a deeper and more liquid client base. It enables a greater access to market, greater competitiveness and economies of scale, implementation of higher transparency, and ultimately an avenue to compete internationally. The first steps in this direction have been taken in the availability of data on SMI at a single place like Vienna or Sofia Exchange, as well as in the SEE link project that connects the smaller SEE markets for data sharing. A more significant step may be to allow cross-membership on SEE regulated exchanges to reach intermediating cost efficiency, diversified service, and ultimately to integrate the Exchanges to the extent of free trading between the listed counterparties already operating or striving to operate in a single economic zone. Available simultaneous cross-listings on two or more exchanges, as is the case for NYSE and Nasdaq exchanges, may be an avenue to move in the direction of integrating the markets to reap better efficiency and enable higher growth prospects. From another point of view, a deeper market may enable companies' growth through better allocated access to capital, a greater participation of private capital, and better candidacy to trade on SEE exchanges' prime markets. It improves transparency and corporate governance of the listed entities and all stakeholders. In addition, such a standard directs the domestic companies on a more competitive base to readily contest in advanced economies' markets that are already operating at the highest standards.

References

Books and Chapters in Books

Eric, D., & Stosic, I. (2012). Development of the European financial system: Challenges for Balkan countries integration process. In *European integration process in Western Balkan countries*, 114–143.

Goldsmith, W. R. (1969). *Financial structure and development*. Yale University Press.

Levine, R. (2005). Finance and growth: Theory and evidence In P. Aglu & S. Durlauf (Ed.), *Handbook of economic growth* (1st ed., Vol. 1, Chapter 12, pp. 865–934). Elsevier.

Ramaswamy, S., & Scott, R. (2005). Managing a multi-currency bond portfolio. In F. Fabozzi, *Indexing, structured and active bond portfolio management: State-of-the-art* (Chapter 19). Wiley.

Academic Articles, Working Papers and Studies

Alberola, E., Erce, A., & Serena, J. M. (2014). International reserves and gross capital flows. Documentos de Discusion 01148 FLAR. *Fondo Lationamericano de Reservas - FLAR*.

Ariel, R. (1990). High stock returns before holidays: Existence and evidence on possible causes. *The Journal of Finance, 45*(5), 1611–1626.

Barbic, T., & Condic-Jurkic, I. (2011). Relationship between macroeconomic fundamentals and stock market indices in select CEE countries. *Ekonomski Pregled, 62*(3–4), 113–133.

Bayraktar, N. (2014). *Measuring relative development level of stock markets: Capacity and effort of countries*. Borsa Istanbul.

Beck, T., & Levine, R. (2002). *Stock markets, banks, and growth: Panel evidence* (Working Paper 9082). National Bureau of Economic Research.

Beck, T., Levine, R., & Loayza, N. (2000). Financial intermediation and growth: Causality and causes. *Journal of Monetary Economics, 46*(1), 31–77. Elsevier.

Billet, M. T., Flannery, M. J., & Garfinkel, J. A. (1995). The effect of lender identity on a borrowing firm's equity returns. *The Journal of Finance, 50*(2), 699–718.

Bossone, B., Mahajan, S., & Zahir, F. (2003). *Financial infrastructure, group interests, and capital accumulation* (IMF Working Paper). International Monetary Fund 2003 (024).

Bossone, B., & Lee, J.-K. (2004). *In finance, size matters: The "systemic scale economies" hypothesis* (IMF Staff Papers, Vol. 51, No. 1). International Monetary Fund 2004 (001).

Bossone, B., & Promisel, L. (2012). *Strengthening financial systems in developing countries*. The World Bank.

Canales-Kriljenko, J. I. (2004). *Foreign exchange market organisation in selected developing and transition economies: Evidence from a survey* (IMF Working Paper No. 04/4). International Monetary Fund 2004 (004).

Cetorelli, N., & Goldberg, L. S. (2011). Global banks and international shock transmission: Evidence from the crisis. *IMF Economic Review, 59*(1), 41–76.

Chen, N.-F., Roll, R., & Ross, S. A. (1986). Economic forces and the stock market. *The Journal of Business, 59*(3), 383–403.

Cojocaru, L., Falaris, E. M., Hoffman, S. D., & Miller, J. B. (2015). Financial system development and economic growth in transition economies: New empirical evidence from the CEE and CIS countries. Bankable Frontier Associates, University of Delaware, Gallaudet University.

Crane, D. B., Froot, K. A., Scott, P., Mason, André Perold, R. C., Merton, Z., Bodie, Sirri, E. R., & Tufano, P. (1995). *The global financial system: A functional perspective*. Harvard Business School Press.

Dahiya, S., Puri, M., & Saunders, A. (2003). Bank borrowers and loan sales: New evidence on the uniqueness of bank loans. *The Journal of Business, 76*(4), 563–582.

Dodig, A. (2020). Relationship between macroeconomic indicators and capital markets performance in selected southeastern European countries. *Zagreb International Review of Economics & Business*, 55–88.

Dodig, A., & Bugarcic, M. (2022). Extended relationship between macroeconomic indicators and capital markets performance in selected southeastern European countries. *Economic Thought and Practice, Dubrovnik*.

Drucker, S., & Puri , M. (2005). On the benefits of concurrent lending and underwriting. *The Journal of Finance*, 2763–2799.

Dumas, B., Harvey, C., & Ruiz, P. (2003). Are correlations of stock returns justified by subsequent changes in national outputs? *Journal of International Money and Finance*, 777–811.

Fama, E. F. (1990). Stock returns, expected returns, and real activity. *The Journal of Finance, 45*(4), 1089–1108.

Ferrucci, G. (2003). *Empirical determinants of emerging market economies' sovereign bond spreads* (Working Paper No. 205). Bank of England.

Fink, G., Haiss, P., & Vuksic, G. (2005). *Importance of financial sectors for growth in accession countries*. ECBOeNB/CFS—Conference on European Economic Integration, Vienna.

Flannery, M. J., & Protopapadakis, A. (2002). Macroeconomic factors do influence aggregate stock returns. *The Review of Financial Studies, 15*(3), 751–782.

Fungacova, Z., & Hanousek, J. (2011). Determinants of firm delisting on the Prague stock exchange. *Prague Economic Papers, 2011*(4), 348–365.

Griffin, J., & Baltagi, B. (1997). Pooled estimators vs. their heterogenous counterparts in the context of dynamic demand for gasoline. *Journal of Econometrics, 77*(2), 303–327.

Halilbegovic, S., & Mekic, A. (2017). Usage of derivatives in emerging markets: The case of Bosnia and Herzegovina. *Asian Economic and Financial Review, 7*(3), 248–257.

Hasseeb, M. K. (2015). *Impact of the real economy on stock market performance: Evidence from Arab countries* (Master's Thesis). The American University in Cairo.

James, C. (1987). Some evidence on the uniqueness of bank loans. *Journal of Financial Economics, 19*(2), 217–235.

Karamustafa, O., & Kucukalle, Y. (2003). *Long run relationships between stock market returns and macroeconomic performance.* University Library of Munich.

King, R., & Levine, R. (1993). Finance and growth: Schumpeter might be right. *The Quarterly Journal of Economics, 108*(3), 717–737.

Koivu, T. (2002). *Do efficient banking sectors accelerate economic growth in transition countries?* (BOFIT Discussion Papers [14]) Bank of Finland, Institute for Economies in Transition.

La Porta, R., Lopez-de-Silanes, F., Shleifer, A., & Vishny, R. (2000). *The economic consequences of legal origins.* Harvard University.

Lazarov, D., Miteva-Kacarski, E., & Nikoloski, K. (2016). An empirical analysis of stock market development and economic growth: The case of Macedonia. *South East European Journal of Economics and Business, 11*(2), 71–81.

Lee, Y.-M., & Wang, K.-M. (2015). Dynamic heterogenous panel analysis of the correlation between stock prices and exchange rates. *Economic Research-Ekonomska Istraživanja, 28*(1), 749–772.

Levine, R. (1997). Financial development and economic growth; views and agenda. *Journal of Economic Literature, 35*(2), 688–726.

Levine, R., & Zervos, S. (1998). Stock markets, banks, and growth. *American Economic Review, 88*(3), 537–558.

Lien, D., & Zhang, M. (2008). A survey of emerging derivatives markets. *Emerging Markets Finance and Trade, 44*(2), 39–69.

Megaravalli, A. V., & Sampagnaro, G. (2018). Macroeconomic indicators and their impact on stock markets in ASIAN 3: A pooled mean group approach. *Cogent Economics and Finance, 6*(1), 1–14.

Naceur, S. B., Ghazouani, S., & Omran, M. (2007). The determinants of stock market development in the Middle-Eastern and North African region. *Managerial Finance, 33*(7), 477–489.

Nijam, H. M., Ismail, S., & Musthafa, A. (2015). The impact of macroeconomic variables on stock market performance; evidence from Sri Lanka. *Journal of Emerging Trends in Economics and Management Sciences, 6*(2), 151–157.

Olgic Drazenovic, B., & Kusanovic, T. (2016). Determinants of capital market in the new member EU countries. *Economic Research—Ekonomska Istrazivanja, 29*(1), 758–769.

Philips, S., & Clifford, S. (1980). Trading costs for listed options: The implications for market efficiency. *Journal of Financial Economics, 8*(2), 179–201.

Pilinkus, D. (2010). Macroeconomic indicators and their impact on stock market performance in the short and long run: The case of the Baltic states. *Technological and Economic Development of Economy, 16*(2), 291–304.

Plihal, T. (2016). Stock market informational efficiency in Germany: Granger causality between DAX and selected macroeconomic indicators. *Procedia—Social and Behavioral Sciences, 220*, 321–329.

Roll, R., Chordia, T., & Subrahmanyam, A. (2008). Liquidity and market efficiency. *Journal of Financial Economics, 87*(2), 249–268.

Samargandi, N., Fidrmuc, J., & Ghosh, S. (2014). Is the relationship between financial development and economic growth monotonic? Evidence from a sample of middle income countries. *World Development 68*(C), 66–81.

Tsuyuguchi, Y., & Wooldridge, P. (2008). The evolution of trading activity in Asian foreign exchange markets. *Emerging Markets Review, 9*(4), 231–246.

Reports and Other Sources

International Monetary Fund. (2017). *Global financial stability report: Is growth at risk?* World Economic and Financials Surveys.

International Monetary Fund. (2022). *Database*. Retrieved January 9, 2022, from https://data.imf.org

Mckinsey and Company. (2017). *Mckinsey global institute: "The new dynamics of financial globalization"*.

McLannahan, B. (2018, March 16). US bank derivatives books larger since rescue of Bear Stearns. *Financial Times*.

Munchau, W. (2018, August 28). Tinkering will not deliver a stronger role for the Euro. *Financial Times*.

Republic of Serbia Securities Commission. (2017). *2016 Annual report*. Belgrade.

The Economic Times. (2016, February 08). Retrieved February 8, 2016, from https://economictimes.indiatimes.com/p/put-call-ratio/articleshow/50901067.cms

The International Country Risk Guide (ICRG). (2018). Retrieved October 12, 2018, from PSR Group: https://www.prsgroup.com/explore-our-products/international-country-risk-guide/

World Bank (2022). Retrieved November 10, 2018, and on January 8, 2022 from https://datahelpdesk.worldbank.org/knowledgebase/

CHAPTER 3

Individual Southeast European Capital Markets Profiles

3.1 Capital Market in Croatia

3.1.1 *Historical Overview*

In profiling the individual capital markets this review starts with **highlighting the market in Croatia due to its historical and ongoing role as the recognized regional leader amongst the selected SEE countries.** The leader role pertains to the level of capital market development, to regional capital markets integration through ZSE's 2015 acquisition of LJSE, and to ZSE's innovation through transparency and corporate governance standards in listing own shares on ZSE, amongst others. The first record of an organized exchange in Croatia dates to 1750. The Habsburg Empire founded the Exchange in the port city Rijeka. Its function was to trade in sugar commodities sold through a sugar refinery in Rijeka. The exchange-traded business was mostly concentrated in Austria-Hungary, initially in the capital city Vienna as of 1771, and subsequently also in Budapest from 1867. The Rijeka Exchange closed in 1803. In 1907, the Union of Industrialists and Traders of Croatia and Slavonia founded the Zagreb Exchange. Its function was trading physical goods not represented on the Vienna Exchange (Wiener Borse) and the Budapest Exchange. The Zagreb Exchange closed in 1911 during the political turmoil in Austria-Hungary. It reopened after World War I in 1919 to regulate trade of physical goods, securities, and cash. The Zagreb Exchange was organized as a corporation under the authority of

A. Dodig, *Capital Markets in Southeast Europe*,
https://doi.org/10.1007/978-3-031-07210-9_3

the Ministry of Trade and Industry of the Kingdom of Serbs, Croats, and Slovenes. Paid membership was available to natural persons/retail entities and to legal entities, who would elect the Exchange Committee to supervise the work of brokers. Under fiduciary duties, brokers could not trade for their own account and needed to post margin guarantees for a successful performance. The Exchange boasted diversified trade, including that of **(a)** the Kingdom's commercial papers, **(b)** regional commercial papers, **(c)** lottery bonds, **(d)** repatriation bonds, **(e)** stocks of trade and transport companies, **(f)** commodities securities, etc. In 1920, the newly founded National Bank in the Kingdom monopolized all foreign exchange trade, thus depriving the Zagreb Exchange of servicing the trading venue role. In 1945, the Zagreb Exchange ceased its operations under the planned economy in the newly established country, Yugoslavia. Because the Exchange was marked speculative in nature it had no place in the socialist society.

In 1991, with the emergence of the independent Republic of Croatia, twenty-five banks and two insurance companies re-established the Zagreb Exchange. In 1993 the alternative OTC market was established in the nearby city of Varazdin. It predominantly registered the closed-end investment funds and other companies not meeting the listing requirements for the ZSE. The Varazdin Exchange became a regulated exchange market in 1998, featuring very few illiquid listings. Nonetheless, in 2007 Varazdin Exchange capitalization reached Euro 9.8 billion (roughly US$ 6.7 billion). In the initial years of its operations, the ZSE had only a rudimentary role with sporadic annual open outcry transactions. Its first listing included SOEs such as the airline Croatia Airlines and the first travel companies such as Arenaturist or Jadranka. Commercial papers and other debt securities were not initially listed but emerged on both the Exchanges in the mid-1990s. Primary trading encompassed privatization funds' securities, securities issued by the Ministry responsible for reconstruction and development of the war-torn infrastructure, securities issued by state agencies for bank savings repatriation, etc. In 1994 electronic trading system was introduced in the ZSE and caused nine hundred eighty-three percent growth in capitalization through 2000. In a similar fashion, electronic trading was introduced in the Varazdin Exchange. ZSE development continued with 1997 real-time electronic trading implementation, while in 1999 an automatic order matching system was introduced. In 2007 the ZSE merged with the Varazdin Exchange and in the same year, NASDAQ X-Stream trade platform was introduced. The first exchange indices in Croatia were CROBEX with eleven companies in the index and Varazdin Index (VIN) with seven privatization funds and Ericsson Nikola Tesla shares in the index. CROBEX was introduced in 1997 and had its peak value in 2007, the same year when VIN was dissolved. The ZSE regulated market features the following instruments: **(a)** ordinary and preferred shares, **(b)** investment fund shares, **(c)** corporate bonds, **(d)** Government and municipal bonds, **(e)** money market instruments, **(f)** treasury bills, and **(g)** structured products.

Key growth driver for the capital market in Croatia was the initial wave of privatizations. The early listed companies were state-owned banks' and insurance companies' own stock exchange listings, followed by strategic companies such as the pharmaceutical giant Pliva, food manufacturer Podravka, shipyard Viktor Lenac, etc. Thereafter, the first investment funds arose in the likes of private players; yet, by market share, Government privatization funds played the dominant role. The 1990s war participants gained coupon rights in over four hundred and seventy companies in the country with nominal value of roughly ten percent of the national GDP of the time. The program's target was to attract strategic investors and pay out the initial owners (Alajbeg & Bubas, 2001). Thus, in the mid-1990s, nearly six hundred thousand small investors were present largely due to the coupon privatization process in bottom-up capital market development. The process was marked by a slow in parallel evolution of institutions' techno-managerial skills and corporate governance. The second wave of capital market growth emerged upon the pension system reform. It was implemented in 2002 and created new market institutional players such as mandatory and voluntary pension funds. The specificities of the pension funds' lower risk profile and inherent investment risk limitations prioritized the largest concentration of investments in Government's debt securities, followed by local municipal and SOEs' securities, OECD countries' securities, etc. The pension assets constituted around US$ 15.2 billion or roughly twenty-six percent of national GDP at the year-end of 2017. Given the surge in demand, which was coupled with a lack of liquid supply in the capital market, by mid-2003 the Government of Croatia decided to impose a requirement for mandatory shares listing on all companies with more than one hundred shareholders or with more than thirty million Croatian Kuna (HRK) in the capital[1] (Seba, 2017). From 2003 to 2007, partial privatizations of oil and gas company INA, telecom operator Hrvatske Telekomunikacije, and pharmaceutical giant Pliva enabled an increase in the number of new small shareholders. However, it was only a gateway to new abrupt privatization and later for strategic foreign investors who would consolidate ownership concentration. At the year-end of 2016, by capitalization INA and Hrvatske Telekomunikacije together represented 30.5% of the ZSE capitalization. INA's free float is only six percent versus forty-two percent for the latter. The top two banks, Zagrebacka and Privredna Banka Zagreb, add another 22.3% to the capitalization, yet representing an immaterial free float. In trading turnover, Hrvatske Telekomunikacije is the top performer with nineteen percent of the total ZSE turnover, followed by three private conglomerates operating in the tourism and fast-moving consumer goods industries. Initially, equity share ownership was the predominant asset class security. Thereafter, debt securities ownership rose to a proportional representation of close to a third of the total ZSE market value. Nonetheless, most traded securities are debt securities; yet the trade occurs mostly on the primary market and in the Government debt assets. Corporate debt securities are rather closely held and seldom traded.

In 2015 the ZSE acquired the LJSE and took the role of the initiator of regional exchange-traded capital markets integration. In 2015 the ZSE was the first regional exchange to adopt a legal entity identifier (LEI) service with a local operator and LEI issuer status granted by the global regulatory oversight committee (ROC). The LEI system was developed by the 2011 G20[2] countries in response to the inability of FIs to globally identify legal entities uniquely. Such incapacity made it difficult to track financial transactions in different national jurisdictions. It formed challenges in counterparty and concentration risk calculations. ROC, a coalition of seventy-one public authorities, financial regulators, and central banks encourage the expansion of LEI, which is already implemented in the advanced economies. In the same year, EBRD bought minority ownership in ZSE.

[1] Roughly US$ 5.2 million.

[2] EU and Argentina, Australia, Brazil, Canada, China, Germany, France, India, Indonesia, Italy, Japan, Mexico, Russia, Saudi Arabia, South Africa, South Korea, Turkey, the United Kingdom, and the United States.

In mid-2016 the listing of ZSE shares on its own exchange made the ZSE the first regional stock exchange with shares listed on a regulated market. ZSE increased its capitalized in part with a new public offering and thus paved an exemplary role and regional leadership in capital raising, transparency, and corporate governance standards. Later in 2016 the ZSE and Funderbeam Markets jointly launched a listed Special Purpose Vehicle (SPV)[3] crowdfunding platform for startup assessment and financing, the first of the kind in the region. In 2017 the ZSE incorporated WBAG Xetra trading system platform, which allows remote investor access and is a co-shared platform with the Wiener Borse and the Deutsche Borse. In 2020 ZSE bought minority ownership in Macedonian Stock Exchange.

3.1.2 Contemporary Setting

The capital market in Croatia continues to lead as the most advanced stock exchange amongst the observed SEE countries. **ZSE represents the largest capitalization and the most diversified spectrum of the traded financial instruments on the regulated, multilateral trading facility, and OTC markets.** The predominant market players are institutional entities, while the predominantly traded securities are those of Government debt. The role of the private sector has not been very influential. ZSE is owned by fifty shareholders (including banks, brokers, insurance companies, and industrials) and has thirty-seven banks and brokerage companies as registered participants in a continuous order-driven and automatic matching trading. Trading hours are on business days from 09:00–16:30, continuous trading is from 09:15–16:30, and "T+2" (two additional business days from trade day to settlement day) settlement period.

At the end of March 2018, by market value, local legal entities owned roughly forty-eight percent of the traded assets, followed by non-residents at roughly twenty-four percent, local natural persons/retail entities' market players at roughly fourteen percent, and others for the remainder. A slight upsurge is observable in the resident natural persons/retail entities' market players' share *vis-à-vis* others. Market share of custody and

[3] A Special Purpose Vehicle, also called a special purpose entity (SPE), is a subsidiary company created by a parent company to isolate financial risk. Its legal status as a separate company makes its obligations secure even if the parent company goes bankrupt.

portfolio accounts is at roughly thirty percent. Basic accounts represent fifty-seven percent of the market and joint and representative accounts eleven percent. Equity shares form roughly seventy percent of the total market value (at roughly US$ 49.5 billion), debt bonds form twenty-three percent (at roughly US$ 16.5 billion), and debt bills form seven percent (at roughly US$ 5.2 billion). Debt securities are predominantly held to maturity rather than traded. This composition review uses a point in time sample for the first three months of 2018, when **(a)** debt bonds formed seventy-one percent of transactions, valued at roughly US$ four billion; **(b)** debt bills formed twenty-three percent of traded securities, valued at roughly US$ 1.3 billion; and **(c)** shares formed only 5.8% of total transactions, valued at roughly US$ three hundred and thirty million.

The Central Depository and Clearing Company is supported by the existence of the Guarantee Fund and the Investor Protection Fund, which were created through contributions by participants. At the end of March 2018, the value of the Guarantee Fund was roughly US$ eleven million, consisting of one-third in cash and the remainder in irrevocable bank guarantees. Investor Protection Fund coverage is capped at roughly Euro twenty thousand per member (Central Depository and Clearing Company Inc., 2018).

A decade later the ZSE trading scope has not returned to the levels it had before the 2007/2008 crisis, as shown in the total annual regulated trading turnover to GDP reaching roughly 6.9% by the end of 2007, but only 1.1% at year-end 2016 (Jaksic & Puric, 2014). Capitalization and trading in bonds increased relative to stocks. At year-end 2016 ZSE capitalization stood at roughly US$ 32.38 billion, while total turnover was roughly US$ five hundred and fifty-two million or 1.7% of the capitalization level (Zagreb Stock Exchange, 2017). OTC turnover is markedly higher at close to US$ 2.75 billion. Again, the debt securities turnover is ninety-eight percent concentrated on sovereign-related bonds and associated national or municipal companies. The remainder of OTC turnover mainly pertains to FIs, hospitality companies, telecommunication companies, and transport companies. ZSE streams eleven market indices, with CROBEX being the oldest. The other indices have a narrower market coverage that is principally related to various single industry performance. ZSE has the largest number of market indices amongst the observed SEE countries. ZSE regulated market includes the prime, the official, and the regular market. The requirements to list on the ZSE regulated tradings include a minimum fifteen percent free float shares for the regular market, or twenty-five percent for the official market and the prime market. Minimum capitalization starts in the official market at HRK eight million (or roughly US$ 1.2 million) or in the prime market at HRK one hundred million (or roughly US$ 15.1 million).[4] Trading on a multilateral platform was conducted on CE Enter market, managed by the ZSE. In 2018 the Progress market tool replaced CE in closer compliance with MiFID II requirements. Stock lending and short selling are permitted but are seldom used.

Asset-backed securities, in specific, covered bonds, as a product are not specifically regulated in the legal and regulatory framework and this creates an insurmountable hurdle for potential investors in this product type. The covered bonds potential in Croatia attracts an increasingly marketable interest for several reasons. First, there is a growing demand in the trade of debt securities locally. Secondly, the market is opening to a deeper base of investors. Lastly, there is a sufficient depth of the local banking market to underwrite and standardize the product base and structure covered bonds. However, regulatory uncertainty impedes growth due to hurdles of, for example, elements such as **(a)** segregation and transfer of covered pool assets, **(b)** insolvency ring-fencing, **(c)** priority of netting in financial transactions upon insolvency regimes, or **(d)** the applicability of set-off in financial transactions in insolvency regimes, etc. Having in mind that private debt securities are also the largest and fastest-growing financial component globally,[5] such regulatory bottlenecks impede the potential of streamlining the development of the capital market in Croatia. In the global arena, the capital market international issuances of debt outpace local issuances. Such a trend increases competitive pressure on smaller capital markets' need to operate more efficiently in search to compete for international placements. Debt securities are an advantageous product in addressing full economic cycle needs, be it in bridging international expansion to pioneer markets or in custom resolving distressed assets positions. The local market players in Croatia conduct public issuances via depository receipts on foreign exchanges, but the reverse trend of international companies' listings in the ZSE

[4] For purpose of listing countervalue in US$, year-end 2019 exchange rates are used.

[5] Sourced on April 25, 2018, from Mckinsey Global Institute report "US$ one hundred and eighteen Trillion and Counting: Taking stock of the World's Capital Market." Mckinsey sample research shows that private debt securities add roughly twenty nine percent to growth of global financial stock (Mckinsey and Company, 2005).

is less frequent. For example, INA d.d., Hrvatski Telekom d.d., and Agrokor d.d. have reached out to the LSE in both equity and debt securities issuances to attract the interest of foreign investors and to increase liquidity on own stocks. On the local market though, the scalable initial listings may eventually come from initiation by evolving institutions such as supranational developmental institutions. For example, supranational entities recently issued local currency securities in the Romanian and Serbian capital market in search to add to the depth of the market and increase the stability of the local currency. In the growing globalization, an effective capital market enables both local and international companies to place initial and follow-on debt securitizations using capital market platforms. In Croatia, the primary local candidates, due to the elementary size and scope of the matter, include large corporations and commercial FIs. An opportunity exists to establish mortgage-backed securitizations and to add to the diversification of risk amongst issuers and investors. Banks benefit from using mortgage-backed securities through released capital, which may then be deployed for traditional lending support to natural persons/retail entities, enterprises, and corporations.

The non-bank financial segment in Croatia is rather underdeveloped and, not accounting for the presence of insurance companies, is represented by only a marginal existence of private sector players. Non-traditional sources of financing, such as **(a)** private equity investing, **(b)** initial public offerings (IPOs), **(c)** venture capital investing, **(d)** high net worth individuals' investing, **(e)** or similar, are limited. Global Entrepreneurship Monitor[6] ranks financial support availability in Croatia at the rating of two out of a maximum of five for the non-traditional sources (Kelley et al., 2015). Greater liquidity is an elementary prerequisite for a sustainable introduction of financial derivatives on an organized exchange. Follow-on steps tend to involve an introduction of futures on indices as well as the introduction of regulated options and warrants. **The capital market in Croatia is marked by high concentration risk and a questionable protection of minority ownership rights.** Only in mid-2002 were the first corporate governance principles introduced prescribing quarterly financial reports disclosure for the majority of publicly listed companies. The 2016 World Bank Group Doing Business report ranked Croatia with a rating of 6.5 out of ten for the strength

[6] The Global Entrepreneurship Monitor research project is an annual assessment of the national level of entrepreneurial activity in multiple, diverse countries.

of minority investor protection, and at three out of ten for the extent of disclosure to investors (World Bank, 2016).

The financial system breakdown by total assets shows a large prevalence of the traditional commercial banks, which represented roughly seventy-one percent of the total at the end of 2016.[7] Commercial banks are active in the capital market primarily as investors in liquid assets and predominantly in Government debt securities. The four mandatory pension funds are the second-largest type of financial system operators. The total assets of the pension funds represent roughly eighteen percent of the total financial system's assets. The risk-averse nature of these funds limits a minimum of fifty percent of investment assets to be held in Croatia's Government debt securities. Most of the other investments are in direct municipal debt, corporate debt, or large infrastructure equity positions. Therefore, the participation of institutional investors in capital markets is concentrated on the same type of product as is largely the preference case with commercial banks. Banks and pension funds together represent close to ninety percent of the financial system's assets (Fig. 3.1).

The third-largest operators in the financial system are insurance and reinsurance companies. They represent roughly seven percent of the total financial system's assets. That ratio increased from five percent representation a decade ago. Insurers, again due to their investment appetite for long-term products and due to the risk-averse investment profile invest a large majority of their own assets in sovereign debt securities. The small representation by other players includes, by decreasing market share order, the following: **(a)** leasing companies, **(b)** investment funds, and **(c)** microfinance segment. Microfinance and private funds' investments in Croatia are largely underdeveloped. The private equity and venture capital segments are on their own indirectly reliant on Government or supranational involvement in the form of Croatian Bank for Reconstruction and Development (HBOR) investments in open-ended funds, which represent roughly 0.5% of the financial system by total assets size. These funds have historically yielded negative financial results. In addition, the pioneer corporate governance profile is questionable as the initial few funds were liquidated and general partners were removed. Other private equity placements are very sporadic and do not form a trend. The structure of funds is dominated by money market investments, though the representation

[7] Total assets are estimated at US$ 81.4 billion in the end of 2016 by own calculations.

ZSE*:

Market capitalization_– US$ 41.2 billion on regulated exchange.

Annual trading turnover – US$ 382 million on regulated exchange, US$ 0.3 million on MTF market, and US$ 1.1 billion on OTC trading.

Market share in regulated trading by security type – ninety percent shares, nine percent bonds, and one percent alternative products.

**

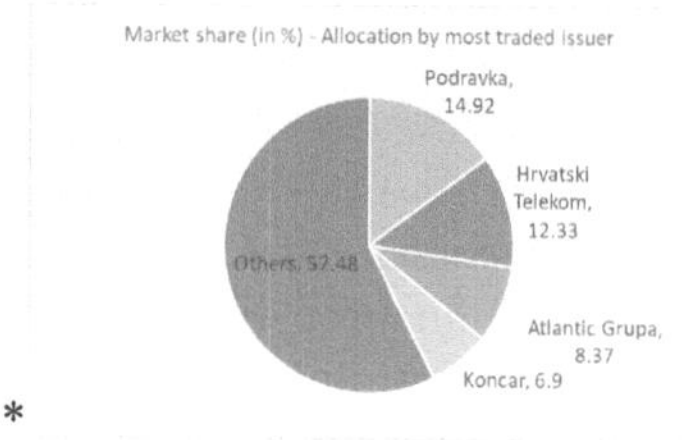

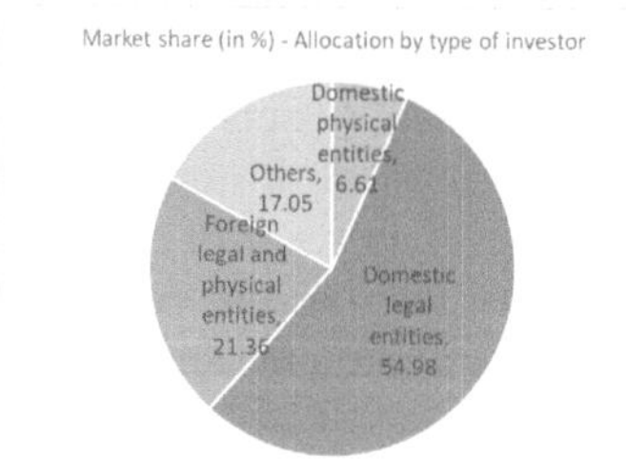

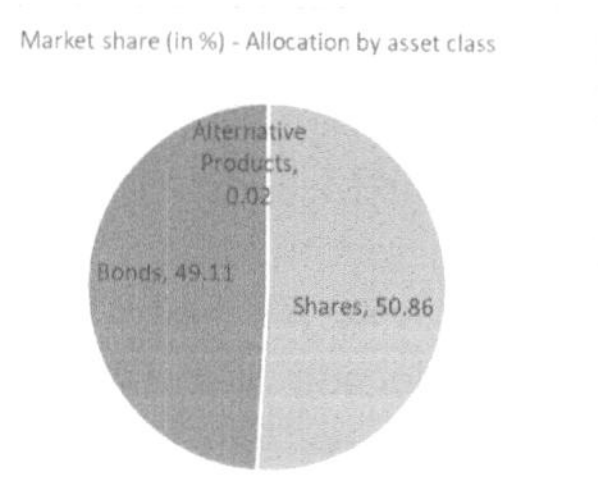

**Year-end 2021 or latest available data sourced from Zagreb Stock Exchange (2022) and 31.03.2018 data sourced from Central Depository and Clearing Company Inc. (2022).*
***ZSE regulated market only and last quarter of 2021 data.*

Fig. 3.1 Characteristics of capital market in Croatia

includes bond funds and equity funds alike, whose performance has been the weakest of the three (Curkovic & Kristo, 2017). Equity capital market performance has historically shown weak results and has a high correlation with poor corporate governance and management. More recently EU capital markets plan convergence has generated increasing funding interest by sovereign and supranational developmental institutions. The leasing sector features about twenty companies with a product concentration on transport vehicles. The prevalent microcredit institutions are credit unions. Local microfinance institutions were only allowed to be organized as credit and savings institutions and largely did not exist due to complex conditions either in the tax system on grants, the need to reorganize the legal form, or similar. The financial system environment appears to have room for improvement through greater involvement of the private sector. **More importantly, the financial system lacks diversified local investment opportunities, and these may be a prerequisite for greater development of the capital market. In the future, it is expected that pension funds and insurance companies may increase the scope of their involvement in the capital market due to the inherent demographic change of an aging population that needs to ensure greater income in old age.** In 2016 the Republic of Croatia introduced capital gain taxation at twelve percent. This is expected to create a short-run slowdown in the trading turnover. Nonetheless, the performance of the capital market in Croatia largely carries a spillover from more developed markets and particularly from the EU, directly and indirectly.

3.1.3 Legal and Regulatory Framework

The legislative and regulatory development pathway follows the transitory phase from planned to free-market economy. The more recent adjustment is to European *acquis* under the path to joining the European Union, which happened in 2013. In 1996 the Croatian Securities and Exchange Commission (CROSEC) was founded as the first independent regulatory institution supervising issuances and trading, proposing legislation and development of capital markets, and reporting to the National Parliament. CROSEC issued operating licenses, authorizations, and approvals. It also monitored the work of central depository, capital market exchanges and market participants including investment services providers, advisors, issuers, management companies, funds, etc. The Agency for Supervision of Pension Funds and the Insurance Companies Supervisory Authority coexisted with CROSEC before the three entities merged into a single entity, Croatian Financial Services Supervisory Agency (HANFA), in 2005. HANFA monitors **(a)** capital market institutions, **(b)** insurance companies, **(c)** leasing and factoring companies, **(d)** investment funds, and **(e)** their managing companies. It also oversees takeovers of joint-stock companies, amongst others. The Croatian National Bank (HNB) regulates the commercial banks in the country and the Ministry of Finance proposes new legislation.

The analysis of the accounting framework in Croatia is not included due to the shorter scope of research and the fact that the financial system of the country is practically fully harmonized with the latest global standards (Table 3.1).

3.2 Capital Market in Slovenia

3.2.1 Historical Overview

The first traces of the exchange-traded business in Slovenia date back to the period of the Kingdom of Serbs, Croats, and Slovenes from 1924 to 1941. The Ljubljana Exchange was established by industrialist Dragotin Hribar, who presided over the Exchange. The establishment of the Ljubljana Exchange followed soon after the set-up of the Zagreb Exchange. It similarly handled the trade in **(a)** physical goods, mostly in commodities; **(b)** securities, primarily those of FIs and industrial enterprises; and **(c)** cash by intermediation of professional brokers in open outcry trading. The National Bank in the Kingdom then monopolized all foreign exchange trade, thus like the Zagreb Exchange, the Ljubljana Exchange was deprived of its trading platform role. In 1927, foreign exchange dealing was allowed again and thereafter reached ninety percent of the total turnover (Ljubljana Stock Exchange, 2018). Subsequently, in 1941, the Ljubljana Exchange stopped operating because of World War II and remained thereafter closed due to the transition to the planned economy and the socialist society in the newly established Yugoslavia.

The Ljubljana Exchange is amongst the first stock exchanges to be established in the post-communist transition economies in CEE. LJSE was established in December 1989, preceding **(a)** the Budapest Stock Exchange, which was established in June 1990, **(b)** the Warsaw Stock Exchange, which was established in April 1991, and **(c)** ZSE, which was established in 1991, etc. The Securities Market Act and Capital Market Act were adopted in 1989 providing the legal basis for the re-establishment of LJSE. In 1992 the Stock Exchange Depository and the Precious Metals Market were introduced. In 1993 LJSE started daily price listing, with trades two times a week. Multilateral cash netting started on a "T+2" settlement basis as the first open outcry trading sessions took place. In 1995 the Government of Slovenia adopted a decree on dematerializing securities and establishment of the Central Securities Clearing Corporation (KDD). In the same year, open outcry trading ceased to exist.

Table 3.1 Key legal and regulatory developments in the capital market in Croatia

Year of application	*Development*	*Novelty*
1993	Law on foundations of foreign exchange system, of foreign exchange and gold transactions	Permission for international investors to buy and sell local securities
1995	Law on investment funds	Regulation on the foundation of closed-end, open-end, and real-estate investment funds
1996	Act on issuance and trade of securities	1. CROSEC establishment 2. Regulation on listed and investment companies' rights and obligations, on IPOs and listings prospectus content, and on investor protection
1997	1. Law on privatization investment funds 2. Amendment to the Act on issuance and trade of securities	Exerted the launch of mass privatizations based on free allocation of shares to the population segments. Establishment of Croatian Central Depository and Clearing Company (CDCC). Classification of successful public offering if more than eighty percent of subscription is successful. The maximum subscription period is set at six months for public and at three months for private offerings
2000	Law on mandatory and voluntary pension funds	Addon to the law on investment funds in the establishment and operations of pension funds and pension funds' management companies

(continued)

Table 3.1 (continued)

Year of application	*Development*	*Novelty*
2002	1. Securities Market Act replacing Act on issuance and trade of securities 2. Takeover Act 3. Law on Banks amendment (final amendment in 2015 with Credit Institutions Act in line with the EU acquis)	1. Introduction of the mandatory shares listing for strategic companies 2. Introduction of takeover rules including setting of lowest takeover prices for joint-stock companies, rights and obligations of participants, and procedures and supervisions 3. Amongst others an introduction of an increase in minimum capital base to HRK forty million (US$ 6.04 million).[8] The change leads to further industry consolidations
2003	Law on foreign exchange transactions	Set up of regulations on international issuances and resident to non-resident cash flows
2006	1. New law on investment funds 2. Amendment to Securities Market Act	1. Introduction of venture capital funds 2. ZSE capital base increased from HRK one million (US$ one hundred and fifty-one thousand) to HRK twenty million (US$ 3.01 million)
2007	Corporate Governance Code creation	Voluntary code presented by ZSE

[8] For purpose of listing countervalue in US$, year-end 2019 exchange rates are used.

Year of application	*Development*	*Novelty*
2009	Capital Market Act*	1. Adoption of the EU ***acquis*** Lamfalussy directives[9] 2. Differentiation between small and institutional investors 3. Derivatives and structured products introduction to trading 4. ZSE capital increased to HRK forty million 5. Introduction of the Investor Protection Fund
2010	1. Amendment to Company Act 2. Amendment to Corporate Governance Code	1. Management and supervisory board statements were made integral to the annual reporting of publicly listed companies 2. Introduction of sixty-eight main questions disclosure questionnaire to publicly listed companies

(continued)

[9] The Market in Financial Instruments Directive within the Lamfalussy process provides legal framework for securities markets, investment intermediaries, and trading venues.

Table 3.1 (continued)

Year of application	*Development*	*Novelty*
2013	1. Adjustment to the Takeover Act 2. Alternative Investment Funds Act	1. Novelty in that stock market price prevails in that the bidder is obliged to offer the average market price in the period three months prior, except when there was no trading in over one-third of trading days. A mandatory takeover offer is required for ownership equal to or above twenty-five percent. Special permissions from HANFA are required for ownership of more than ten percent of financial companies 2. Prescription of conditions for establishment and operation of alternative investment funds and management companies
2016	Introduction of capital gains tax at twelve percent rate that is applicable for holding period under two years	Other tax rates include: 1. Dividend rate at twelve percent, none on interest on bonds for non-resident legal entities and resident natural persons/retail entities, else twelve percent rate applies, 2. Twelve percent on other interest or fifteen percent for non-resident legal entities

Year of application	*Development*	*Novelty*
2017 amendment	Prevention of Money Laundering and Terrorist Financing Act	1. A decreased threshold of reporting to Euro fifteen thousand (US$ 13.4 thousand) and mandatory customer due diligence for occasional transactions exceeding Euro one thousand (US$ nine hundred) or for betting transactions more than Euro two thousand (US$ 1.8 thousand) 2. Establishment of the Registrar of beneficial owners
2021	CCP Board Establishment	On August 20, 2021 HANFA informed its public about establishing the Board of regulators of the CDCC – CCP Smart Clear company. The member list of CDCC-CCP Board of regulators which was founded as: 1.HANFA, as the competent authority of the CCP in accordance with Article 18 (2) (b), (d) and (f) of the EMIR 2. ESMA (Chairman or one of the independent members of the Supervisory Committee for CCPs referred to in Article 24a (2) (a) and (b) of the EMIR), in accordance with Article 18 (2) (a) 3. HNB, in accordance with Article 18 (2) (c) and (h) of the EMIR, and 4. ECB, in accordance with Article 18 (2) (c) of the EMIR CDCC will transfer the settlement activities to the CDCC-CCP within a maximum of two months from the enforcement of the decision on approval for a license Having in mind the regulatory procedure and deadlines, the beginning of operations of the CDCC-CCP is likely scheduled at the end of 2021 or later

(continued)

Table 3.1 (continued)

Year of application	*Development*	*Novelty*
Conforming stage to the EU *acquis*	1. Capital Requirements Directive IV 2. MiFIR** 3. Short selling and stock lending 4. CCP 5. Transparency, Market Abuse, and Prospectus standards 6. Bank Recovery and Resolution Directive 7. Transparency, Market Abuse, and Prospectus standards 8. European Market Infrastructure Regulation	1. Basel III standards 2. Record keeping, transaction reporting, market transparency, admission of financial instruments to trading, etc 3. 2012 ESMA and EU regulation. Permitted 4. 2017 settlement standards for CCDC. Croatia does not have a qualified central counterparty entity needed for clearing higher risk transactions including financial derivatives 5. 2015 EU standard on transparency of securities financing transactions and reuse 6. 2016 EU standard 7. 2016, 2014, and 2017 respective EU standards 8. 2016 EU standards on OTC derivatives, central counterparties, and trade repositories***

Source Author's selection on showcase regulation and legislation.Seba (2017)

*Complete information on regulatory coverage is available on HANFA website at http://www.hanfa.hr/capital-market/

**MiFIR II compliant since January 2018. HANFA approved ZSE as Approved Publication Arrangement for OTC transaction information

***Not compliant with T2S settlement eliminating differences between local and cross-border settlement using central bank money. In addition, the shallow market, smaller equity and liquidity base have not yet resulted in creation of central counterparty to traded contracts and ensuring the performance of such

In 1996 the first dematerialized privatization of shares was completed in the transaction for Kolinska, a food processing company. In 1997 SKB and BTC, two local commercial banks issued depository receipts on the LJSE and in the same year the first block trading occurred. Again in 1997 the Government introduced a tax on capital gains. The National Bank of Slovenia (BSI) first obliged foreign investors to keep local custody accounts and to maintain foreign exchange reserves on local banks' balance sheets, but then relaxed the rule by mandating a non-sale period of the first seven years from the initial investment date. In 1999 LJSE started publishing the closed-end investment fund index, PIX, which was terminated in 2008. LJSE launched six industries' indices in 2000, but only dropped them in 2005. LJSE then published the blue-chip index SBI20 in 2000, which was reorganized into SBITOP in 2006.

In the privatization process, first, the decentralized and gradual commercial approach failed, then the centralized and mass approach failed, and as a compromise of the two approaches, at the end of 1992, the Law on Transformation of Social Ownership[10] was passed. The compromise featured a process in which **(a)** approximately up to forty percent of social capital was to be transferred indirectly to the Government of Slovenia in direct ownership by restitution, development, or pension funds, **(b)** twenty percent transfer was to be executed through coupon ownership certificates to be allocated to natural persons/retail entities including employees, and **(c)** the remaining forty percent was to be ceded on commercial terms to any buyers, most frequently again to the preferred Government-owned development funds (Mencinger, 2006). Government-owned privatization investment funds were the primary intermediaries and received a minority stake in numerous enterprises. These funds later evolved into corporations consolidating minority interests, operating under strong political influence, and managing to expand businesses to become one of the largest players in Slovenian insurance, pension assets' management, and investments funds' management industries. Simultaneously, private asset management companies emerged in the lucrative environment of managing the Government-owned funds

[10] Three other laws added to the scope of privatization: **(a)** the Housing Act enabled privatization of approximately one hundred thousand apartments; **(b)** the Denationalization Act introduced the restitution of nationalized property, and **(c)** the Law on Cooperatives assigned forty percent of shares in food processing enterprises to the farmers' cooperatives.

and under the process of transforming the capital into private hands. The transformation was conducted through exchanging shares between management and owners, and in parallel between the funds themselves to decrease the overall funds' size and with the intention to progress further privatization. However, the internal interference was high, and the process was prolonged to last a full decade. Over that time the consumption of management entitled fees amassed while enterprises were burdened with lapsed resources.

In 2000 Slovenia undertook pension system reform to introduce a voluntary private pension system creating a market that reached roughly US$ 2.5 billion of assets under management at the year-end 2016. Pension companies, insurance companies, and pension funds are subject to asset investment limitations of up to (**a**) thirty percent in equity, (**b**) ten percent in real estate, and (**c**) a minimum of forty percent in Government bonds. Roughly seventy percent of pension assets are invested in sovereign bonds.

In 2001 the BSI lifted restrictions on foreign portfolio investments in the capital market and in the same year KDD officially introduced an OTC market. In 2002, because of the Novartis Group takeover of Lek pharmaceuticals, LJSE booked a record turnover. In 2004 Slovenia joined the EU after which several EU entities, in particular asset management companies and new funds, entered the market through common EU passporting rights. Local players reacted by increasing the product scope offer and the overall capital market grew very quickly thereafter. In 2005 the first auction trading was launched for less liquid securities. In 2006 the first ETF was launched, MP-Eurostock, with a portfolio of stocks from the thirty largest European corporations. In 2007 the first non-resident issuer placed a bond on LJSE. The nature of growth was largely concentrated on equity products. Thereto, the 2007/2008 crisis aftermath left deep repercussions, halving the value of the regulated stocks' prices.

In 2008 the Vienna Stock Exchange became the majority owner of LJSE. In 2009 LJSE admitted its first remote members, namely Austrian commercial banks, and in the same year LJSE became approved as the officially appointed mechanism for central storage of regulated information. In 2010 LJSE started trading on Xetra trading platform. In 2012 the first commercial paper security was listed. In 2015 ZSE finalized takeover of the LJSE.

3.2.2 Contemporary Setting

The capital market in Slovenia operates under the EU legal and institutional framework. The market liquidity and turnover are shallow. Investors' perception of the market points to relative uncertainty. Besides, the market is still strongly influenced by Government-controlled capital. Government ownership concentration is significant in the total LJSE capitalization and turnover. Two important factors defining the capital market environment in Slovenia are the scale of involvement of Government capital and the predominance of select financial intermediaries. In the banking sector, Nova Ljubljanska Banka, a Government-controlled bank, accounts for roughly a third of the market by assets size, while the second-largest bank, Nova Kreditna Banka Maribor, was privatized in 2016 by the sale to Apollo Fund and EBRD. In the insurance sector, Triglav d.d., a Government-owned insurance company, holds roughly a third of the total market by premiums. Triglav is also one of the biggest players in the investment funds' market. The outlook therefore implies that the privatization cycle has not been completed in a scale comparable to the other researched SEE countries. Another implication is that one may expect a next level of the privatization cycle under compliance with the EU requirements that were imposed as one of the criteria in the ex-post 2007/2008 crisis EU funding support. Privatizations to date are overshadowed by low-scale progress and slow process in the 1990s transition, which meant a lesser impact on a concentrated development of the capital market in Slovenia (Fig. 3.2).

The trend of new privatizations in the more recent period is visible in transactions for other non-strategic Government-owned companies, as witnessed in the sales of stakes in Ljubljana airport to Fraport in 2014, Mercator food retailer to Agrokor in 2014, Pivovarna Lasko to Heineken in 2015, etc. In the most recent case of a large market and non-privatization related capital market transaction, in May 2018, Hisense, one of China's and the global largest producers of white goods, provided a public offer for Gorenje. The public offering price exceeded LJSE's listed Gorenje market price by more than one hundred percent. In this block transaction trading, Gorenje's stock was suspended on LJSE. Such a valuation discrepancy yet again points to a lack of liquidity on the LJSE to better reflect the transaction value ex ante.

LJSE*:

Market capitalization – US$ 50.1 billion.

Annual trading turnover – US$ 430.3 million on regulated exchange and US$ 37.3 billion on OTC trading and off-market**.

Market share in regulated exchange trading by security type – 99.9 percent shares and the rest in bonds and structured products.

***

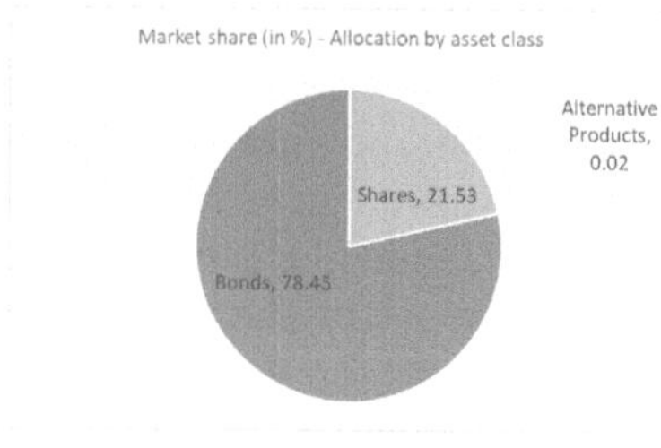

***

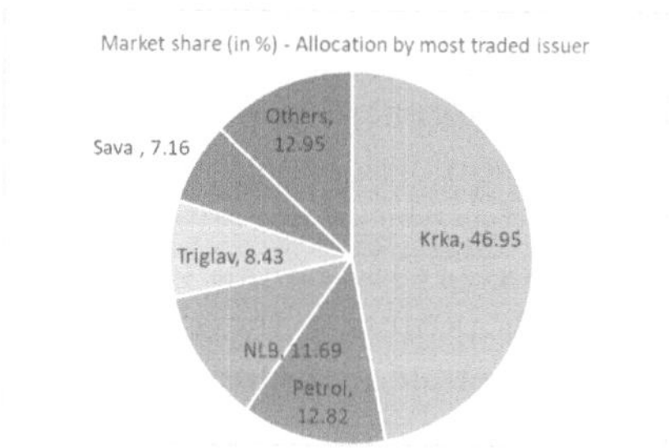

***

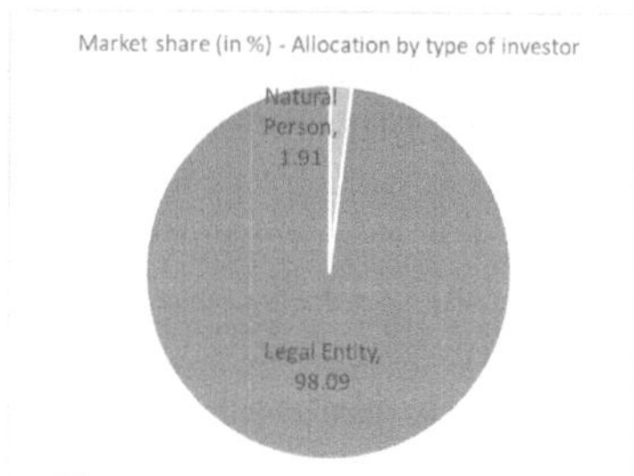

**MTF capitalization and trading data are publicly NA.*
***Year-end 2021 data sourced from Ljubljanska Stock Exchange (2022) and KDD Centralna Klirinsko Depotna Druzba d.d. Ljubljana (2022).*
**** Data per LJSE regulated market.*

Fig. 3.2 Characteristics of capital market in Slovenia

Krka pharmaceuticals is the dominant LJSE listed company representing thirty-five percent of the year-end 2016 turnover and capitalization. Petrol, a gasoline trading company, follows with eighteen and fourteen percent, respectively, and Triglav, insurance company, with eleven and nine percent, respectively. Krka shares are owned by government fund, Kapitalska, institutional investors, and thirty-nine percent by individual investors. In the latter two companies, Government fund has the largest and controlling ownership stake. **The preference for internal Slovenian economic players in the privatization process, the continued control predominance of government capital, and questionable insider information access have deterred continuous large-scale foreign investments.**

In 2018 the first regulated real estate alternative investment fund, KD Adriatic Value was launched. The Fund was launched in cooperation with Peakside Capital, an international real estate investor, and KD Funds, an asset manager emerging from the former Slovenian privatization funds. Under a relatively smaller market size, the rise of asset-backed securities such as mortgage-backed has less potential in comparison with the markets in Croatia or Serbia. LJSE market is insufficiently liquid, and IPOs are not utilized due to cost non-effectiveness and in preference for private transactions. The regulated market features the following instruments: **(a)** ordinary and preferred shares, **(b)** investment fund shares, **(c)** corporate bonds, **(d)** sovereign bonds, **(e)** money market instruments, **(f)** treasury bills, and **(g)** warrants.

KDD, the central clearing agency, is integrated into the harmonized European settlement infrastructure and is an accredited LEI provider. The scope of KDD services is limited by not having a banking license to take credit risk and to act as a CCP in settlements. KDD's scope of work includes providing services of **(a)** maintaining decentralized securities, **(b)** serving issuers for securities share ledge, **(c)** custody for takeovers, **(d)** calculating and settling stock exchange and off-market transactions, and **(e)** assigning identity codes. KDD provides settlement protection for the LJSE regulated market transactions with **(a)** the Liquidity Reserves Fund, **(b)** the Guarantee Fund, **(c)** partial settlement and cancellation of trade, **(d)** buy-in/sell-out procedure, and **(e)** pledge of securities on members' proprietary accounts. For the Liquidity Reserves Fund, respective KDD members contribute when daily net cash obligations exceed an amount equal to twenty-five percent of the initial principal of the Guarantee Fund plus its additional contribution. Securities Market Agency, Agencija za Trg Vrednostnih Papirjev (ATVP), supervises the Slovenian capital market and issues authorizations to **(a)** stock exchanges, **(b)** depositories, **(c)** brokerage companies, and **(d)** management companies, amongst others. The LJSE regulated market consists of the prime, standard, and entry markets, while SI Enter is the MTF market. Requirements for listing on the prime market include minimum capital of Euro ten million (roughly US$ 9.1 million in year-end 2019) and twenty-five percent free float. The business days working hours are 08:00–16:00, with continuous trading from 9:30–14:30. All on-exchange trades are settled in one batch on “T+2” time settlement.

3.2.3 *Legal and Regulatory Framework*

BSI licenses and supervises the banking system and foreign exchange market in Slovenia. ATVP, founded in 1994, independently regulates the capital market and market participants in Slovenia. It has the authority to grant licenses to brokers, and fund managers, approve public offerings, investigate, and prosecute. Insurance Supervision Agency oversees the insurance market and pension companies and their operations. The key market legal and regulatory developments are summarized in Table 3.2 as follows.

The accounting framework in Slovenia is not analyzed in the study due to the shorter scope of research and the fact that the financial system of the country is practically in its entirety harmonized with the latest global standards.

3.3 Capital Market in Bosnia and Herzegovina

3.3.1 *Historical Overview*

There is almost no evidence of capital market developments in B&H before the establishment of the modern-day country under the constitutional framework of the 1995 Dayton Agreement. The first stock exchanges were set up in 2001 and 2002. The first trading occurred in 2002. As in the comparable regional examples, the capital market developed as a platform for privatizations under economic transition from planned to free market. Economic transition in B&H followed the centralized mass voucher ownership of certificates privatization process. From 2003 the process was largely conducted through the participation of closed-end privatization investment funds. In 2006 first SOEs were listed on the stock exchanges. **However, the closed-end funds failed to restructure the former SOEs due to discount pricing, negative returns, and lacklustre efficiency in the process. In response investors’ confidence and trust in the B&H capital market was low from the initial days of its establishment.** Furthermore, the inefficient process was marked by minority owners’ inability to exert positive

Table 3.2 Key legal and regulatory developments in the capital market in Slovenia

Year of application	*Development*	*Novelty*
2007 alignment with the EU 2015 amendment	Banking Act	1. Alignment with the EU Directives. Regulates set-up and operating conditions of credit institutions in Slovenia 2. Authorizes ECB exclusive authority to grant and withdraw licenses. Exclusive direct supervisory authority on systemic banking institutions. An example is observable under the case of the creation of state "bad bank" following the 2007/2008 crisis. Expanding Bank for International Settlements (BIS) supervisory role on further risk management and reporting
2007	Market in Financial Instruments Act*	Aligns with MiFID directives. Regulates the financial instruments market, the required reporting, investment services, exchanges operations, etc
2005	The Investment Funds and Asset Management Companies Act	Alignment with the EU Undertakings for Collective Investments in Transferable Securities (UCITS) Directive on conditions to establish funds and management companies, public offerings, vendors, supervision, etc

(continued)

Table 3.2 (continued)

Year of application	*Development*	*Novelty*
2015	Alternative Investment Fund Managers Act	Alignment with EU Alternative Investment Fund Management (AIFM) Directive. Regulates private investment funds and alternative funds, custodian establishment, operations, and liquidation
2006 entry 2015 amendment	Takeover Act Amendment	Applicable to public companies, companies trading on regulated markets, or joint-stock companies with at least two hundred and fifty shareholders or equity larger than Euro 4.1 million (roughly US$ 3.7 million)[11] 1. Regulates the obligatory takeover procedure when an investor acquires more than fifty percent ownership rights 2. Use of pledge collateral is prohibited as means of acquisition payment

[11] Year-end 2019 exchange rate is used in Table 8.

Year of application	*Development*	*Novelty*
2006 entry and 2015 amendment	Companies Act Amendment	Regulates the rules for economic and commercial activities of commercial companies, proprietors, related parties, subsidiaries, etc. Novelties in year 2015 include: 1. Obligatory reporting on related entities 2. Restrictions on withdrawal of minimum capital value for newly established companies 3. Additional regulations to the institutionalization of internal audits 4. Implementation of EU Directive 2013
2015 amendment	Book-Entry Securities Act	Regulates corporate actions and access to data with central registrars Harmonizes with the EU standards for purposes of joining "T2S" single market infrastructure for a more cost-efficient manner delivery-versus-payment settlement in central bank money

(continued)

Table 3.2 (continued)

Year of application	*Development*	*Novelty*
2016 amendment	Prevention of Money Laundering and Terrorist Financing Act	A decreased threshold of reporting to Euro fifteen thousand (roughly US$ 13.4 thousand) and mandates customer due diligence for occasional transactions exceeding Euro one thousand (roughly US$ eight hundred and ninety-three) or for betting transactions more than Euro two thousand (roughly US$ 1.8 thousand). Establishment of register of beneficial owners
	Tax rates:	1. Fifteen percent on interest while deposits and bonds are exempt 2. Fifteen percent on dividends 3. Capital gains tax is applicable by assessment. Non-applicable for non-resident natural persons/retail entities unless owning more than ten percent or if fifty percent of sold entity assets derive from immovable property. For resident natural entities and non-resident legal and natural entities with permanent establishment in Slovenia it is twenty-five percent, decreasing progressively with time after five years. Ordinary income tax, at progressive rate starting from sixteen percent, applies for resident legal entities

Year of application	*Development*	*Novelty*
Conforming stage to the EU *acquis*	1. Capital Requirements Directive IV 2. MiFIR* 3. Short selling and stock lending 4. CCP 5. Transparency, Market Abuse, and Prospectus standards 6. Bank Recovery and Resolution Directive 7. European Market Infrastructure Regulation.**	1. Basel III standards 2. Recordkeeping, transaction reporting, market transparency, admission of financial instruments to trading, etc. 3. Short selling is in general restricted and proceeds according to ESMA reporting standards. Securities lending is possible on a bilateral basis 4. KDD does not provide a netting service which limits the central counterparty role. In addition, lack of equity base prohibits EMIR margin requirements on ninety-nine percent confidence level, fund size, and collateral amount buffers for other market players 5. Stronger compliance standards to Croatia and higher violation up-front monetary fine consequences 6. 2016 EU standard

Source Author's selection of showcase regulation and legislation
*MiFIR compliant. MiFID Two still non-compliant and pending Parliament approval on transpositions to local legislation
**Compliant with "T2S" settlement eliminating differences between local and cross-border settlement using central bank money

returns through privatization sales or through conversions into open-end funds that allow redemption. The process has also revealed problematic anti-money laundering accusations, subpar privatization funds' manager's selection, etc.

Sarajevo Stock Exchange (SASE) was established as a joint-stock company in 2002 in accordance with the Federation of B&H's (FB&H) Law on Securities, which was adopted in 1998. Eight brokerage companies contributed a total share capital of Bosnia-Herzegovina's Convertible Mark (BAM) three hundred thousand (c. US$ one hundred and sixty thousand at the time). The first trading on the SASE took place in April 2002. The first SASE index was created in 2003 under the name B&H Investment Funds Index (BIFX). Thereafter the following indices were established: **(a)** SASX-10 in 2006, **(b)** SASX-30 in 2009, **(c)** SASX-BBI Islamic index in 2016, and **(d)** SASX-FN index in 2017, based on the most profitable companies in the real sector. In 2008 the following developments were introduced on the capital market scene: **(a)** corporate governance rulebook, **(b)** IPO and special auctions rulebook, **(c)** off-market trading rulebook, **(d)** the first IPO, and **(e)** the first bond listing. The first international investors were the nearby regional counterparts, primarily Croatian and Slovenian companies. The 2007/2008 crisis impact on the SASE regulated exchange capitalization and turnover resulted in plummeting by more than fifty percent (Sarajevo Stock Exchange, 2018).

Banja Luka Stock Exchange (BLSE) was established as a joint-stock company in 2001 in accordance with the Republika Srpska's (RS) Entity Law on Securities, which was adopted in 1998. Eight banks and one brokerage company were the initial owners and founders of BLSE. The first trading took place in 2002 using the LJSE's electronic trading system and under close cooperation of the two exchanges. In 2003 the privatization investment funds, Government-owned company, namely Oil Refinery Modrica, and local banks' shares composed in entirety of the listings on the BLSE. The first index, BIRS, was established in 2003. It was followed by the establishment of the investment funds' index, FIRS, in 2004, and of power utilities companies' index, ERS10, in 2005. In 2008 the first IPO was done by a private local company. In 2009 corporate governance scorecards were adopted. Both BLSE and SASE ownership was demutualized in 2008, allowing non-members to take ownership stakes (Banja Luka Stock Exchange, 2018).

The first single country B&H index, BATX, was established on the Vienna Stock Exchange in December 2009 for listing and investments, including embedded multi-currency and derivative products.

Capital market development in B&H fell behind the comparable regional SEE markets and many of the first milestones were achieved only in the late 2000s. Unfortunately, the early development faced brisk stalling in the aftermath of the 2007/2008 crisis spillover. Post-crisis recovery started with the initial emergence of Entity Government level (Federation B&H and RS) debt securities that were structured through the conversion of old currency savings and war repatriation debt into receivables. The year 2011 marked the start of Entity Government level treasury bills issuances and listings. First established in 2009, open-end investment funds developed with an investment strategy to invest in Government securities. The appearance of Entity Government level funding through debt securities issuance was more prevalent in RS and on the BLSE, which then led to BLSE's turnover surpassing SASE's turnover and in the existence of bonds secondary market trading in BLSE versus large non-existence on SASE. In 2008 the first municipal bonds were listed. Municipal bonds, however, entail Entity Governments' performance guarantees. In 2013 the first corporate bonds were listed by local banks and local corporations. The issuances were executed in very small financial amounts and with a narrow investor base. As such, they rather appeared as bilateral loans that are only routed through exchanges to achieve disclosure and statutory reporting purposes. While a fair number of banks are listed on both exchanges, the underlying causes of the listings may have been legal and statutory requirements for receiving parent bank funding; as opposed to primarily utilizing the BLSE and the SASE as an alternative source of funding (World Bank, 2015). No real sector company is simultaneously listed on both the SASE and the BLSE. The two exchanges exhibit different legal and regulative requirements. In 2014 the first repurchase agreement (REPO) trading operations were conducted with Government-owned closed-end funds and corporate securities. In 2016 "T+2" settlement period was introduced, versus the prior "T+3" timeline.

3.3.2 *Contemporary Setting*

Capital market in B&H is characterized by ambiguities and a lack of investor trust under complexities associated with split Entity Governments' structure, amidst unstable and fragmented politics, weak structural reforms, and weak corporate governance, amongst others. The current environment is categorized by the following issues: (**a**) low private real sector participation (**b**) an absence of institutional investors *vis-à-vis* Slovenia and Croatia, (**c**) an emigratory "brain drain," (**d**) delicate institutional policies capacities, (**e**) a weakened public sector companies' capacities and financial results due to operational inefficiencies, and (**f**) an increasing pressure on small enterprises' financial contribution to the large public sector and the social spending apparatus. On the progress side, recently in the RS, but not in the Federation B&H, an advancement was achieved in reorganizing legacy closed-end privatization funds to the open-ended kind and/or joint-stock companies. In 2019 in the RS some ten percent of minority ownership holders have been paid out; namely in two funds, OMIF Future and OMIF Maximus, which emerged as open-end funds from the former closed-end Zepter fund. Non-performing assets were allocated to closed-end funds with intention of later liquidation. Opportunities for improvements may exist in harmonizing legal adjustment between the Entity Governments. This would allow imminent investment funds mergers and a more straightforward route for the market entrance of foreign institutional market makers, brokers, asset management companies, and real sector investors, at first, and then the local and international natural person/retail investors. At present, investors are deterred by small and fragmented markets. On the higher priority importance, consideration might be given to allowing payments in kind to try to revitalize liquidity on formerly failed investments. Besides, large-scale privatizations could be implemented to attract new investments and new capital. In addition, the pension system might be reformed to enable internal institutional direct investment placements via local capital markets. Nonetheless, reforming the pension system will require a very significant policy push in an environment of fragmented and conflicting politics and a very high level of unemployment at close to thirty percent, or more than fifty percent for youth. Besides, mandatory contributions to the first pillar of the pension system are already high, amounting to up to 18.5%. Finally, in B&H the environment is characterized by aging population, high emigration trend amongst youth, and fiscal deficits funded by borrowings.

Pension funds in OECD markets invest forty-four percent of assets on average in stock exchange-listed shares (Rakocevic, 2016). This figure appears whopping in comparison to B&H, where only a fractional portion of pension system assets are placed in listed shares. In the RS there is a unique Pension Reserve Fund at the Entity Government level, established with the intention to receive ten percent holding of all companies to be privatized. At present, it participates in fixed-income securities purchases on the capital markets, though at a low base of under US$ seventy million. In 2017 the Pension Reserve Fund, EBRD, and Slovenian asset management company Skupna d.d. teamed up to **establish a private pension fund management company for voluntary pension contributions**. The initial capital injected was BAM 4.4 million (c. US$ 2.7 million at the time), following which large corporations started subscribing to the fund. Another capital market advancement opportunity may exist in the closer integration of the two Entity level capital markets to then achieve better economy of scale efficiencies for wide stakeholders. B&H has the lowest comparable country debt to GDP ratio in the region, though it increases fractionally by way of public debt financing in the form of municipal and Entity Government borrowings utilizing regulated exchanges. Although B&H sovereign level Government is empowered to borrow locally, to date it has not done so. Investors in an Entity Government level securities benefit from preferential tax treatment but simultaneously face higher uncertainty from public sector performance due to frequent and direct political interference. Government securities are almost exclusively held to maturity with minimal secondary trading. In addition, investors remain cautious of the risk profile and debt repayment viability of low transparent funded sub-projects. In any case should GDP not grow by a rate higher than that debt, the risk profile may change swiftly. An exemplary comparable trend was apparent in Serbia, where public debt grew from roughly thirty-three percent of GDP in 2009 to roughly seventy-five percent in 2015 due to poorly managed sovereign spending and weak sovereign fiscal control.

The capital market in B&H is regulated at an Entity level by two separate securities commissions, each with its own set of broadly similar laws and regulations. The two commissions often face limitations in resources and through political interference. An exemplary case occurred in 2009 with the long-standing failure to appoint Federation B&H Securities Commission executive management due to political deadlock. For the equivalent reason, the Commission did not operate from October 2019 to September 2020. **Integrating the two Entities' exchanges to closer and uniform cooperation and single economic space** may be plausible economically and socially. Electronic routing links for inter-depository transfers may have been established between the BLSE and the SASE imminently after an agreement on a common platform for trading was signed in 2012. In the respective replicative cases, the SASE linked with the Istanbul Exchange and the BLSE linked with the Athens Exchange. Cooperation between regulatory agencies is subpar and regulatory differences spur further market obscurity. Such a barrier may yet be partially overcome by having an intermediary securities administrator role, even in an informal association format, and one supervising enhanced coordination and cooperation to allow for a continuous informational exchange and for cross-checks. Eventually, the integration would allow free investors' passporting between the two Entities' authorities.

From the perspective of corporate governance and regulatory effectiveness, ambiguity still looms over the market on fallacies in insider information trading and in related parties' transactions. In certain market examples, there are subpar standards for advanced economies on **(a)** investor protection, **(b)** corporate governance, and **(c)** disclosure requirements. In the current environment the involvement of natural persons/retail entities in trading, both resident and non-resident, is marginal. More so, SASE provides regular and coherent data publications while BLSE does not, which points to room to improve transparency. According to the Securities Commission of the Federation B&H, fines for public non-disclosure range from BAM fifteen thousand (roughly US$ eight thousand five hundred and seventy-one) to BAM two hundred thousand (roughly US$ one hundred fourteen thousand two hundred and eighty-six) for legal entities and from BAM five hundred (roughly US$ two hundred and eighty-five) to BAM ten thousand (roughly US$ five thousand seven hundred and fourteen)[12] for natural persons/retail entities. Foreign issuers face a further disadvantage in that the legislation does not require listed companies' public reporting in English or another foreign language. From the available data, the predominant trade in securities is

[12] Year-end 2019 exchange rate is used for all of the shown stock exchanges requirements. BAM is pegged to the Euro at a rate of 0.5113.

in fixed-income issuances, at eighty-one percent of total turnover in the BLSE. SASE shows a greater predominance of equity turnover and equity representation in the asset class breakdown by capitalization size. The involvement of foreign institutional investors is barely existent, though foreign and mostly regional investors own listed equities at a ratio of roughly forty percent of the total, and in fixed-income securities at under fifteen percent of the total (World Bank, 2015) (Fig. 3.3) .

Market capitalization–

SASE at US$ 3.1 billion.

BLSE at US$ 2.4 billion.

Annual trading turnover* –

SASE at US$ 311.6 million on regulated exchange and US$ 1.9 million on OTC and off-exchange trade.

BLSE at US$ 34.2 million.

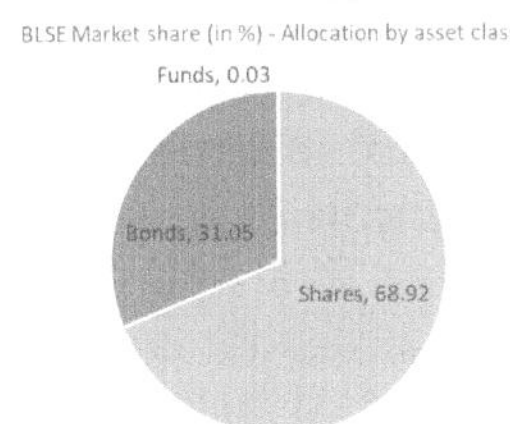

SASE Market Share (in %) - Allocation by type of investor		
Group	Buy-side	Sell Side
Domestic investors	30.70%	15.97%
Foreign investors	7.98%	24.29%
Custody investors	61.32%	59.73%

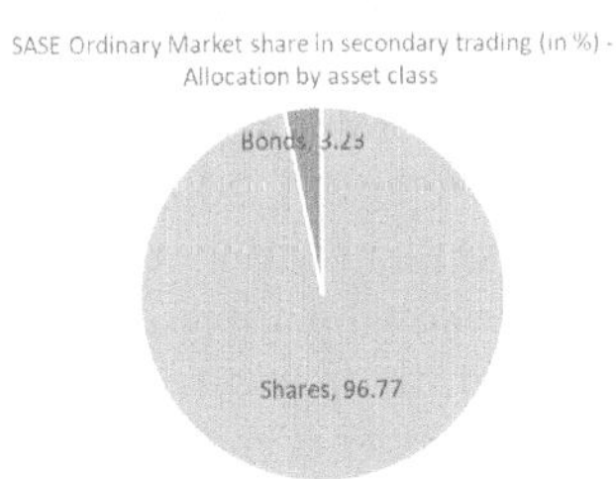

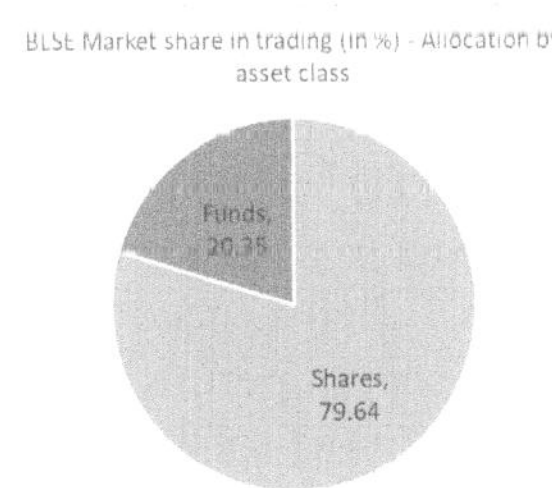

**Year-end 2021 data sourced from the Banja Luka Stock Exchange (2022) and year-end 2020 data from the Sarajevo Stock Exchange (2022). MTF data is unavailable.*

Fig. 3.3 Characteristics of capital market in B&H

The financial sector's assets in B&H are approximately worth US$ 15.5 billion. The insurance market is rather small, at roughly four percent of B&H's US$ 16.4 billion GDP, versus seven percent in Croatia and ten percent in Slovenia, and forms less than five percent of the total financial assets in the country. Leasing companies form roughly 1.5% of the financial sector assets, microcredit institutions another 2.3%, and investment funds 2.8%. Insurance industry exhibits a growing trend in an environment with a low level of life insurance or voluntary insurance participation. Commercial banks capture the remaining and the predominant portion of the financial system assets in B&H (Central Bank of Bosnia and Herzegovina, 2016). The banking sector is dominated by the UniCredit and Raiffeisen subsidiaries, together holding roughly one-third of banking industry assets.

The survey in B&H (Kozarevic et al., 2014) indicates a lack of supply of financial derivatives and similar innovative financial instruments. The researchers found that only a quarter of the surveyed banks hired staff certified with ACI[13] dealing certificates and that only little over half of the surveyed user companies have risk management departments in their organizational structure. It points to a lack of awareness of the characteristics and benefits of financial derivatives and innovative financial products. Other market limitations identified in the survey are: **(a)** frequent need for cash cover as deposit collateral, **(b)** requirement on large client turnover, **(c)** lack of need to use differing currencies, and **(d)** frequent requirements to post margins. These findings coincide with the research in Serbia (Marinkovic & Skakavac, 2010). The financial derivatives providers in B&H are almost exclusively Western European commercial banks, which introduced such products to the market. Findings of this research point to the EU MiFID legislation (DIRECTIVE 2004/39/EC, 2004) directing that companies who participate in capital markets, in order to qualify as professional clients, need to meet two of the following three characteristics unless special permission is granted based on trading turnover. These conditions are **(a)** total assets of more than Euro twenty million (roughly US$ 17.9 million), **(b)** total turnover of more than Euro forty million (roughly US$ 35.7 million) and, **(c)** total capital of more than Euro two

[13] Association Cambiste Internationale—international non-profit, non-political association of wholesale financial market professionals. Members of ACI FMA are to a large extent engaged in professional trading, broking, operations, regulatory and compliance activities in foreign exchange, money fixed-income and derivatives markets.

million (roughly US$ 1.8 million).[14] The SEE pool of companies meeting the total assets and/or total turnover and/or total capital requirements today is relatively small. Nonetheless, special permissions do exist and are widely used. In addition, companies may participate as non-professional clients under a few additional restrictions. SASE and BLSE provide official market and free market continuous trading in equity shares, closed and open-ended investment funds' shares, bonds, and other debt securities, etc.

General criteria for admission to the official market include **(a)** minimum capital of BAM four million (roughly US$ 2.5 million)[15] at the SASE while the BLSE requires BAM ten million (roughly US$ six million), **(b)** minimum twenty-five percent free float with a book value of BAM two million (roughly US$1.25 million) or BAM 3 million (roughly US$1.9 million) for bonds on the SASE while the BLSE requires fifteen percent free float and BAM one million listing value (roughly US$ 0.6 million), **(c)** three years of audited reports, and **(d)** minimum of one hundred and fifty owners on the SASE while the BLSE requires one hundred owners. Free market requirements are lower at **(a)** minimum twenty-five percent public listing with a book value of BAM two million on the SASE while the BLSE requires fifteen percent and BAM 0.5 million (roughly US$0.3 million), **(b)** two years of audited reports, and **(c)** minimum thirty owners as required by the BLSE. SASE business days' trading hours are 9:00–13:30, with continuous trading starting at 10:00. BLSE business days' trading hours are 8:00–13:00, with continuous trading starting at 09:30.

3.3.3 *Legal and Regulatory Framework*

Central Bank of Bosnia and Herzegovina (CBB&H) and the B&H Deposit Insurance Agency operate at the sovereign country-level versus the Entity level. In the FB&H, the securities market is regulated by the Securities Commission of the FB&H, which was established in 1998 pursuant to the FB&H Securities Market Act. In the RS, the capital market is regulated by the RS Securities Commission, which

[14] Year-end 2019 exchange rate is used. BAM is pegged to the Euro at a rate of 0.5113.

[15] Year-end 2019 exchange rate is used. BAM is pegged to the Euro at a rate of 0.5113.

was established in 1999 pursuant to the RS Law on Securities. In the Brčko District, an independent securities commission oversees the district-related securities market. Similarly, each Entity has its own banking industry supervisory agency. Dematerialized electronic registration of financial securities, securities safekeeping and data maintenance, and clearing and settlement of all transactions in securities traded through the BLSE and the SASE are undertaken by Entity level Central Registries of Securities. Both registrars were established as joint-stock companies under the auspices of the FB&H's and the RS' Securities Market Laws. The two registrars have sufficiently diversified public and private ownership structures to ensure that they are able to operate independently from the exchanges in the respective Entities. In the current environment, dividends are processed by issuers or custody banks directly, while in the future one might expect such a function to be transferred to the central registries, which are the paying agents for interests on bonds. Depository guarantee funds are established at the individual registry level. Guarantee funds are made up of member contributions for BAM five thousand (roughly US$ five thousand eight hundred and fifty-seven in year-end 2019), in addition to the share of transaction volume payments. Both contributions serve to cover any losses of participants and brokers during settlements. The registrars also keep reserve funds of twenty-five percent of annual income to cover operating losses.

The analysis of the accounting framework in B&H is not included due to the shorter scope of research and the fact that the financial system of the country is to a great degree synchronized with the latest global standards (Table 3.3).

3.4 Capital Market in Serbia

3.4.1 Historical Overview

In 1886 the National Assembly of the Kingdom of Serbia adopted the Stock Exchange Law as proposed by the Serbian Trading Association. Eight years later the Belgrade Stock Exchange was founded for the purpose of promoting, facilitating, and regulating trade in (a) various commodities, (b) cheques and coupons, (c) cash and equivalents, and (d) other, predominantly in Government debt financial securities. With an increase in trading, the Belgrade Stock Exchange introduced two separate trading platforms, the Commodity Stock Exchange and the

Table 3.3 Key legal and regulatory developments in the capital market in B&H

Year of application	*Development*	*Novelty*
2016 2017	Banking Act amendment in RS Banking Act amendment in FB&H	Largely in line between the two Entities, the Acts are the first amendments in close to twenty years after Basel I implementation. The amendments follow the failures of two commercial banks in the RS in the recent three years. Main novelties rest on: 1. Better alignment with the EU regulation on CRV ID Four and CRR capital requirements 2. A supervisory review process and increasing power to the regulating agencies and banks' supervisory boards. The increased capacity and power of supervisory agencies address resolution and restructuring processes. Locally owned banks face hurdles to meet the new demands such as internal, risk-based approaches, stress testing, and larger safekeeping and disclosure compliance 3. The record date for shareholders meetings is shortened to thirty days from forty-five days in advance. Unforeseen shareholders meetings are to be published at the latest fourteen days prior and with a quorum at fifty percent, versus seventy-five percent earlier

(continued)

Table 3.3 (continued)

Year of application	*Development*	*Novelty*
2017 2021	Law on Securities in FB&H amendment Law on Securities in RS amendment Law on Securities in RS amendment	1. Both entities: Novelty for legal entities and natural persons/retail entities approval threshold to acquire or increase their qualified share (ten, twenty, thirty (thirty-three in RS) or fifty (sixty-six percent in RS)) in the capital of professional intermediaries or of exchange 2. FB&H: Allowing banks and insurance and reinsurance companies to participate in off-exchange transactions mediated by brokers; however, investment funds, pension funds, fund management companies and intermediaries are prohibited to transact 1. RS: Shareholders in a stock exchange may be both local and foreign natural persons/retail entities and legal entities. Previously, the right to own such shares was restricted to professional intermediaries only. The restriction that the participation in the capital of a stock exchange by a single investor may not exceed twenty percent has been removed 2. 2021 Amendment in RS: Brokerage houses may also perform ancillary activities related to the core business that do not adversely affect its performance. Examples include (a) advising companies on capital structure and business strategy, (b) providing legal or financial advice in the field of corporate governance, (c) research and financial analysis in the field of investment, (d) performing technical, fundamental, and other analysis, (e) preparation of business plans, (f) participation in the preparation of legal and other documents and other similar activities. Brokerage houses can also perform custody services if they obtain the approval of the securities commission. Brokerage houses that perform more than one business are obliged to provide share capital according to the highest prescribed amount for the business it performs and an additional BAM one hundred and fifty thousand (roughly US$ seventy thousand in year-end 2019) if it performs custody business

Year of application	*Development*	*Novelty*
2017	Law on insurance in FB&H amendment	The provision has been adopted regarding the obligatory separate performance of the activities of life insurance and non-life insurance entities
1999	Law on Business Companies in FB&H Law on Business Companies in RS	Regulates the rules for economic and commercial activities of commercial companies, proprietors, related parties, subsidiaries, etc.
2015	Amendment to Law on Investment Funds in RS and FB&H	1. Novelty in that the Securities Commissions are to approve potential shareholders and board members 2. In RS, closed-end privatization investment funds are to be reorganized to open-end funds in a timeline of up to three years
2013	Takeover Act amendment in FB&H and RS	Natural or legal persons shall be obliged to announce a takeover bid, where they have acquired rights exceeding a threshold of thirty percent of voting shares of the target company
	Tax rates: 1.Dividends 2.Interest income on bonds 3.Capital gain 4.VAT	1. Dividends are taxable only for foreign legal entities at a rate of five percent in FB&H and ten percent in RS 2. Interest income from fixed-income listed securities is taxable only for foreign legal entities at a rate of ten percent in FB&H and in RS 3. Applicable on foreign legal entities in FB&H at a rate of ten percent and on resident and non-resident natural persons/retail entities in RS at a rate of ten percent 4. Seventeen percent in FB&H and RS

(continued)

Table 3.3 (continued)

Year of application	*Development*	*Novelty*
Conforming stage to the EU *acquis*	Capital Requirements Directive IV MiFIR Short selling and stock lending CCP Transparency, Market Abuse, and Prospectus standards Bank Recovery and Resolution Directive* European Market Infrastructure Regulation*	1. Stricter than Basel I. Basel II and III non-compliant 2. OTC trades require client ID reporting 3. Short selling is restricted. Securities lending is possible on bilateral basis 4. Central Registrars do not have a netting service 5. Low compliance standards in RS and medium compliance standards in FB&H

Source Author's selection on showcase regulation and legislation
*Na

Currency Exchange. The Belgrade Stock Exchange continued operations until 1953 when it was closed upon the introduction of the planned socialist economy. It was reopened in 1989 after the adoption of the Law on Capital Markets in Yugoslavia. Thirty-two biggest banks in the country established the Yugoslav Capital Market Exchange, thereafter, renamed the Belgrade Stock Exchange (BSE) in 1992.

Following the reopening, initial trading started in 1990. The first Government debt securities were traded and thereafter the first equity shares were traded in 1991. Nevertheless, the trading was shallow and more significant trading activity emerged only in the twenty-first century, in 2000, when equity shares entitled from the privatization process became available in the secondary trading. In the same year the first Treasury notes were issued. In 2001 the Government issued bonds for the purpose of recovering the legacy debt that is related to the lost foreign currency savings in the prior transitioning and war period. These issuances were then listed onto and boosted trading volumes on the BSE. The final series of the foreign currency savings bonds were excluded from the BSE in May 2016 upon the final maturity repayment. A total of fourteen bonds were traded in an amount of roughly US$ 1.3 billion, of which more than eighty percent of trading was through the OTC market. Continuous and remote trading was introduced on the BSE in 2004. The first published index was BELEXfm, a broad market index introduced in 2004. BELEXline index in 2007 replaced BELEXfm. Another BSE index, BELEX15, was established in 2005 to represent the fifteen most liquid companies in continuous trading. In 2006 the first open-end investment funds were listed. In 2008 BELEXFIX, new information and trading system was launched to allow electronic order routing. In 2012 the pioneering primary issuance and trading was conducted with respect to corporate bonds. In 2014 the first municipal bonds were listed on open market segment listing. However, the municipal bonds were delisted as soon as 2015 to be moved to the multilateral trading platform due to illiquidity in trading. In 2015 new long-term local Government bonds were admitted to the BSE prime listing. In 2016 EBRD issued a Republic of Serbia Dinar (RSD) denominated bond also on the prime listing. Fixed-income securities listed on the BSE are predominantly concentrated in the Government securities, of which ninety-nine percent are either settled at maturity or are traded exclusively through non-regulated platforms. In 2018 BSE in a joint program with EBRD and the accounting and consulting company PricewaterhouseCoopers (PwC) launched the "Serbia IPO Go" project.

In this joint effort program companies interested in listing on the BSE are to be provided with free support from PwC experts in successfully carrying out the process of preparation for listing on the BSE (Belgrade Stock Exchange, 2018). While this effort is a positive development, work akin to "moving a mountain" still lies ahead.

1990s privatization process in Serbia followed the centralized mass voucher ownership approach where **(a)** sixty percent of capital went to employees and ex-employees; **(b)** thirty percent of capital was assigned to the Government run fund for citizens; and **(c)** ten percent of capital was assigned to the Government run pension fund. The process was conducted on a voluntary basis upon the initiative of a company itself. Consequently, this approach created room for prolongations such as intermediation by insider trading and thereafter frequent loss in company valuations. In 2001 an alternative to the privatization process was introduced in passing the Law on Privatization, which allows for the privatization transactions via public auctions.

In comparison to the SEE region, the capital market development in Serbia emerged relatively later and is marked by an aggressive initial growth, which was soon followed by a strong stalling in the aftermath of the 2007/2008 crisis and from which the market has largely still not recovered. In 2002, the first year of free float shares trading, the turnover reached an amount of roughly US$ one hundred and twenty-one million for the year. Thirteen years later, in 2015, BSE's annual turnover reached roughly US$ one hundred and fifty-four million. From 2011 to the end of 2017 the number of listed joint-stock companies decreased from roughly two thousand six hundred to one thousand five hundred. In a similar trend the first licensed asset management company appeared in 2007. Two years later nineteen licensed companies existed in the market. However, in 2018 four such companies continued to operate. The 2007/2008 crisis aftermath featured frequent liquidations of companies and continued ownership concentration by local sponsors who tended to de-list from the BSE in search of lower corporate governance requirements. In this process, growing concerns emerged on minority ownership rights protection. In Serbia, shares are considered liquid for a proxy transaction price if in the prior six months 0.5% of the listed shares were traded, or 0.05% of the listed shares were traded in the prior three months. Therefore, in takeover procedures "squeeze outs" of minority owners may occur through related party influence or transactions lowering prices to below the book and/or fair value. The capital market in Serbia illustrates a high concentration of ownership of listed shares amongst a small number of market players with frequently related party interactions.

It is imperative to introduce the theme of the rise of gray economy in the 1990s, which may create a significant economic factor in a wide array of industries and policies. The scale of cash flows of this origin may be high. Yet, the limitations in entering the regulated exchange-traded market largely deter such capital from fuelling otherwise a very illiquid small economy's capital market. Such surrounding is replicative to a lesser or greater extent in all the researched SEE countries.

GDP of Serbia is more than seven times greater than the regulated exchange-traded market capitalization. The banking sector assets in Serbia, represented by thirty banks, form close to eighty percent of GDP in value. In the recent period the banking sector banks' failures (e.g. four banks, including Agrobanka, Vojvodjanska Razvojna Banka, Privredna Banka Beograd, and Univerzal Banka, have lost licenses since 2012) and more frequent market consolidating mergers and acquisitions are apparent (e.g. OTP and Findomestic merger in 2015, OTP acquisition of NBG Vojvodjanska in 2017 and of Societe Generale in 2019, AIK Banka acquisition of Piraeus Bank in 2017, Halyk Bank Turkey acquired Cacanska Banka in 2015, PPF Group acquired Telenor Bank in 2018, in 2019 NLB acquired Komercijalna Banka, and in 2021 Raiffeisen acquired Credit Agricole and Direktna Banka and Eurobank merged).

3.4.2 Contemporary Setting

In the current environment, SOEs form a significant depth to the BSE capitalization; however, the liquidity of these listings is trivial. SOEs and consolidated local sponsored corporate holdings' performance are curtailed by low transparency. The Capital Market Law is still to evolve beyond the basic content and toward a more comprehensive one that captures asset-backed securities, financial derivatives executions in netting, in close-offs, in settlements, etc. ISDA agreement was signed with the Ministry of Finance in 2018. It enables hedging capacities and the utilization of products non-deliverability function. The capital market in Serbia bears the trademark of presence of informational asymmetries that is frequent in frontier markets, of weak corporate governance, and, an overall of high ambiguity sentiment. The Government support in improving the market environment, through effective legislative and judiciary role, may be critical to ensure progress.

At the year-end 2016 value of financial sector assets stood at US$ 30.5 billion, which was equivalent to eighty-five percent of GDP value. Per sectoral representation breakdown the banking industry assets form ninety-one percent of the financial sector's assets. In the banking industry the five largest banks are Western European subsidiaries that jointly represent more than fifty percent of total assets. Banks are the dominant players in the capital market as **(a)** direct investors in predominately local Government debt securities, **(b)** self-listed companies, **(c)** third party custodians, **(d)** asset management companies, and **(e)** indirectly as crucial lenders in the market, amongst other. Euro-denominated loans are predominant in an otherwise a Euroized economy despite the increasing but still a marginal role of RSD currency. NPLs were reduced from twenty-two percent of gross loans in 2014 to nine percent at the end of March 2018 because of increased provisions, write-offs, and entrance to the market of debt servicing and NPLs turnaround companies. The NPLs trading market is constrained to turnover in the legal entities space only as the Consumer Act prevents foreclosure and collection of natural persons'/retail entities' assets, and the Banking Act the transfer of natural persons'/retail entities' NPL assets to a non-financial institution entity. In other parts of the financial system, the insurance industry holds six percent of the sectorial assets, with this share continuously growing, for example, from four percent in the year-end 2010. The leasing sector represents two percent of total financial sector assets. Seven voluntary pension funds, being managed by insurance or commercial banks' four management companies, represent one percent of the sector. The pension funds' assets portfolio is invested primarily in Government bonds and roughly thirteen percent in savings with commercial banks. In the Fund management industry, management service fees are capped at 1.25% of the net value of assets under management. Lastly, by comparative size to the financial sector, the microfinance industry is completely immaterial (National Bank of Serbia, 2016).

Government bond securities are proportionally the largest product segment in the capital market. Commercial banks are the dominant investors in government bonds. Other institutional investors, such as insurance companies or pension and investments funds, and natural persons/retail entities alike, represent only a small proportion of the total. While the public sector is deepening the base of debt securities listings, interest from foreign investors remains low. In addition, non-residents have ownership restrictions to own solely short-term fixed-income securities. Respectively, foreign entities show a lack of interest in both fixed-income and equity investments alike. Announced privatizations of cornerstone companies, Telekom Srbija, one of three telecom operators in the country, and Elektroprivreda and Elektromreze Srbije, national electricity generation, distribution and supply, and transmission companies, respectively, might spur turnover and capitalizations in the near future in case these processes are inclusively conducted through the BSE.

BSE has a diversified ownership structure with roughly forty owners; however, the controlling stake is in the hands of the Government. More recently, in August 2021, Athens Stock Exchange acquired a ten percent ownership stake in the BSE. Moreover, trading activities were transferred to the trading platform of the Athens Stock Exchange in a progress akin to the aforementioned benefit of integration that strengthens infrastructure capacity and adds to liquidity. The Central Securities Depository and Clearing House is one hundred percent owned by the Government. The Central Securities Depository and Clearing House Guarantee Fund consists of contributions by members, for an aggregate amount of RSD five million (roughly US$ fifty thousand at year-end 2017). The Investor Protection Fund was enacted and implemented in 2011, after the introduction of the Capital Markets Law. The Fund provides reimbursements of up to Euro twenty thousand equivalent in RSD per active member. Settlement occurs in the "T+2" time horizon, other than "T+1" in the case of equity shares acquisitions. BSE showcases **(a)** prime, **(b)** standard, **(c)** SMart listing, **(d)** open market, and **(e)** unofficial MTF market for trading on business days from 09:00 to 14:00, or in continuous trading hours from 09:30 to 14:00. Prime listing requirements include: **(a)** minimum capital of Euro three million (roughly US$ 2.7 million), **(b)** minimum Euro two million (roughly US$ 1.8 million) nominal value and twenty-five percent free floating shares representation, **(c)** minimum five hundred shareowners, and **(d)** daily average liquidity of minimum RSD five hundred thousand (roughly US$ four thousand and three hundred or Euro four thousand and seven hundred) trading and minimum five trades for the past six months.

Standard listing requirements are lower for **(a)** minimum Euro two million capital, **(b)** minimum Euro one million (roughly US$ 1.1

Market capitalization – US$ 3.1 billion.

Annual trading turnover –US$ 361.8 million on regulated exchange, US$ 33.7 million on MTF, and US$ 28.1 billion on OTC** trading.

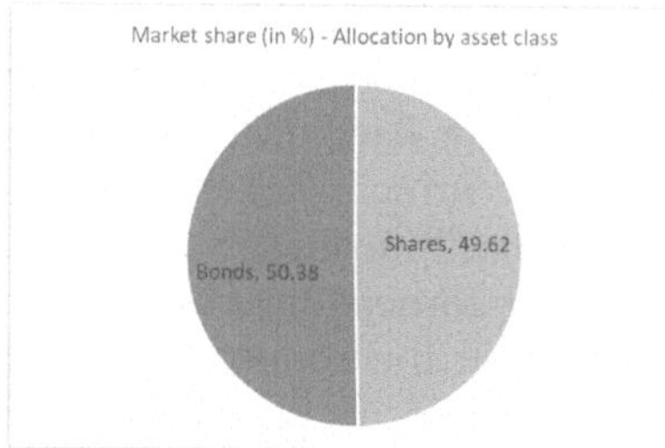

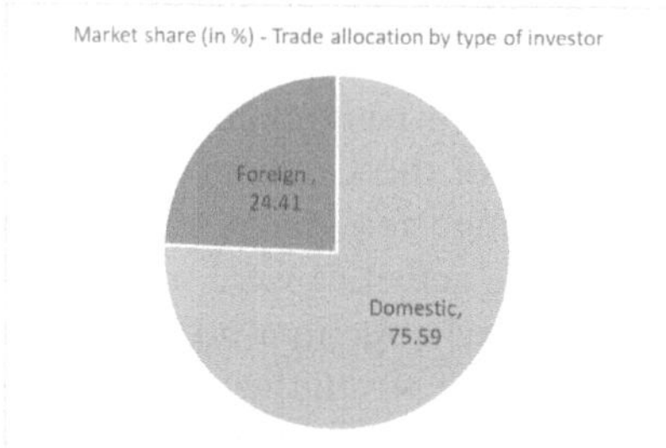

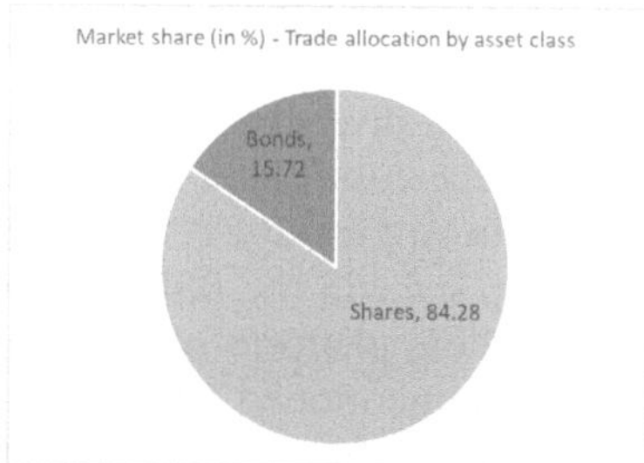

**Data sourced from the Belgrade Stock Exchange (2022).*
***Year-end 2016 annual report data from the Republic of Serbia Securities Commission (2017). Large majority of recorded OTC transactions involves Central Bank repo transactions and primary sales transactions.*

Fig. 3.4 Characteristics of capital market in Serbia

million) and twenty-five percent free floating shares, and **(c)** minimum three hundred shareowners. SMart requires minimum Euro 0.5 million (roughly US$ 0.55 million) capital, and free float of twenty-five percent of shares and minimum Euro one hundred and fifty thousand (roughly US$ one hundred and thirty-three thousand) in nominal value (Fig. 3.4).[16]

3.4.3 *Legal and Regulatory Framework*

The National Bank of Serbia (NBS) **(a)** determines and implements monetary and foreign exchange policies, **(b)** manages foreign exchange

[16] All listed exchange rates for listings requirements are as of year-end 2019.

reserves, internal and cross-border transactions, and (c) maintains financial system stability in the country. NBS licenses and controls the activities of (a) banks, (b) insurance companies, (c) fund management companies, (d) payments companies, and (e) leasing companies. The Central Securities Depository and Clearing House registers titles of financial instruments and serves for clearing and settlement of financial instruments transactions. Pursuant to the Law on Capital Markets in Serbia, the Republic of Serbia Securities Commission is the regulatory supervisory body for the Central Securities Depository's and Clearing House's activities. The Ministry of Finance proposes laws regulating investment firms, whereas the Securities Commission participates in the drafting of laws.

This study does not include the analysis of the accounting framework in Serbia due to the shorter scope of research and the fact that the financial system of the country is largely synchronized with the latest global standards (Table 3.4).

3.5 Capital Market in North Macedonia

3.5.1 Historical Overview

In 1995, thirteen banks, three insurance companies, and three savings houses founded and became the first members of the joint-stock company Macedonian Stock Exchange (MSE), the first organized securities exchange in the history of North Macedonia. The first trading, in an open outcry, occurred in March 1996. The 1997 Law on Issuance and Trading in Securities mandated that all financial securities transactions in North Macedonia are realized through the MSE. The Law Amendment in 2002 required mandatory listing for companies meeting the MSE criteria and such action laid the ground for an increase in the MSE capitalization. MSE capitalization at that time was under one percent of the value of GDP in North Macedonia. In comparison, other researched SEE stock exchanges' capitalization was roughly around ten percent of the respective GDP. In 1998 block trading was introduced and soon after ownership consolidation and transactions were amassed. Following the dematerialization of securities and the introduction of centralized record keeping, in 1999 the Central Securities Depository was established. In 2001 electronic trading was introduced on the back of a technical assistance arrangement with the LJSE. In the following year the Takeover Law was introduced. In 2004 the first local Government bonds were listed.

Table 3.4 Key legal and regulatory developments in the capital market in Serbia

Year of application	*Development*	*Novelty*
2006	The Investment Funds and Asset Management Companies Act*	Partly aligned with the 2009 EU UCITS Directive on conditions to establish funds and management companies, public offerings, vendors, supervision, etc 1. Fund management company may be registered in joint-stock form with minimum capital of Euro two hundred thousand (roughly US$ one hundred and seventy-nine thousand). A single person may not have more than a ten percent stake in more than one such company. Portfolio manager may oversee no more than one fund and each fund must have one manager and auditor at a minimum 2. Open-end fund may be established with minimum Euro two hundred thousand capital, and a private limited liability company fund with Euro fifty thousand 3. Maximum ten percent of investment fund's assets may be invested in securities or financial derivatives of a single issuer or related issuers 4. Maximum twenty percent of investment fund's assets may be deposited with a single bank or related banks 5. Maximum thirty-five percent of assets may be invested in securities issued by the Republic of Serbia or NBS 6. Open- and closed-end investment funds may not acquire more than twenty percent of share capital or voting shares in a single company 7. Closed-end fund may not invest more than twenty percent of its assets into a single real property 8. No investment restrictions apply to private funds

Year of application	*Development*	*Novelty*
2005	Voluntary Pension Funds Law	1. Maximum five percent exposure in securities issued by the organizer of pension scheme who joined the fund 2. Maximum ten percent exposure in single entity, with the Republic of Serbia and the NBS excluded from the restrictions 3. A fund may withdraw up to thirty percent of pooled funds as lump-sum payment
	Takeover Act	Applicable to listed companies with more than one hundred shareholders and with capital above Euro three million (roughly US$ 2.7 million) 1. Takeover offer is mandatory upon reaching or surpassing twenty-five percent ownership 2. "Squeeze out" rights are achievable upon reaching ninety percent ownership
	Prevention of Money Laundering and Terrorist Financing Act	Non-disclosure investors are to pay a penalty between RSD five hundred thousand and three million (US$ 4.8 thousand or Euro 4.4 thousand, and US$ 28.6 thousand or Euro twenty-six thousand, respectively, at the end of year 2019)

(continued)

Table 3.4 (continued)

Year of application	*Development*	*Novelty*
2011	Company Law amendment	1. Legal persons may represent a company; however, a company must have at least one representative of natural entities 2. Base capital to be denominated in RSD and not Euro 3. One- or two-tier corporate governance bodies. One tier is for shareholders assembly and directors. Two tiers include supervisory board requirements and an executive board instead of directors for joint-stock companies 4. Criminal liability is introduced for representatives including imprisonment, fines, and prohibitions to work 5. Minimum capital for limited liabilities companies is RSD one hundred (roughly US$ nine hundred and fifty-four or Euro eight hundred and sixty-six at year-end 2019) and RSD three million (US$ 28.6 thousand or Euro twenty-six thousand at year-end 2019) for joint-stock companies 6. Introduction of the requirement to publish draft merger agreements

Year of application	*Development*	*Novelty*
2015	Banking Act amendment	Increased supervisory capacity in alignment with the EU Bank Recovery and Resolution Directive and in principle relating to the measures of early intervention including provisional administration, the "bail-in" tool, and establishment of state asset management special vehicles

(continued)

Table 3.4 (continued)

Year of application	*Development*	*Novelty*
2011	Law on Capital Markets Amendment**	1. Enabling international FIs to issue debt securities in the Republic of Serbia 2. Introduction of forward contracts, commodity derivatives, and credit default swaps
2021	New Law on Capital Market	1. Harmonizing local legal and institutional framework with the EU rules inclusive of MiFID II, prospectus, investor-compensation schemes, transparency, securities settlements, and market abuse. The rules concern: (a) dematerialized securities and operations of entities authorized to perform transactions with financial instruments, (b) data reporting services provider, (d) improvement of the quality of the information received by clients regarding investment services, (e) greater regulatory requirements with regard to trading platforms and high-frequency and algorithmic trading, (f) the obligations of participants in the capital market regarding market abuses, and (g) the wider supervisory obligations and sanction powers of the Securities Commission

Year of application	*Development*	*Novelty*
2017	Bankruptcy Law amendment	1. Creditors' board must have one secured creditor member 2. Secured creditor to approve underlying asset lease 3. Secured creditor can exercise set-off on claim in public sale 4. Secured creditor has pre-emptive sale right
2018	Law on Foreign Exchange amendment	1. Residents may invest in long-term EU or EU registered entities' financial securities 2. Liberalization for short-term portfolio investments cross-border sale for residents and non-residents 3. Cross-border loans from EU are allowed for credits of up to one year
	Tax rates:	1. Twenty percent for institutional investors on interest, dividends, and capital gains 2. Fifteen percent for natural persons'/retail entities' investors on interest, dividends, and capital gains 3. Income tax is progressive up to fifteen percent 4. VAT is twenty percent for most and eight percent for certain goods

(continued)

Table 3.4 (continued)

Year of application	*Development*	*Novelty*
Conforming stage to the EU *acquis*	1. Capital Requirements Directive IV 2. MiFIR 3. Short selling and stock lending 4. CCP 5. Transparency, Market Abuse, and Prospectus standards 6. Bank Recovery and Resolution Directive 7. European Market Infrastructure Regulation***	1. Basel III standards as of end of June 2017 with Republic of Serbia considered risk-free and Government securities treated as highly liquid assets and exempt from exposure limits. Phased out gradual period for removal of local regulator special provisions 2. In large extent compliant with MiFID 3. Short selling is restricted. Securities lending is possible 4. The Central Securities Depository and Clearing House does not have a netting service 5. 2003 EU standards. Non-compliant with Directive 2014/57/EU on buy-back programs and stabilization of financial instruments 6. 2016 EU standard

Source Author's selection of showcase regulation and legislation

*Non-compliant with alternative investment fund managers act and 2011 EU Directive. Cross-border mergers are not allowed and master-feed structures non-compliant

**Convertible bonds may be transacted in cash or money only. Underwriting fees are capped

***Largely aligned with settlement finality but only moderately with financial collateral arrangements with mismatch on pledge of movable assets and bankruptcy concerns

In 2006 the Corporate Governance Code was established. In the same year, the Government processed significant large privatizations. A transaction that stands out is the in block trade sale of vertically integrated electricity distribution and supply company, Elektrani na Severna Makedonija, to Austrian Energie Versorgung Niederösterreich, in a transaction worth over US$ two hundred and fifty million. That single transaction exceeded the aggregate of all prior FDIs in the country through the end of February 2002, which equalled US$ 260.6 million in total (Macedonian Privatization Agency). In the same year, 2006, the Government sold its remaining shares in telecommunications company, Makedonski Telekom. In 2006 mandatory pension funds appeared on the capital market, whereas in 2009 two voluntary pension funds also emerged. In 2007 record takeovers occurred on the back of the introduced Takeover Law, successful privatizations, and an overall increased foreign investors activity on the MSE. In 2011 the first IPO was conducted by the local kiosk operator company, Tobacco. MSE nowadays streams three indices. MBI10 index was introduced in 2005 and it tracks the top ten companies by capitalization. MBI10 is the inheritor of broad MBI index that was established in 2001. In 2006 OMB index was established to track the most liquid bonds. In 2007 MBID index was established to track the biggest publicly held companies (Macedonian Stock Exchange, 2018).

Analogous to what happened in the comparative SEE economies, in the 1990s transition process North Macedonia's economy experienced a decline due to the loss of traditional trade markets in the former Yugoslavia. Moreover, due to a dispute with Greece over the name "Macedonia," the two neighboring countries engaged in a hostile eighteen-months long trade embargo. In the transition from planned to free market economy North Macedonia implemented the mass privati zation approach through the internal issuances of shares to respective member companies. These shares were then acquired by employees at a discount of thirty percent; in addition, fifteen percent of total shares were automatically transferred to the Sovereign Pension Fund. In 1993 the new Privatization Law was enacted, though it was only implemented in 1995. The new Privatization Law aimed to transform the initial mass privatization concept to one which allowed freedom for enterprises to directly structure the preferred privatization process. In the amended process, a single entity could directly acquire the controlling company stake (Arsov, 2005).

MSE's function as the intended platform to process the transition from state to private ownership was not exclusive. Trading on the MSE emerged only in 1996, which was late into the privatization process that per se had started years earlier. MSE's initial performance in the first three years was immaterial, and only from 1999 through 2005 first larger privatizations were realized through the MSE. These include the sales of Makedonski Telekom to Hungarian Magar Telekom, an affiliate of T-Mobile, and of Stopanska Banka to the National Bank of Greece. These transactions manifested in block trades characterized by the absence of direct market quotations. In 2005 repo transactions were established, yet the market never picked up broad momentum apart from the National Bank of Republic of Macedonia (NBRM) and commercial banks related transactions. The period from 2005 to 2008 was characterized by amassing FDIs, further privatizations, and the record MSE capitalization level. Market turnover reached roughly US$ one billion, which is more than ten times greater than the year-end 2017 turnover value of roughly US$ 92.2 million. Fast growth in a short time span before the financial crisis also led to the 2007/2008 crisis amplified impact in loss of more than two-thirds in the MSE's value in both capitalization and turnover. Financial indicators on the MSE thereafter and to date have not significantly changed. In terms of growth, the number of listed companies in 2013 increased to one hundred and sixteen from thirty-two in the previous year, and the number has not changed much through the most recent data. Yet, capitalization and turnover on the MSE are lower compared to the year-end 2008 respective values. Initial privatizations in the 1990s and early 2000s were sluggish and, as a by-product, investment funds' emergence was also slow. The first funds and the first groundbreaking FDIs appeared in 2005, only to be deterred soon by very negative returns in the 2007/2008 crisis aftermath. At year-end 2016 MSE had ten members, six of which were brokers and four commercial banks. In January 2017 Sparkasse Bank Macedonia Skopje joined the MSE, thus becoming the first new member to join in the past few years. On the MSE, as of February 2018, the previous "T+3" timeframe was transferred to "T+2" settlement timeframe.

3.5.2 *Contemporary Setting*

The capital market in North Macedonia exhibits (a) weak turnover, (b) small free float ratio, (c) high concentration in capitalization and

turnover to a small number of companies, (d) investors' perception of market obscurities, and (e) unstable political environment. The four largest companies on the MSE form thirty-three percent of capitalization and fifty-one percent of regulated prime market turnover. The largest listed companies are Alkaloid, a pharmaceuticals production company, and three commercial banks, namely Komercijalna, NBG Stopanska, and NLB Tutunska. MSE Corporate Governance Code was established in 2006; nonetheless, twelve years later the progress on successful implementation is rather meager. Only a minority of the ten largest listed companies disclose having committees including audit, remuneration, and nomination committees, or having independent board members. Similarly, only the minority of the ten largest listed companies provide public disclosure on committee meetings and activities, or on-board work evaluations. Only ten percent of the listed companies provide recent financial statements and only four of the ten largest listed companies provide audited reports on the companies' websites (European Bank for Reconstruction and Development, 2017).

The total assets of the financial sector at year-end 2016 amounted to roughly US$ nine billion. The banking sector with fifteen active banks dominates the financial system. The banking sector represents eighty-five percent of the total financial assets and seventy-three percent of the nominal national GDP value. The four largest banks, Komercijalna, NBG Stopanska, NLB Tutunska, and Sparkasse Ohridska jointly hold the majority of the total banking assets. Most of the banking sector is owned by Western European parent banks. Savings houses represent less than one percent of the total banking assets. Pension funds represent 9.4% of the financial system assets. Mandatory pension funds represent ninety-eight percent of the total pension funds' assets. Pension funds' assets have more than doubled in value in the past five years; however, the pension funds' scale of involvement in MSE remains paltry. The pension funds primarily invest in sovereign debt securities, wherein a rising share is invested in the exchange-traded funds in the United States and in US$. Under ten percent of the total funds' investment is in listed shares, of which less than half is invested in shares that are listed on the MSE. Nonetheless, the legal limit for pension funds to invest in equities, including ETFs, is thirty percent of total net assets value under management. The pension funds' growth is attributable to the increasing number of members and paid-in contributions that form roughly two-thirds of net assets value addition. The insurance sector represents about 3.5% of the total financial assets. Other investment funds represent roughly 0.7% of the total financial assets. The remaining financial system assets belong to savings houses, leasing companies, microfinance companies, etc. In the capital market, there are five fund management companies that manage fifteen open-end funds. Foreign investors are the predominant owners in all but the savings industry within the financial system. Commercial banks are the largest direct owners of asset management companies and at the same time are large investors in the investment funds (National Bank of the Republic of Macedonia, 2016).

The origin of most foreign investments stems from the neighboring countries, which symbolizes, amongst others, that North Macedonian economy is marginally visible globally. In this respect, nascent MBI10 index ETFs in the Sofia and Frankfurt Exchanges contribute to better market visibility. However, that visibility remains limited to attracting passive index investors via the regional or global indexes. Foreign investors enjoy equal ownership treatment as local investors, such as free funds repatriation, tax exemption if investing under Technological Industrial Development Zones,[17] and an overall investor-friendly business environment. Still, a substantial increase in investments has not followed. North Macedonia ranked tenth in the 2017 World Bank Doing Business report. That ranking is the highest comparable amongst the observed SEE countries. Strong performance areas include the segments of **(a)** starting a business, **(b)** getting credit, **(c)** trading across borders, and **(d)** minority investors' rights protection. Segments of property registration, electricity supply, and contract enforcement rank relatively weaker. North Macedonia is the smallest economy amongst the observed SEE markets and represents a case with a relatively larger share of trade with neighboring nations versus global or continental counterparts. An opportunity to increase visibility may exist in improving transparency and governance standards that may eliminate market research filtering barriers. North Macedonian economy exhibits **(a)** a high unemployment of roughly twenty-two percent, **(b)** almost ten years long continuing fiscal deficit, and **(c)** excessive political divisions which prolong

[17] Investors in these zones may benefit from ten years tax holidays under the Government's aim to develop a modern technologies industry amongst other strategic fields.

operational inefficiencies of the public sector. The 2007/2008 crisis aftermath is rather more prolonged on the MSE and therefore investors' sentiment is still one with a strong negative collective memory. Closed-end funds are not present on the market, though, together with the private equity industry, such entrants may provide for improvements in management standards, governance, institutionalizations, and continuous investments inflow, amongst other.

The primary market is predominately represented by the Government debt securities that large commercial banks and pension funds invest in. In 2016, secondary market trading formed 2.1% of GDP, with seventy-two percent of trade occurring on sovereign securities OTC market transactions. Otherwise, local legal entities remain the major investor in secondary stocks' trading and investment funds' portfolios. MSE streams **(a)** official super listing, **(b)** regular market listing, **(c)** unofficial free market, and **(d)** market for public companies' listings. Requirements for super listing involve **(a)** twenty percent free float, **(b)** minimum two hundred shareholders, **(c)** minimum Euro ten million (US$ 11.2 million) capital, **(d)** profitable former three fiscal years operations, and **(e)** a website in English and the Macedonian. Regular listing requirements are **(a)** two years of audited statements, **(b)** minimum Euro five hundred thousand (US$ 0.56 million) capital, **(c)** fifteen percent free float, and **(d)** minimum of one hundred shareholders (Fig. 3.5).

Bonds' listings require **(a)** minimum nominal value of Euro five hundred thousand (roughly US$ four hundred and forty-six thousand),[18] **(b)** at least twenty-five percent public placement, and **(c)** minimum of fifty investors. Investors' compensation fund is prescribed by law but is not yet implemented. The Exchange uses BEST trading system, which is the system formerly used by LJSE before the transition to the Xetra trading system in 2010. Official business days' trading hours are 09:00 13:00, with continuous trading starting at 10:00.

3.5.3 *Legal and Regulatory Framework*

The Securities and Exchange Commission in North Macedonia is the financial regulator and licenser for capital market transactions. The

[18] Year-end 2019 exchange rate is used for listing comparative values.

MSE:

Market capitalization

– US$ 4.45 billion.

Annual trading turnover –

A – US$ 236.4 million on regulated exchange of which US$ 123.9 million on regulated trading non-inclusive of block trades and auctions.*

B - US$ 2.1 billion on OTC trading.**

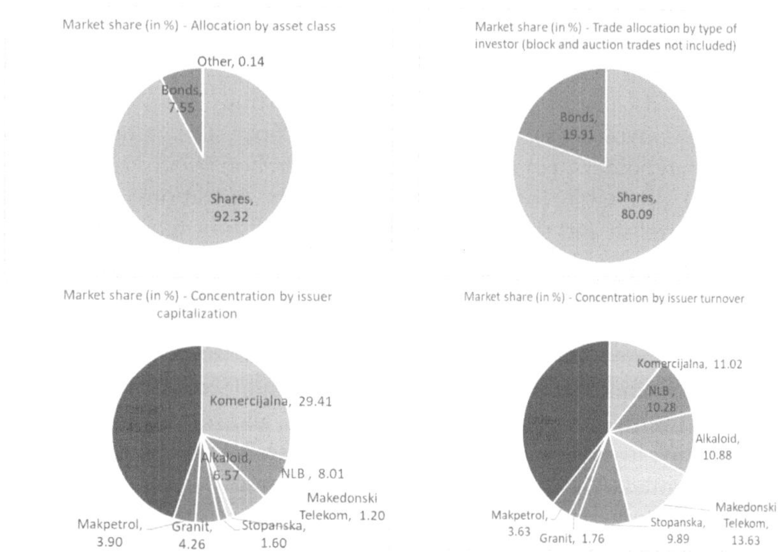

**Year-end 2021 values. Data sourced from Macedonian Stock Exchange (2022).*
***Data sourced from year-end 2016 Annual Report, Central Securities Depository of the Republic of Macedonia (2017)*

Fig. 3.5 Characteristics of capital market in North Macedonia

Commission authorizes and monitors investment funds and asset management companies. NBRM regulates the banking, leasing, and NBFIs in North Macedonia. NBRM main role is to maintain price stability. The local currency, Denar, is pegged to Euro. The Ministry of Finance regulates non-deposit-taking financial companies, and the Agency for Insurance Supervision oversees insurance activities. The Agency for Supervision of Fully Funded Pension Insurance regulates and supervises mandatory and voluntary pension companies and their funds' operations. The Central Securities Depository, established in 2001 and predominantly owned by commercial banks, provides centralized registrar, clearing, and settlement services.

The analysis of the accounting framework in North Macedonia is not included due to the shorter scope of research and the fact that the financial system of the country is closely synchronized with the latest global standards (Table 3.5).

3.6 Financial Derivatives in Southeast Europe

This study does not empirically test the implications of the presence of financial derivatives due to the absent regulated exchange-traded usage and to the simultaneous very low scale of use and often unavailable OTC market data in the SEE economies. Nonetheless, it recognizes the global importance of financial derivatives' use to the capital markets' environment and development. It accounts for financial derivatives' product structures, global trends in use, and an assessment of the selected SEE business environment conduciveness. Metaphorically speaking, to research the dynamics of capital markets and of the relationship with macroeconomic indicators without providing context on the importance of and the characteristics of financial derivatives would be the same as discussing the dynamics of the automotive industry without dwelling on the characteristics of engine innovation and prospects. The **main perspectives for the development of financial derivatives' markets** pertain to **(a)** the type of instrument to develop first, **(b)** institutional arrangements to govern the trade, **(c)** policy support and infrastructure establishment, **(d)** the necessity of scalable liquidity, and **(e)** the importance of the market risk factor.

Over seventy percent of US$ 20.7 trillion OTC gross market value, or of US$ 544.5 trillion OTC notional outstanding volume market, and

Table 3.5 Key legal and regulatory developments in the capital market in North Macedonia

Year of application	*Development*	*Novelty*
2005 establishment and 2015 amendment	Securities Law	Introduction of common representative for owners of secured bonds. Requirement for joint-stock and limited partnership companies which meet special criteria for listing on MSE
Part of Securities Law	Market in Financial Instruments Act*	Aligns with MiFID directives. Regulates the financial instruments market, the required reporting, investment services, exchanges operations, etc
Effective since 2004 2006 establishment of Central Register	Company Law	Allows trade company registration in central registrar's one-stop-shop system that enables registration in under four hours for under Euro fifty (roughly US$ forty-five).[19] Foreigners enjoy same treatment as local investors
2011	Law on investment funds	Regulates foundation and operations of investment funds and investment funds management companies, on issuance, redemption, and sale of stocks and shares, and on activities performed by third parties on behalf of investment funds and depository banks. Foreign investors enjoy equal treatment as local investors in not needing additional approvals

[19] Year-end 2019 exchange rate is used in Table 11.

Year of application	*Development*	*Novelty*
2002	Law on mandatory pension funds	Lays the foundation of investment limitations and requirements for pension asset management companies and funds. Each mandate lasts up to ten years before a new public tender process.
2008	Law on voluntary fully funded pension insurance	Regulates establishment, operation, and winding up of voluntary funds, companies, membership, reporting, fees, rules, etc
	Takeover Act	Required for ownership stakes above twenty-five percent.; fifty percent in the case of banks
	Tax rates	1. Personal and corporate income, and dividend at ten percent 2. No capital gains tax for legal entities. For individuals no capital gains tax until end-2018; thereafter the rate will be ten percent 3. MSE and investment firms' transactions are VAT exempt. Otherwise, VAT tax is eighteen percent 4. No interest income tax

(continued)

Table 3.5 (continued)

Year of application	*Development*	*Novelty*
Conforming stage to the EU *acquis*	1. Capital Requirements Directive IV 2. MiFIR* 3. Short selling and stock lending 4. CCP 5. Transparency, Market Abuse, and Prospectus standards 6. Bank Recovery and Resolution Directive 7. European Market Infrastructure Regulation**	1. Basel III standards compliant as of March 2018 2. Short selling is NA and stock lending is available 3. Central Securities Depository does not have a netting service and does not serve as central clearing counterparty guaranteeing transactions with own capital or requiring open positions collateral posting 4. Compliant with European Directive 2005/60/AC and FATF. Required for transactions greater than Euro one thousand (roughly US$ eight hundred and ninety-three). Any cross-border transactions reported for statistical purposes only 5. Non-compliant with expected compliance to the EU Directive 2014/59 by the end of 2018

Source Author's selection of showcase regulation and legislation
*MiFIR compliant. MiFID Two still non-compliant
**Compliant with cross-border settlement using central bank money

close to ninety-eight percent of daily turnover in exchange-traded derivatives are in interest rate contracts. Exchange-trade in financial derivatives is at US$ 67.7 trillion open interest and US$ 7.3 trillion daily turnover.[20] Global OTC market outsizes **(a)** estimated global GDP of US$ 75.6 trillion (World Development Indicators database, 2017),[21] **(b)** aggregate global stock exchange market capitalization that is estimated at US$ sixty-nine trillion[22] (Desjardins, 2017), and **(c)** regulated exchange-traded derivatives market. OTC markets often serve as the preferred avenue to overcome a lack of infrastructure capacity, liquidity, and stricter transparency and regulation in the regulated organized exchanges. Therefore, OTC markets chronologically tend to develop ahead of organized exchanges. Halilbegovic and Mekic (2017) research survey quotes that hedging risk is the primary purpose for financial derivatives use in B&H. In the market, the prevalent products are OTC currency and interest rate swaps.

Though with conflicting results, the previous empirical work does point out that the introduction of financial derivatives works in favor of reducing or does not affect variances of stocks listed on regulated exchanges (Claessens & Varangis, 1991; Gerber, 2008; Hernandez-Trillo, 1999; Samitas & Kenourgios, 2004; Tobias & Song, 2009). Findings in the case of a market without a clearinghouse, as in Mexico, do not show a favorable impact on the reduction of the regulated exchange's listed stocks' volatility following the introduction of financial derivatives. Hernandez-Trillo (1999) utilized GARCH process to generate, from second level/transformed data, a conditional time-series measure of regulated exchange listed stocks' return variances with and without derivatives use. In that sample case derivatives are traded on the inherent stock exchange and not on a separate derivatives' exchange. In such a case credit risk is covered through a direct delta hedging model versus

[20] BIS semi-annual survey: Quoted data are for statistics as of end of June in 2016. Exchange-traded derivatives statistics complete the coverage of the derivatives markets by providing information about the size and structure of organized futures and options markets. The statistics data are compiled by the BIS from commercial data sources and capture the turnover and open interest of interest rate and foreign exchange derivatives traded on derivatives exchanges.

[21] World Bank estimate for year-end 2016.

[22] Visual Capitalist estimates. Over ninety-three percent of global stocks' value is divided between North America (roughly forty percent of total), Asia (roughly thirty-three percent of total), and Europe (roughly twenty percent of total).

utilizing a central clearinghouse. The study period covered one hundred and seventy-eight instruments, primarily puts and warrants, in the period from 1992 to 1996. which included the well-known 1994 Mexican Peso or the "Tequila" crisis.[23] The Hernandez and Trillo research results are prone to empirical sample specifics due to the model case that has no clearinghouse that otherwise is a catalyst to more scalable and meaningful use. Otherwise, financial derivatives tend to reduce market risk in a case of crisis.

OTC contracts encompass a wide range of privately negotiated agreements that are not exclusively related to a bank and a non-financial firm relationship as the two opposite counterparties and as claimed in a previous B&H research survey by Rovčanin and Hanić (2014). Rather, financial firms, banks, and NBFIs, often inter-arrange OTC contracts to hedge and diversify own risk, primarily through interest rate and currency swaps. North America's capital market is home to close to seventy percent of the total financial derivatives market. The US$ and Euro stand out as the most frequent currency counterparty pair and as the two most internationalized foreign currencies.

Considering the types of instruments and based on prior exemplary market development trends, an introduction of financial forwards and swaps tends to precede financial options, and financial futures come into play chronologically as last. Due to simplicity in structure such an order is somewhat natural. Institutional arrangements vouch for the easier rise of OTC markets before the infrastructure, standard contracts' specifications, clearing and settlement system operationalization, and trade volume are adequate for an introduction of derivatives on a regulated exchange market. The function of risk is present in equity products, interest rate products, and currency and commodity value, amongst others. The survey in Serbia in the research paper by Marinkovic and Skakavac (2010) considers such a risk as valid for all cases other than for equity products due to illiquidity in the regulated exchange-listed market. Under a perspective of a larger, more liquid, and more effective capital market, the selected SEE markets integration comes into focus. The research to date does not elaborate on this trend despite the selected SEE countries' historical tendency for economic convergence and for the simultaneous

[23] Crisis was sparked when Mexican Government suddenly devalued the local currency, Peso, against US$ causing one of the first international financial crisis ignited by capital flight.

presence and prevalence of the equivalent large market players. In further review, counterparty risk is often an overlooked risk factor, though quickly growing in importance in stressed markets. Counterparty risk provides another opportunity to utilize hedging tools and financial derivatives' capacity.

Past data have shown that almost half of the global interest rate derivatives' OTC market value is in Euro. As mentioned before, the Eurozone is an economic area overshadowing the economic environment in the selected SEE countries. As all the five selected countries converge on the EU membership it is likely that eventually they will also join the Eurozone. Slovenia already has, B&H local currency is pegged to the Euro, and in 2018 the Croatian Central Bank announced its strategy for meeting the Maastricht currency convergence criteria with expected inclusion as of 2023 at the earliest. In addition, North Macedonia manages local currency value in relation to the Euro value. An impact of coherent currency convergence is in the diffusion of current local currency added risk. For the selected SEE markets, the improved liquidity in and a more efficient means of managing counterparty credit risks are important for the development of the financial derivatives market. The natural further development sequence may be the first to advance the existing forwards, swaps, warrants, and options markets for underlying assets with local characteristics, namely power and gas, agriculture, and tourism-related aspects.

As regulators have proclaimed speculative banking as the consuming origin of market uncertainty and a later collapse, questions remain as to whether regulatory and legal frameworks prevent a future crisis. In practice, restrictions are imposed to prevent non-knowledgeable or speculative factors from causing a destructive impact. Restraints are therefore more a detaining and less a knowledge sharing tool. Legislative and regulatory constraints, large financial value, frequent negative publicity, and flexibility of action are factors identified to constrain the use of financial derivatives in risk management (Claessens & Varangis, 1991). Claessens and Varangis discussed SOE's use of futures and options in the oil trade. The two researchers performed one-year trading simulated scenario analysis which showed potential coherent gains through risk reduction.

Comparing the movement of the Athens Stock Exchange's three-month futures price versus cash market index's price, Dimitris Kenourgis discovered in his research that futures contracts were a focal point of information assimilation, fulfilling the price-discovery function (Samitas &

Kenourgios, 2004). Kenourgis utilized study data from August 1999 to June 2002 using Granger, Johansen, and OLS techniques and methodologies to determine the relationship of three-month index futures with the spot index itself. Daily average trading volume exceeded two thousand in each observed year. The testing results proved statistical bi-directional causality in the short run for predictability from lagged to current values. Such implication however pointed to opportunities for arbitrage profits which thus denies the hypothesis of an efficient capital market. Broker-dealer balance sheets have grown to increasing importance through the supply of credit securitization market-making and underwriting. As such, contractions in broker-dealer balance sheets tend to precede declines in real economic growth (Tobias & Song, 2009).

Over the past decades, financial derivatives and financial securitizations have evolved from straightforward deals to highly complex transactions with difficult to predict outcomes (O'Harrow, 2010). Financial innovation evolves in parallel to increase in globalization that stems from faster technological advancements allowing for knowledge sharing and from easier capital and labor mobility. Imbalances amongst various development stages in global economies demand swift risk-sharing and reduction as modern finance continues to evolve in seeking responses. Capital markets and financial derivatives are characterized by structural efficiency at shifting risk amongst counterparties. **Legal development, regulatory development, and global standardization tend to follow behind the global growth in the use of innovative products and the evolvement of financial innovation.** Aggressive market-making may undermine the stability of an exchange rate system through speculative attacks on a weaker emerging market currency. Such speculative attacks are often triggered through the excessive supply of puttable options, spot trade, central bank action, and forward sales, and result in capital outflows (Gerber, 1998).

Gerber's 1998 research exemplifies a series of case studies on financial derivatives' impact in enabling greater cross-border cash-flows exchange, which then on a gross basis gets reflected on the national balance of payments. Gerber uses a plain example of vanilla bond issuance by a corporation in one country but in another country's currency to attain cost reduction and portfolio diversification. Such contracts are then hedged through financial swaps with market providers. However, developing markets frequently impose regulatory constraints on capital flows and exchange rate flexibility. An overly constraining regulation frequently transfers cross-border cash flow from onshore to offshore destinations. On the constructive side, the **creation of a well-functioning and diversified money market provides a barometer sense of elementary funding conditions in search for long-term price discovery, secondary market build-up, and market stability**.

3.7 The Outlook for the Selected Reviewed Markets

The selected SEE countries are joined under the umbrella of "Euroized" economies due to trade interdependencies between each other and with the Eurozone countries[24] alongside geographical, social, and cultural ties. Western European banks' subsidiaries are predominant operators in the banking industries in the selected SEE countries. For the same markets, the flow of trade is the greatest with the EU. The depth and breadth of cooperation at the intra-country, intra-regional, and intercontinental levels may spur capital markets' transactional and informational cost efficiencies. The five SEE countries observed in the review share traits on the aligned paths toward the EU membership. Croatia and Slovenia are already part of the EU and the other countries are signatories of the active Stabilization and Association Agreement status providing nonreciprocal free access to the EU markets through autonomous trade preferences. Further integration may unlock additional investments and the growth potential. All the selected SEE countries are constituents of the EU promoted efforts to create a single EU capital markets union. In 2015, European Commission adopted Action Plan on building a single market union. At year-end 2016, corporate debt financing in the EU was sourced seventy-five percent from bank lending funding versus from debt securities funding, compared to the United States, where the ratio is twenty percent bank lending versus eighty percent funding from debt securities. EU listed stocks' market capitalization stands at fifty-five percent of EU's GDP. In the United States that replicable ratio is at one hundred and forty-seven percent.

The level of capital market investments in the EU is still below the 2007/2008 crisis level. The plan for the EU capital markets union is based on the following pillars:

[24] Countries who use the Euro. In 2021 a total of nineteen countries uses the Euro.

1. Adjustment of investment environment so as to meet the needs of a more diversified financial system wherein developed capital markets complement bank financing. With the adjustment:
   a. Remove cross-border investing hindrance including securities' ownership rights in case issuer and investor are in different countries or when claims are used as cross-border collateral.
   b. Establishment of a pan-European personal pension fund to allow voluntary pension scheme to be managed at a pan-European scale.
   c. Harmonize regulation and enhance ESMA supervision ability.
2. Implementation of Euro three hundred and fifteen billion (roughly US$ two hundred and eighty-one billion at year-end 2019 exchange rate) investments package co-financed with the private sector. European Fund for Strategic Investments offers Euro twenty-one billion worth guarantees to fund digitalization, transport, energy infrastructure, and education. Research and resources innovation window is to be deployed by European Investment Bank and small and medium-size enterprises support window is to be deployed by European Investment Fund.
3. Unlock the frozen capital, including the resolution of NPLs.

In the SEE capital markets' outlook the high illiquidity is a direct indicator of a poorly performing industry in fulfillment of its efficient price discovery and resources allocation role. Some possibilities to alleviate the existing market uncertainties may exist in improved corporate governance, increased transparency, and in predictable enforcement. If investors' trust is successfully restored, potential elements to increase liquidity may exist in increasing efforts to list and trade first governments' debt securities, then corporate debt securities, and possibly structured products such as asset-backed securities as well. Even further broadening and deepening of the market liquidity may come from more significant input by cornerstone institutional investors. If successful in reforming, these markets may increase integration into the global markets that then enables higher exposure and more competition through more diverse offer. In the medium-term horizon identifiable market hurdles are apparent in structural deficiencies, in specific through pension systems' reforms and legal adjustments that include convincing taxation policies, *ceteris paribus*. In order to build the long-run horizon growth the SEE countries need to overcome the vast hurdles that exist. These hurdles are exacerbated with time in deteriorating demographics and high emigration that calls for pivotal need to strengthen the wider environment, education and awareness, and to invest in and attain human resources.

Harmonization of market conditions in the selected SEE countries may be fast sped due to joint path to the EU membership and the inherent high level of links between the underlying micro- and macroeconomic structure. Therefore, providing access to capital for micro- and small- enterprises, and later inclusion of natural persons/retail entities in the opportunities for the placement of their savings and investments to capital markets seem critical to achieve inclusive growth and a greater participation rate in the selected capital markets. The initial lack of capital for micro- and small-enterprises to invest in research and development may adversely affect the liquidity and the cost of raising capital for these enterprises upon their evolution to larger companies. The benefits for SEE enterprises converging from private and bank funding to public listings may coincide with general capital markets' advantages. These advantages include **(a)** better transparency and investors' interest, **(b)** better liquidity access, **(c)** opportunity for labor force increasing integration, and **(d)** further supply chain benefits. Financial securitizations via capital markets may reduce cost of funding and may contribute to a better diversification of funding base that then improves capital efficiency and risk allocation. In this respect, in example of FIs additional capital is freed for later allocation to real sector investments. In follow-on supply chain, the real sector companies may spur opportunities for a larger inclusion of micro and small enterprises in the financial system. Taking a closer look at the SEE securitizations market, the asset-backed securities are noticeably not present and may emerge as an accessible and important channel for alternative longer-term financing. In another example, covered bonds allow FIs to channel credit to the real estate markets at a larger scale and more efficiently. Legal and regulatory changes are moving to closer inter-alignment between the SEE countries and with the EU. Recent legislation in the SEE capital markets is shifted toward the holistic definition of financial derivatives and structured products and alignment with complementary laws regarding insolvency regimes, taxation, and pension system reform.

Greater intra-regional integration may benefit local businesses' supply chains as markets become more competitive and lay roots to the potential rise of regional enterprises. Regional enterprises' champions thereafter might become more competitive in the EU and global markets and, overall, open doors for larger and greater capital utilization. The specific characteristics of the selected SEE countries make the area particularly well suited for consideration to integration. The countries were previously part of a single Yugoslav economy. Following the breakup in the 1990s today the same countries jointly continue toward the process of economic reintegration. Significant gains exist in just reintegrating fragments of regional systems such as **(a)** power grids, **(b)** rail networks, **(c)** supply chains, **(d)** brand recognition, etc. Geographic and cultural proximity and a common path toward the EU membership add tailwind to the integration trend to continue. The selected SEE capital markets chronically exhibit low liquidity and consideration of improvements validates the question about the need for the integration of exchanges and for the increased inclusion of financial derivatives and structured financial instruments products. In periods of high market volatility, liquidity first, and solvency next are amongst the primary stressed performance indicators. Economic performance in these periods greatly benefits from an availability of liquid capital markets' capacity to catalyze the recovery process. In the selected SEE markets illiquidity prevails throughout and the wide bid-to-ask price spreads further evidences these inefficient terms. Otherwise, in a liquid and orderly market, financial derivatives' price discovery capacity may **(a)** signal securities' intrinsic value, **(b)** attract further involvement of market makers, and **(c)** add to development stage of a financial market. On the contrary, an illiquid environment causes capital crunch. In theUnited States, despite the higher stage of economic and capital markets development, in the periods of high market volatility even the iconic FIs could not withstand the stressed performance. In less developed market the stressed performance is more destructive and prolonged. In aftermath stressed performers often see mergers for better capital and operating efficiencies. In the case of capital markets, the global trend of integration continues, from demutualization of trade exchanges, to increased indexation offerings, and to recent mergers of continental exchanges toward global entity exchanges. In disruptive innovation technology has altered and accelerated the terrain for traditional stock markets' operators. Electronic trading is increasing in use rapidly and companies build footprints in asset classes other than stocks. In response, operators and inter-dealer industry face a trend of increased concentration. An example is observable in the Intercontinental Exchange acquisition of New York Stock Exchange Euronext in 2013

(*The Economist*, 2013) to become the largest equity platform operator and the largest global exchange for futures trading, by equity capitalization and value in equities traded. In the same trend, in 2017 the Chicago Board of Options Exchange acquired Better Alternative Trading System. It brought together the largest options trading platform operator with that of the largest ETFs and multilateral trading facility platform. In 2018 the Chicago Mercantile Exchange Group acquired NEX Group in a merger of the leading futures and derivatives central counterparty clearing platform operator with the leading OTC post-trade servicer. In Europe, mergers involving the LSE and Deutsche Borse have been blocked multiple times by the European Commission because of the threat of market monopolization. Ultimately in 2021 LSE acquired Refinitiv, a large data and infrastructure service provider. As part of the same dealings LSE sold Borsa Italiana to Euronext, who consolidates ownership of multiple EU stock exchanges (e.g. Amsterdam, Paris, Dublin, Milan, Lisbon, and Oslo). Expected merger synergies involve not only cost-cutting for the company and end-clients, but also improved offerings and expansion in the geographical and products offering coverage. Yet, the growing ownership concentration increases the possibility of collusions, raises concerns about the possibilities of unfair competition to new reentrants and ultimately the supply-exerted price increases to the end customers. It is certain, however, that dealing with fewer counterparties in the form of (**a**) operators, (**b**) dealers, (**c**) market makers, (**d**) investors, and (**e**) exchange owners bring about higher counterparty concentration risk globally. Examples of market reactions include (**a**) stricter legislations, (**b**) improved regulations, (**c**) and/or a rise of independent exchanges targeting higher regulated exchange inclusion of natural persons/retail entities and OTC clients in the non-discriminatory fashion of favoring high-frequency trading. The Independent Exchange in the United States is an example of such a new exchange. Lower costs open doors for greater direct involvement of natural persons/retail entities' investors. Capital markets feature consistent innovation and it is thus not surprising that in the frontier and less liquid markets the economic cycle turns for a prolonged period. In the case of the selected SEE countries it should be noted that the use of financial derivatives rests predominantly on privately arranged hedging with vanilla swaps and forward products. The reason is that they entail a lower risk speculation component in comparison to default swaps, which exacerbated the downward spiral effect in the 2007/2008 crisis.

References

Books and Chapters in Books

Alajbeg, D., & Bubas, Z. (2001). *Vodic kroz hrvatsko trziste kapitala za gradjane*. Institut za javne financije.

Academic Articles, Working Papers and Studies

Arsov, S. (2005). *Post-privatization retrospective of Macedonia—Could we have done it better?* Ss. Cyril and Methodius University—Faculty of Economics.

Claessens, S., & Varangis, P. (1991). *Hedging crude oil imports in developing countries* (Policy Research Working Paper Series 755). The World Bank.

Curkovic, M., & Kristo, J. (2017). Performance measurement of UCITS investment funds in Croatia. *UTMS Journal of Economics, 8*(1), 11–18.

Gerber, A. (2008). Direct versus intermediated finance: An old question and a new answer. *European Economic Review, 52*(1), 28–54.

Halilbegovic, S., & Mekic, A. (2017). Usage of derivatives in emerging markets: The case of Bosnia and Herzegovina. *Asian Economic and Financial Review, 7*(3), 248–257.

Hernandez-Trillo, F. (1999). Financial derivatives introduction and stock return volatility in an emerging market without clearinghouse: The Mexican experience. *Journal of Empirical Finance, 6*(2), 153–176.

Jaksic, M., & Puric, J. (2014). Uporedna analiza poslovanja Beogradske, Zagrebačke i Varšavske Berze. *Bankarstvo, 43*(6), 86–111.

Kozarevic, E., Kokorovic, M., & Civic, B. (2014). The use of financial derivatives in emerging market economies: An empirical evidence from Bosnia and Herzegovina's non-financial firms. *Research in World Economy, 5*(1).

Marinkovic, S., & Skakavac, A. (2010). Derivatives market in Serbia—current developments and perspectives. *Economics and Organization, 7*(1), 47–59.

Mencinger, J. (2006). Privatization in Slovenia. *EIPF and University of Ljubljana—Slovenian Literature Review*, 3–65.

Rovčanin, A., & Hanić, A. (2014). The use of financial derivatives in risk management purposes of non-financial firms in Bosnia and Herzegovina.

Seba, M. G. (2017). 20 years of the Croatian capital market. *Zagreb International Review of Economics and Business 20 (SCI)*, 41–58.

Tobias, A., & Song, H. (2009). *Money, liquidity, and monetary policy* (Staff Report No. 360). Federal Reserve Bank of New York.

Reports and Other Sources

Banja Luka Stock Exchange. (2018). Retrieved on May 18, 2019, from https://www.blberza.com/Pages/docview.aspx?page=sp4

Banja Luka Stock Exchange. (2022). Retrieved on January 18, 2022, from https://www.blberza.com/periodicalstatreports.aspx

Belgrade Stock Exchange. (2022). Retrieved on January 19, 2022, from https://www.belex.rs/eng/trgovanje/izvestaj/godisnji

Central Bank of Bosnia and Herzegovina. (2016). Retrieved on May 15, 2022, from https://www.cbbh.ba/?lang=en

Central Depository and Clearing Company Inc. (2018). *Quarterly report: I quarter 2018*. Zagreb.

Central Securities Depository of the Republic of Macedonia. (2017). *2016 annual report*.

Desjardins, J. (2017). *Visual capitalist*. Retrieved on July 5, 2017, from http://www.visualcapitalist.com/all-of-the-worlds-stockexchanges-by-size/

European Bank for Reconstruction and Development. (2017). *Corporate governance in transition economies—FYR Macedonia country report*.

Kelley, D., Singer, S., & Herrington , M. (2015). *Global entrepreneurship monitor: 2015/16 global report*. Global Entrepreneurship Research Association.

Ljubljana Stock Exchange. (2018). Ljubljana stock exchange statistics. Retrieved on April 28, 2019, from https://www.ljse.si/cgi-bin/jve.cgi?doc=2330

Macedonian Stock Exchange. (2018). Retrieved on May 18, 2022, from https://www.mse.mk/en.

Macedonian Stock Exchange. (2022). *Annual statistical report*. Retrieved on January 19, 2022, from http://www.mse.mk/en/stats

Mckinsey and Company. (2005). *US$ 118 trillion and counting: Taking stock of the world's capital market*. Mckinsey Global Institute.

National Bank of the Republic of Macedonia. (2016). *Financial Stability Report for the Republic of Macedonia in 2016*.

National Bank of Serbia. (2016). Retrieved on May 18, 2022, from https://nbs.rs/en/indeks/index.html

O'Harrow, R. (2010, April 21). A primer on financial derivatives. *Washington Post*.

Rakocevic, R. (2016). *The impact of global capital markets on capital market in Serbia*. University of Belgrade—Faculty of Political Sciences.

Republic of Serbia Securities Commission. (2017). *2016 annual report*. Belgrade.

Samitas, A. G., & Kenourgios, D. F. (2004, May 28th–30th). Market efficiency and signaling: An event study analysis for Athens stock exchange. In *Proceedings of the1st Applied Financial Economics (AFE) International Conference on Advances in Applied Financial Economics*, (pp. 163–175).

Sarajevo Stock Exchange. (2018). Retrieved on May 15, 2019, from http://www.sase.ba/v1/en-us/SASE/About-SASE/SASE-History

Sarajevo Stock Exchange. (2022). Retrieved on January 15, 2022, from http://www.sase.ba/v1/en-us/Reports/Other-reports/Annual-Reports

World Bank. (2015). *Financial sector assessment program—Bosnia and Herzegovina—Capital markets.*

World Bank. (2016). *Doing business 2016—Measuring regulatory quality and efficiency.* Creative Commons Attribution CC. https://doi.org/10.1596/978-1-4648-0667-4

Zagreb Stock Exchange. (2017). Retrieved on April 21, 2018, from http://zse.hr/default.aspx?id=32877

Zagreb Stock Exchange. (2022). Retrieved on January 14, 2022, from http://zse.hr/

CHAPTER 4

Scientific Research Basis and Empirical Testing Results

4.1 Statistical Approach

4.1.1 Methodologies and Techniques in Use

A complementary set of four distinctive methodologies and techniques are used to empirically and comparably test the meaningfulness of the model relationship between the time-series and the cross-countries diverse data on capital markets and economic indicators. These techniques and methodologies are central to addressing the empirical questions involving static and dynamic attributes, homogenous and heterogeneous interdependencies, and include: (a) bi-variate Johansen long-run relationship cointegration test between a single country macroeconomic indicator and the relevant country's SMI, (b) bi-variate Granger short-run causality relationship test between a single country macroeconomic indicator and the relevant country's SMI and vice versa, (c) multi-variate panel PMG relationship model cointegration test, and (d) multi-variate panel VAR analysis. This research differs from previous studies by applying the most coherent and comprehensive statistical testing of bi-variate and multi-variate model relationships to date for macroeconomic indicators and stock exchange indices in the selected SEE markets.

Johansen cointegration method is used to test for long-run co-movement between capital markets' stock exchange indices and macroeconomic variables at the level of a single country. Testing for long-run cointegration between two variables determines model relationship's

A. Dodig, *Capital Markets in Southeast Europe*,
https://doi.org/10.1007/978-3-031-07210-9_4

statistical significance in the observed period without controlling for the direction of the relationship, its intensity, or predictive power. Johansen cointegration test singles out bi-variate long-run cointegrating model relationship from otherwise more frequent short-term spurious relationship. It is followed by Granger causality method, which tests for the short-term shock response transmission in a bi-variate model relationship between the specific country's SMI and its macroeconomic variable, and vice versa. Granger method tests single direction of the model relationship of spurious short-run fluctuations without statistical predictive capacity or significance in the long run. Besides, in the case where cointegration exists for bi-variate model relationship Granger test is considered miss-specified and seeks alteration via error correction adjustment, in the form of VECM or rather panel PMG for multiple further advantages. For these reasons this research introduces panel PMG estimator technique test and panel VAR predictive explanatory model relationship test. Panel tests resolve the small sample data limitations, which are frequently seen in SEE countries and call for use of panel cross-countries testing techniques and methodologies. As stock exchange markets in SEE countries resemble short-lived existence and are subdued and economically less important, there are restraints in terms of reasonably lengthy data availability and data variance. Panel testing is used to infer statistically more meaningful results. Panel PMG estimates statistically meaningful model relationship between macroeconomic indicators and stocks' indices in various time intervals. Panel VAR test is performed to check cross-countries' data for how much of the forecast error variance of each of the variables can be explained by exogenous shocks to the other variables and to itself.

The selected techniques and methodologies account for bi-variate relationships' causal and dynamic cointegration and for multi-variate time-series' variant statistical predictive association between macroeconomic indicators and SMIs. In the data review the Augmented Dickey-Fuller (ADF) test was performed to determine the presence of non-stationary level time series, which is a precondition for data use validity in the Johansen cointegration test. In the next step ADF is applied to confirm the existence of unit roots in the data set. Confirmation of data stationarity is achievable in case of no unit roots in the differences and stochastic properties. Data stationarity is a required precondition for use of Granger causality method test and of panel VAR to then draw stable results inferences. Panel PMG can treat stationary and non-stationary data simultaneously. In background description, stationary data show characteristic of constant mean and variance over time and of a co-variance with sole difference in the scale of lag.

Numerous evidence links exchange-traded capital markets' prices to macro variables' performance using diverse specifications. Some of these include: (a) theoretical Capital Asset Pricing Model (CAPM), international CAPM for addition of FX risk, Arbitrage Pricing Theory, Present Value Model; (b) modeling using data regression in VAR, VECM cointegration test, OLS estimation, testing cross-countries' group data in panel VAR approach, PMG estimation, mean group (MG) estimation, fixed-effects methods, random effects methods; (c) testing for relationship existence and spurious causality in Johansen long-run cointegration method, Granger short-term relationship causality method; and (d) ARIMA and GARCH for testing conditional volatility in second-level residuals, amongst others.

4.1.2 *Selection of Panel PMG Estimation Technique*

Panel PMG was selected as the most appropriate estimation technique for the purpose of empirical testing. Panel PMG is employed to test dynamic time-series and cross-countries' associating variables' model relationship estimations. This estimation technique is particularly conducive to empirical research of SEE markets due to contemporaneous shared and distinct traits that are broadly and effectively included. Panel PMG has the capacity to fix the long-run coefficients and in that way capture better the shared SEE markets characteristics. Furthermore, panel PMG has the capacity that allows for the short-run coefficients heterogeneity and in that way reflecting varying degrees of single country's state of economic structure and development. Panel PMG accounts for bias and static fixed effects from non controlling factors. This is the preferable approach due to its relevance, completeness, and rigor in addressing the empirical research question that simultaneously involves static and dynamic attributes and homogeneous and heterogenous research interdependencies. This chapter presents in more detail the panel PMG estimation technique. All of the other research methods, e.g. Johansen, Granger, and panel VAR are presented in more detail in Appendices C.1.2, C.1.3, and C.1.4, respectively.

PMG technique pools together the long-run parameters but solves the inconsistency problem due to heterogeneous short-run dynamism. PMG technique relaxes the restrictions on the common coefficients in the short run while maintaining the assumption on the homogeneity of the long-run slopes. Panel PMG technique ensures more robust consistency of estimating coefficients by better resolving the possible presence of an endogeneity problem. This is achieved due to the inclusion of lags of dependent and independent variables and due to the cross-data groups heterogeneity (Pesaran et al., 1999). In addition, panel PMG can simultaneously treat stationary and non-stationarity data that is very pertinent for the limited data availability in the study of the selected SEE markets. Such feature eliminates the necessity for data order transformations and the process related information loss. The main characteristic of PMG is the flexibility to allow short-run coefficients to be heterogeneous across one group of information (e.g. individual countries) while constraining the long-run slope coefficients to be homogeneous across other group of information (e.g. joint set of countries). At the same time PMG allows long-run differences for intercepts and error variances. This characteristic is particularly valuable in considering the facts that certain parameters, or at least a subset of them, may be the same or similar across countries as is the case in SEE due to the shared underlying economic fundamentals and the overall interconnectedness. Individual country's independent values are nonetheless included through heterogeneous differentiations in short-run model relationships. Such PMG features create statistical approach advantage in determining short- and long-run dynamic model relationships. There are several requirements for the validity, consistency, and efficiency of PMG technique. Firstly, the existence of a stable long-run cointegrating model relationship amongst the variables of interest requires the coefficient on the error correction term (ECT) to be negative and not lower than negative two values. Secondly, an important assumption for the consistency of the autoregressive distributed lag model (ARDL) is that the resulting residual of the error correction is serially uncorrelated and that the explanatory variables can be treated as exogenous. Such conditions can be fulfilled by including the ARDL ("p,q") lags for the dependent ("p") and independent variables ("q") in the error correction form. Thirdly, the relative size of time series ("T") and sample size ("N") is important as the use of dynamic panel technique helps to avoid biases in the average estimators by resolving the issue of heterogeneity.

4.1.3 *Analyses of Procedures and Relationship Model Presentation*

Data stationarity is tested for using ADF test, which confirms the presence of unit roots in the data standard level and in the data differences level series (Dickey & Fuller, 1979). The null hypothesis is set that Y = 0. If no unit root is present, data series is considered stationary. On the contrary, the presence of unit root characterizes non-stationarity of data series. The optimum number of time lags is determinable by Schwartz Bayesian Information Criterion (SBIC) test results' guidance.

Bi-variate tests start with cointegration analysis, which is set in an environment where time-series variables exhibit wandering, yet not drifting extensively far apart so as to disturb the long-run equilibrium. In practical words, though short-run deviation in cointegrating movement of two variables may be observed, two variables exhibit cointegrating equilibrium in the long run (Engle & Granger, 1987). Johansen cointegration method allows the analysis of such behavior (Johansen, 1991). The method applies maximum likelihood procedure to determine cointegrating vectors (CE) of non-stationary time series using regression analysis. In-detail information on Johansen model is available in Appendix C.1.2.

Testing causality of the short-term transmission shock in the research model relationship shifts focus to bi-variate Granger test, with model presented in-detail in Appendix C.1.3. Granger procedure is correct if two series are not cointegrated. Engle and Granger argue that causality tests, which ignore ECT from cointegrating relationship, are in fact miss-specified and call for re-parametrization with VECM. The simple error correction model is limited to dealing with single endogenous variable while panel PMG is a more reliable technique for dealing with panel data. This study, due to constraint of cointegrating precedent relationship, opts to reject the available Granger test results due to lesser reliability. Moreover, Granger test utilizes only stationarity data that are in this study sample only reached under second differences transformation of the data. Processes of data differencing transformation causes loss of valuable information and thus reduces the reliability and applicability of practical results. Instead, it utilizes panel PMG estimation technique as the most reliable for the underlying data characteristics and the research scope. Granger testing in effect may be spurious in the significance of results for data series that contain a trend and are otherwise random. Granger test implies that in the bi-variate model relationship single variable's results occur before another variable's results without explicit theoretical support to the model relationship. For this reason, panel PMG and panel VAR are further utilized to determine a more meaningful impact and association in the reviewed model relationships.

Panel VAR provides additional degrees of freedom and allows for heterogeneity spillover test between individual economies. It is achieved by restricting coefficients on variables to mean effects yet capturing variability through regressors combinations. Panel VAR also utilizes only stationarity that then requires standard transformation process which comes with lesser precision due to removal of identifying variance. This reserach defines the panel VAR algorithm more compactly by means of Formula (5) presented in Appendix B.3.

Panel PMG test enables greater consistency and fixes correlations and static testing present in fixed effects and random effects methods. Panel approach resolves the biases for non-controlled fixed factors for country-specific fixed factors such as productivity, or by estimating systemic variations. Furthermore, models with lagged endogenous variables allow variability across countries. Therefore, panel PMG is the preferred estimation technique since it allows the use of level data series.

Cross-countries data testing strengthens the extensiveness of the statistical database while accounting for contagion effects. Moreover, pooling cross-country and time-series data together and utilizing mean coefficients result in increased variability and in efficiency gains. Also, biases are offset due to the heterogeneity of cross-sectional data, wherein panel PMG controls long-run coefficients homogeneity. To assess both the long-run stability of model relationship and the relationship dynamics this research employs PMG estimation developed by Pesaran et al. (1999). Hausman test is applied for model miss-specification to distinguish significant differences and preferences amongst three dynamic model estimators that are (a) PMG, (b) MG, and (c) dynamic fixed effects (DFE). Dynamic model estimators are preferred to static models and to random and fixed effects due to study sample data and model specifics of testing long-run effects and adjustment to a long-run equilibrium. Preference exists due to inconsistencies in other techniques when dealing with a small sample size, non-stationary data, and both endogenous and error term augmented variances.

Other panel techniques (e.g. static estimators, instrumental variables, GMM estimators) normally require a larger sample, of in rule of thumb greater than a minimum of a sample of one hundred as adequate, or sample of four hundred as great. Even so other techniques yet frequently fail in dealing with data of various stationarity characteristics. If Hausman test results point to p-value larger than five percent then PMG model is preferred over MG model, and the same applies to DFE preference over MG. Hausman approach tests in the null hypothesis whether there is homogeneity in the long-run coefficients. If the null hypothesis is not rejected, PMG is preferred over MG. Reasons for choosing PMG over DFE lie in the flexibility for the analysis of dynamic time-interval model relationship. It also allows short-run coefficients heterogeneity across groups while still capturing characteristics of long-run shared group factors. PMG model can incorporate cross-sectional information and can tolerate data heterogeneity. It is therefore suitable to this empirical study of independent and shared SEE markets' traits. The basic assumptions of PMG estimator are as follows: (a) error terms are serially uncorrelated and are distributed independently of the regressors and the explanatory variables can be treated as exogenous; (b) there is a long-run relationship between the dependent and explanatory variables; and (c) the long-run parameters are the same across countries. This estimator is also flexible enough to allow for long-run coefficient homogeneity over a single subset of regressors and/or countries. This approach to estimation can present the multiplicity between the listed stocks' indices and macroeconomic variables while solving the problem of a traditional panel model association. The selected panel PMG model is the following:

$$\begin{aligned} \mathrm{SMI} = {} & \mu_{it} + \lambda_i \mathrm{SMI}_{t-n} + \beta_t \mathrm{GDPPC}_{it-n} + \beta_t \mathrm{FX}_{it-n} + \beta_t \mathrm{MMIR}_{it-n} \\ & + \beta_t \mathrm{HICP}_{it-n} + \beta_t \mathrm{IPI}_{it-n} + \beta_t \mathrm{BOPNFA}_{it-n} + \varepsilon_{it} \end{aligned} \tag{4.1}$$

In Formula (4.1) above β term is the long-run parameter coefficient, λ is scalar value vector, i represents countries, t refers to time, μ refers to the constant value, n represents the number of periods, and ε refers to error disturbances. Since evidence of cointegration in level series data is found, using transformation differences in data would be inefficient because it neglects the information in nominal levels of the different times. Besides, panel PMG estimator has the capacity to treat both stationary and non-stationary data, thus enabling the utilization of the level series data.

4.1.4 *Selection of Variables—Theory and Practice*

This research used the selected macroeconomics' indicators and exchange-traded capital markets' indices for the end of every three months, starting from year-end 2005 through year-end 2016. The data were collected using Eurostat (2018), central banks, International Monetary Fund (IMF), stock exchanges', and national statistical agencies' databases. Proxy indices for B&H's, Serbia's, North Macedonia's, Croatia's, and Slovenia's organized exchange-traded capital market prices are SASX-10 and BIRS, BELEX15, MBI10, CROBEX, and SBITOP, respectively. Given that it was not possible to divide independent B&H country variables at the Entity Government level, a joint B&H index, BATX, was used. It also achieves better data robustness and reliability while maintaining consistency with comparable single country indices in the overall data. The construction of a single common SMI follows the capitalization-weighting approach by including four largest companies from the SASE and two from the BLSE.

The selection of the variables in the analysis was governed by (a) the common times series included in the studies of capital markets' performance, (b) popularity and frequency in research, (c) the state of underlying economies and the relative importance of the selected indicators thereto, and (d) simplicity in accounting standardization and data availability. Capital markets' prices are influenced by company-specific, industry-specific, and other socio-political impacts which are not in entirety controlled for. This research focuses on measuring the overall implied model relationship with the selected individual macroeconomic indicators. **SMIs** are used as proxies for the representation of specific stock exchange's prices. In an efficient capital market, stock exchange's prices should reflect a priori full market information and then future prices follow a random walk from historical ones. Since it was not possible to holistically control all of the external factors' influence on stock exchanges' prices, the robustness of this statistical analysis was limited to the capacities of the chosen methodologies and techniques and the chosen informative role of the included and endogenized macroeconomic indicators. Due to a limited number of observations and limited choice of variables in the study sample to date, future researchers are encouraged to include and endogenize more variables and a longer period of observations that thus may reduce the impact of the potential endogeneity bias on the results. The selected macroeconomic variables in this study are:

GDPPC indicator measures the level of economic development. Countries with higher GDPPC tend to illustrate more advanced, larger capitalization, and more liquid capital markets (as shown in Fig. 3.4), which tend to show lesser correlation with stocks' prices movements

(Morck et al., 2000). The 2010 triennial survey showed that the growth of the financial derivatives' market in EMEs is positively related to the growth in GDPPC. National output growth can generally be treated as a catalyst in promoting financial development, as was proven by Lee and Chang (2009) research in a set of thirty-seven countries using annual data for the period from 1970 to 2002. Lee and Chang utilized panel cointegration and error correction VECM testing on dynamic relationship and causality amongst FDI, financial development (measured as liquid liabilities to GDP and private credit to GDP ratios), and economic output. In general, there is a positive relationship between a country's income level standards and the level of stock exchanges' market development (Bayraktar, 2014).

Morck et al., (2000) empirically proved that stocks' prices move together more in poor economies than in rich economies due to larger systematic component in financial returns' variations. They utilized panel OLS regression on thirty-seven countries' GDPPC and SMIs from 1990 to 1995. Essentially, under auspices of an efficient capital market the economic activity should a priori be reflected in a company's market value (Shapiro, 1988; Fama, 1990). The growing economic output per capita implies an increasing consumption in a longer run and propels demand, which reflects in increasing companies' sales and earnings and thereafter equity valuations. More imminently, direct increase in economic output per capita propels direct investments and demand on stock exchanges. While this rational relationship in general holds, there are apparent bubbles and fads in the causality, which is attributable to specific time periods and the stage of economic development in the observed markets (Binswanger, 1999). The observed SEE countries manifest trends of unstable political environment marked with (a) opaque bureaucracy, adverse policies, wide spread environment of mistrust, (b) falling or stag nant population, (c) somewhat static GDP, and (d) a low level of natural persons/retail entities' involvement in capital markets' transactions.

For GDP data, the study used the expenditure calculation approach under the European System of National and Regional Accounts 2010 (ESA 2010) rules. For B&H, data in this methodological calculation and data on a three-month period basis are unavailable for 2006 and 2007. For Croatia, 2016 data are provisional. Population census data were used in each year as equivalent to the most recent available prior census. The population censuses were conducted in the following order: (a) Croatia in 2001 and 2012, (b) Slovenia in 2002 and 2011, (c) B&H in 1991 and

2013, (d) Serbia in 2002 and 2011, and (e) North Macedonia in 2002.[1] GDPPC values are calculated on a one-year trailing basis for values at the end of every three months.

BOPNFA tracks broad implied economic activity by means of net acquisitions and disposal of financial assets and liabilities. The indicator tracks how net lending to or borrowing from non-residents is financed. BOPNFA' sub-account constituents FDIs, remittances, international borrowings, and national reserves form significant elements in SEE countries' economic structure. The components of net positive claims flow to residents and include direct investments, portfolio investments, and net reserves. BOPNFA exemplary assets' classes include gold, currency, special drawing rights, financial derivatives, equities, and bonds. External financing plays an important role in modernizing a national economy and stimulating growth through the introduction of new processes, know-how transfers, and financial integration for alleviating access to capital (Lee & Chang, 2009). Nonetheless, overreliance on external funding weakens a country's net worth and strength of domestic policy tools in a scenario when it is necessary to adjust to spillovers. A higher risk of spillover in a more integrated market may however be partially offset by lower funding costs and increased competition efficiencies. Liberal national policies pursue to facilitate the flow of capital and trading to help capital market exchanges widen and broaden the investor base and the necessary liquidity. The state of development of an economy, of sub-segment financial system, and of sub-segment capital markets plays a role in market capacity to enhance the relationship with macroeconomic performance locally and internationally. Alfaro et al. (2004) prove that more developed financial markets absorb capital more efficiently as was seen in the results of panel cross-section OLS regression on thirty-nine countries from 1981 to 1997. Their empirical study tested for the impact of investment capital through the prism of financial development that was measured in proxy by the relative value of transactions costs.

Most research focus on the explanatory relationship between FDIs and international reserves to stock exchanges or to economic output. FDIs and international reserves typically have a positive impact on stock exchanges' prices (Barbic and Condic-Jurkic, 2011; Issahaku et al., 2013) and on economic output growth (Lazarov et al., 2016; Lee & Chang,

[1] It should be noted that the population slightly decreased during the observed period and GDP per capita to some degree reflects this.

2009). This research seeks to capture broader interactions between financial assets, portfolio investments, reserve assets, and debt investments with wide-ranging, dynamic, and inter-temporal impact on capital markets' prices. Companies that are reliant on the support by financial assets have a more volatile relationship with stock market performance as has been proven by time-series and cross-sections evidence research by Robert Hall (2001). Frequently used measures of corporate finance availability are based on a cross-sectoral cash-flow movements at a macro sector level and/or on an individual companies' financial statements cash-flows aggregation at a micro sector level. Both approaches face limitations in possibly omitting inter-sectoral flows and in incoherent data aggregation, amongst others. Due to data limitations in obtaining individual components of the BOPNFA indicator this research used an aggregate net value. In this way the study captures the input proxy of international trade flow activity and openness. Further research can add value by individually assessing interactions of balance of payments' individual capital account, current account, and financial account sub-accounts components' relationship with listed stocks' prices. This research is the first to grasp in an empirical model the relationship between portfolio investments, ones with higher sensitivity to risk and liquidity, and ultimately to stock exchanges' movements in the selected SEE markets.

IPI is another popular indicator of aggregate real economic activity. Often the relationship between industrial production and stock exchanges' prices appears to be more significant than the relationship between stock exchanges' prices and growth rates of real GDP (Binswanger, 2001). Domian and Louton (1997) provide evidence on an asymmetry in predictability between IPI and stocks' prices as they point to better indicative predictability of IPI on stocks' prices than vice versa. From a theoretical point of view an increase in IPI indicates a greater activity in capital markets alike through direct contribution, such as better financial performance of listed industrial companies, or indirect contribution, such as a greater disposable income in the market (and vice versa). Many other researchers prove the validity of the relationship and argue that the degree of the association increases with the length of observed time (Fama, 1990; Binswanger, 1999). In EMEs, industrial production carries relatively more predominant influence on economic strength both in the formative share in GDP and in employment than is the case in advanced economies. In advanced economies other sectors such as services and technology often prevail. In case of the selected SEE countries, IPI data are readily available. Nonetheless, industrial production in all the selected markets carries a decreasing importance in its role in the economic development, one less pronounced and further concentrated on foreign versus domestic demand factors.

FX indicator is selected principally to illustrate the level of macroeconomic stability. It measures the expected foreign investors' determination to invest in the currency risk, for change in value, or for regulatory capital flow controls. Moreover, the strength of local currency also measures local companies' competitiveness in an international market and local natural persons'/retail entities' international purchasing power. When purchasing power parity does not hold, investors hold an exchange rate risk when investing internationally and arbitrage pricing bubbles emerge in a disturbed international economic equilibrium. A decrease in the value of a currency (e.g. versus US$ in this research) is expected to imminently adversely impact both equity and debt investors' financial returns and vice versa. Such a performance is of greater significance for shorter-term and portfolio investors. However, on the other side and in the flow-oriented theory, in case of a depreciating local currency, local export-based companies benefit in international competitiveness and performance in a longer run and are thereafter key drivers of an improved performance of local capital markets. This study tests for the significance of the exchange rate short- and long-run model relationship and the associating impact on SMIs. The study used US$ as the foreign currency counter-value in desire to increase data variance and reliability that is unavailable elsewhere. The reasons are the high level of Euro prevalence in the observed markets and the inexistence of fluctuations in Euro foreign currency rate for the cases of B&H and Slovenia. Slovenia adopted Euro in early 2007 and the volatility of the FX regime in 2006 is not considered. B&H local currency, Convertible Mark, is fixed in value to Euro. Nonetheless, the prevalence of the practical relevance of SEE markets on US$ value is very low given the global economic commonness of the "hard currency" and meager importance of SEE markets in the global context of US$ use. SEE markets showcase small and open economies where FX volatilities quickly spill over. At the same time all the markets are extremely Euroized, and thus local currency value is less detrimental and is often replaced with Euro in practical daily uses. In such an environment, Croatia and North Macedonia also show a form of managed float to Euro. Results of former empirical research point to currency depreciation creating a negative effect on stock exchanges' prices and with effect of stronger co-movements in crises periods (Ajayi & Mougoue, 1996; Lin, 2012; Chkili & Nguyen, 2014). Other empirical results point to the existence of a short-run negative relationship but a long-run positive relationship in proof of both portfolio and traditional/flow-oriented investor approach and in measure of policy makers control mechanisms' effects (Lee & Wang, 2015). Similar empirical results repeat in advanced and emerging markets utilizing various methodologies and techniques including VAR, Markov Switching VAR, Vector Error Correction Model, panel PMG, etc.

HICP indicates a stage of inflation in a market and again a level of macroeconomic stability. In general, stock exchanges' prices are commonly found to respond negatively to an unexpected inflation. The US federal reserve system (FED) theory presumes that higher inflation increases yields on bonds, which compete directly with equity for investors' interest and demand. In valuation theory, the unexpected inflation, in its impact on interest rates, decreases the present value of equity. Besides, the expected inflation is adjusted in both discount interest rates and cash-flows rates, then leaving equity prices unchanged. A rise in inflation directly reduces the purchasing power of investors imminently through demand and in the long run through decrease in consumption capacity, and vice versa. In the short run high inflation is expected to deter the activity in capital markets. It is a signal of contemporaneous changes and of future inflation uncertainty, which negatively impacts the dynamism of financial intermediation in that market and its aggregate economic growth (Azar, 2010; Balduzzi, 1994; Campbell & Vuolteenaho, 2004). In an increasing inflation the living costs increase and shift demand from investments to consumption. Costs of borrowings rise and cause downward pressures on financial returns, dividends, and ultimately on equity valuations. In transitioning markets dividend policies are less standardized and higher market uncertainty environment prioritizes sooner payout, through capital gain or dividend (Dodig & Dzidic, 2022). While inflation often occurs in spillovers as in the case of Euro crisis, it is also significantly a local risk. In the case of Turkey recently official and unofficial inflation rates varied significantly. In cases of extreme deviations between black and official market rates, in data analyses researchers have estimated black market premiums. Eurostat classification of goods and services, classification of individual consumption by purpose (COICOP), is used in this research in the classification of data for HICP and the used reference year is 2010 = 100. HICP data are unavailable in B&H and thus the research used a local definition inflation proxy, for which the end of three months data, except for the year-end data, is unavailable for years 2005 through 2010.

MMIR indicator is related to capital markets' performance in several ways. Lower interest rates imply higher liquidity in the market and greater flow of funds onto investments, which increase capital markets' activity and performance. Increasing key interest rates curbs future inflation. Moreover, increased interest rates create an incentive to investors' portfolio rebalancing in favor of fixed-income securities. Interest rates are assumed to contain information on current and future economic activity. Chen et al. (1986) argue that interest rates themselves are relevant in impact on equities' financial returns through yields and default spreads. Darrat and Mukherjee (1986) empirical research found a significant relationship in Indian and African stock exchanges' markets in the 1980s between short- and long-term interest rates and equities' financial returns using principal components analysis. Analyzing effects of the US monetary policy Erhman and Fratzscher (2004) found in their empirical research that on average a monetary tightening of fifty basis points reduced equities' returns by about three percent during the testing period between 1994 and 2003. Erhman and Fratzscher found that in general a poorer credit rating and less indebted companies react more significantly because the unexpected changes in interest rates create more volatility. Companies listed on stock exchanges respond in a more heterogenous fashion to changes in interest rates while those with lesser transparency respond in more negative volatility due to the expectation of stronger constraints in access to capital. In principle, stock exchanges' markets provide a quality and quantity alternative platform for placement of savings. MMIR in that perspective may thus serve as an approximation of a savings rate. Johnson et al. (1999) conducted an empirical research on sixteen industrialized countries using panel VAR regression. Their study confirmed the reaction of stock exchanges' prices to local and US monetary environment, yet without controlling for firm, industry, and event specific events. Barbic and Condic-Jurkic. (2011) empirical research showed a statistically significant cointegrating relationship between MMIR and SMI for the case of Slovenia but not for the case of Croatia in the period from 1998 to 2010. Countries using fixed exchange rate system forfeit independency to move interest rates separately from the anchor currency. The Mundell-Fleming impossible trinity, or policy trilemma theory, discloses limited monetary policy options in that pursuing two of the following three policy objectives excludes the third. The three options are: (a) free flow of capital, (b) fixed exchange rate, and (c) monetary autonomy (Aizenman, 2010). In this research, ECB key rates are used for the cases of B&H and Slovenia.

The shown economic rationale supports links between performance of exchange-traded capital markets and each of the selected macroeconomic indicators. Bearing in mind the limitations of the influence by other factors on capital markets' performance and bearing in mind constraints on the availability of data, the selection of indicators is considered justified. This empirical research covers eleven-year long period in an approximately full economic cycle ensuing from the peak in 2007, the subsequent recession, the recovery, and the kick-starting of growth before the new stalling.

While bi-variate Johansen and Granger models interchangeably test the bilateral country macroeconomic indicator's model relationship with SMI pair, multi-variate panel PMG and VAR relationship models include the full set of variables which are:

Independent variables—Quarterly (end-December, end-March, end-June, and end-September) selected SEE macroeconomic indicators including GDPPC, FX, MMIR, HICP, IPI, and BOPNFA;
Dependent variables—Quarterly (end-December, end-March, end-June, and end-September) selected SEE stock exchanges' traded markets indices (BATX, BELEX15, MBI10, CROBEX, and SBITOP, respectively);
Sample and data source—Data are based on quarterly frequency for year-end 2005 to year-end 2016 for the selected SEE countries using Eurostat (2018), central banks', stock exchanges', and national statistics agencies as data sources. Tables and figures showing values of these indicators for SEE countries are provided in Appendix A.1.

4.2 Panel Pooled Mean Group Test Results

4.2.1 *Homogenous Aggregate Southeast European Results*

The results of the aggregate sample data panel PMG test are presented in Appendix C.1.5. In Table A.18, the ECT term is negative and statistically significant at the ninety-nine percent confidence interval. In particular, the results suggest that under the estimating impact of macroeconomic indicators around 19.5% short-run deviation from the SMI equilibrium value is adjusted for every three months until reaching the long-run model relationship's equilibrium level. IPI indicator's positive estimation coefficient in the model relationship is statistically significant while impacts by other selected macroeconomic indicators are statistically non-significant. More to, the constant term is significant and adds to model environment. In the short run the results indicate that slope coefficients of all the selected model macroeconomic indicators are statistically non-significant. A decreasing influence of macroeconomic indicators in the long run would be in accordance with the expected relationship's behavior of return to equilibrium if long-run correction measures are present. In that scenario individual countries take control actions which result in the model relationship impact slowdown through the error correction mechanism. Otherwise, scenarios where the long-run impact of the estimating coefficient is stronger than in the short run might signify deeper asymmetries of market-specific underlying structure and the inherent irrational investors' behavior. In other aspects such scenarios may signify stronger market inefficiencies.

In other words, while test results point to non-significance of IPI indicator in the short-run, an increase in IPI value in the long run causes a fall in SMI value again in the long run and without clear implications on the corrective measures presence. Results of this research can be considered as sample data specific to an environment where capital markets exhibit a high concentration toward a few large corporations in industry and frequently to high government ownership and with possible distortions in market time reaction. In EMEs, industrial production holds a relatively more important influence on economic output both in the formative share in GDP and in employment than is the case in advanced economies. In advanced economies other sectors such as services and technology often prevail. If individual country results are considered then it becomes more apparent that only for B&H and Serbia the ECT term is significant and confirms long-run relationship stability. As such input from these countries is likely the driving factor on group results. At individual country in both markets governments' owned industries are greater formative factors on the economies and on SMI constituency. Indicatively at the group and individual country level these results are aligned with other researchers claiming the validity of the IPI relationship with SMI through increasing degree of association with increasing length of observed time (Fama, 1990; Binswanger, 1999). However, while other researchers in EMEs also point to existence of long-run relationships the direction of estimating impact by increasing IPI is typically aligned with theory and manifests in positive increase in SMI (Abu et al., 2016).

In comparison to prior empirical research on the equivalent model and markets I have tested then available shorter time span data with test results again confirming markets inefficiencies due to presence of short- and long-run relationships, but in lesser instances and with different significance of indicators (Dodig, 2020; Dodig & Bugarcic, 2022). Having extended the captured statistical data from eleven to almost sixteen years of information the model environment is both more extensive and standardized. Vis-à-vis the results show a single statistically significant variable in the long run against then shown three and two statistically significant variables in the short run at an individual country level against then shown three variables which all-together may allude to improved market performance. In the long run anlaysis the group data then established estimators were negative coefficients HICP and MMIR and positive coefficient BOPNFA. Similarly, Megaravalli & Sampagnaro (2018) showed a statistically non-significant impact of inflation indicator and a statistically significant positive long-run impact of FX indicator on three Asian countries' SMIs in the period from 2008 to 2016. However, in that research the FX indicator impact was not observed in the short run. The results of the research presented in this book also point to non-significance in the short-run relationships at a group level, yet, at individual country level for Croatia and Serbia the short-run testing results on FX relationship show significance establishment (for more details see Annex C.1.1.5, Table A19). The results for Croatia have repeated compared to prior research. The FX coefficient results are in alignment with the portfolio theory that an increasing value of the currency is favorable for portfolio investors to rebalance their portfolio positions in a more valuable currency (Ajayi & Mougoue, 1996; Lin, 2012; Chkili & Nguyen, 2014; Lee & Wang, 2015). Even so, a positive FX coefficient contradicts the traditional theory that an increase in the value of a local currency hurts exports and the flow-on effect on the performance of the stock prices of export-dependent companies. In an overall, the limited impact of U.S. dollars, as the FX indicator currency pair, on the local economies must be kept in focus when interpreting the importance of the test results of the FX coefficient.

Moreover, in this book the research results also show MMIR positive estimating coefficient on SMIs in the short run at an individual country level for Slovenia. Thus, these results are in contradiction again with the research findings in Ghana and with the portfolio theory of contracting monetary policy creating a shift of investors' portfolio preference away from equity assets and toward fixed-income assets. The results are also in contradiction with a traditional market approach due to an increased uncertainty on market performance under increasing interest rates. Implication on the direction of the relationship impact of the MMIR factor is in contradiction with the common research findings for higher returns in more expansive monetary policy (Johnson et al., 1999; Erhmann & Fratzscher, 2004). In the aligning empirical research finding, Pilinkus (2010) shows decreasing money supply positively impacting stock exchange prices in his study on the case of Estonia in the period from 2000 to 2008. As apparent, empirical researches in frontier markets exhibit varying results that are largely representative of the wider specific environment. For example this may be in inefficiency of bank intermediary role to relay interest rates effect to the real sector, in discrepancy between official and unofficial inflation and FX rates, in large structural lag in market reaction, etc.

In more of the comparable empirical panel research on the CEE countries Drazenovic and Kusanovic (2016) studied annual data from 1995 to 2010 utilizing the fixed-effects method and have found non-significance in the relationship of stock market size with GDP growth and with inflation indicators. Fink et al. (2005) confirmed non-significance in the relationship of stock market size with GDP growth indicator. Yet, Lazarov et al. (2016) pointed to the significant relationship of stock market capitalization to GDP growth in Central and Southeast Europe but non-significance in the impact of inflation and FDI indicators.

The different research reached contradicting results. The research pertained to different study periods, different countries, utilized different methods and techniques and, overall, called for updates in research to reach further consistency. In a comprehensive review, the statistical testing results point to cointegrations and causality of macroeconomic indicators for listed stocks' prices performance thus providing evidence on the failure of the weak form of capital market efficiency. Besides, further statistical evidence is provided for profiling individual capital markets, which points to the presently (a) low turnover liquidity, shallow and concentrated investors base, (b) weak assets class diversification, (c) subpar corporate

Table 4.1 Summary of existent PMG pair relationship

Country	*SMI*	*Panel PMG estimation on significant short-run relationship existence from macroeconomic indicators onto individual country's SMI*	*Aggregate regional data panel PMG estimation on significant long-run relationship existence from macroeconomic indicators onto SMIs*
B&H	BATX		IPI-
Serbia	BELEX15	FX +	
North Macedonia	MBI10		
Croatia	CROBEX	FX +	
Slovenia	SBITOP	MMIR +	

Note " + " sign marks positive relationship direction, and "-" sign marks negative relationship direction

governance, (d) regulatory inefficiencies, and (e) insufficient infrastructure and political support. Individually and jointly, all of them may cause market performance asymmetries and specifics (Table 4.1).

Summary of the existent bilateral Johansen and Granger pair relationship is presented in Appendix.

Additional data can be found in Table A.14 in Appendix C.1.3

While panel PMG results are preferable for being the best applicable and the most reliable in the research environment, other methodologies yield complementary information. Amongst the panel empirical findings, this book presents panel VAR test results for which in-detail review is available in Appendix C.1.4.

4.2.2 Heterogenous Southeast European Individual Countries' Results

The in-depth analysis of individual country results utilized panel PMG consistency quality in allowing short-run heterogeneity and cross-country differing in intercepts, coefficients, and in error terms variances. Test results reveal the statistical significance of ECT scores in the cases of B&H and Serbia but not in the cases of Croatia, Slovenia, and North Macedonia. Statistically significant ECT results suggest a stable long-run cointegration between macroeconomic indicators and SMIs in which the short-run deviation under the impact of the estimating macroeconomic indicators is adjusted in return to long-run relationship equilibrium.

ECT adjustment coefficient is prominent at a scale of thirty-nine percent correction and thirty-two percent quarterly correction in respective cases of B&H and Serbia. In the cases of Croatia, Slovenia, and North Macedonia it is possible that the short-run estimating relationship impact by macroeconomic indicators rather causes increasing long-run relationship deviation from the equilibrium relationship balance with the respective SMI value. The prominent individual countries' estimating coefficients for macroeconomic indicators which are statistically significant in the short run are to a large extent specific for individual markets' environment and are unique for the short-run time horizon.

The case of positive estimating impact by FX indicators' on SMIs in Croatia and in Serbia is first singled out. The FX indicator coefficient is in alignment with the portfolio theory of increasing currency value calling in favorable portfolio investors' rebalancing and improvement of stock prices (Ajayi & Mougoue, 1996; Lin, 2012; Chkili & Nguyen, 2014; Lee & Wang, 2015). However, it contradicts the traditional theory of increasing currency value, which hurts exports and the flow of business and determines companies' stock price performance. Therefore, the result for the estimating coefficient significance may be plausible due to variability in that the two countries are the only ones, together with North Macedonia, to run a somewhat independent currency regime. In precedent testing Johansen cointegration confirmed FX and SMI relationship in Serbia and the descriptive statistics have shown that FX in Serbia had the greatest relative changes in the covered time period. However, the relationship direction may be rather specific for an individual market and calls for an extended and updated local risk analysis. Nevertheless, results of panel VAR test for FX indicator show little evidence of the importance of this indicator through forecast error variance decomposition (FEVD) explanations, which reveals that FX indicator accounts for under percent of error variance decomposition of SMI in any period under the eleven-years study horizon.

In the case of Slovenia the result for estimating MMIR coefficient is significant and positive in the short run. Johanes cointegration also showed relationship between MMIR and SMI in Slovenia. The direction of the statistically established relationship is in contradiction to traditionally viewed increase in uncertainty on market performance under increasing interest rates. It is also in contradiction with the common research findings for higher returns in more expansive monetary policy (Johnson et al., 1999; Erhmann & Fratzscher, 2004) but is in alignment with empirical research finding in Estonia (Pilinkus, 2010) then proving that varying results are largely representative of the wider specific environment. In case of Slovenia an example may be in transition to ECB key rate during the observed period and possible structural lags in manifestation through the relationship.

In the case of B&H and Serbia the results for estimating coefficients of all short-run macroeconomic indicators relationship appear non-significant as is the case for the aggregate group results. However these are the only two countries with stable long-run relationships due to significant ECT. Such results point to greater long-run inefficiencies in established IPI indicator estimating coefficient significance and in market environment where government-owned industry is a greater formatting factor of SMI.

4.3 Summary of Empirical Findings and Conclusions.

In the current stage of the development of the observed capital markets in SEE, the focus of this book and the inherent research is in creating new information, new data, and new knowledge. The empirical research utilizes the available data and through statistical testing creates new learning on the selected capital markets' performance in relationship with essential macroeconomic indicators. In addition, this research provides an in-depth profiling of the structural dynamics and trends of each individual and of coherent SEE capital markets. The research implications are intended to increase the awareness of the diverse components embedded in the surrounding financial and economic system. The presented assessment sets fundamental elements for a closer market perspective and a comparative outlook in researching the SEE emerging markets. The study of the relationship dynamics between macroeconomic fundamentals and regulated stock exchanges' performance in the selected SEE countries paradigms a comparative basis to the research in other emerging and advanced economies. These by large assess the nexus of stage of capital market development to economic growth (Fink et al., 2005; Lazarov et al., 2016; Drazenovic & Kusanovic, 2016) and impact of macroeconomic indicators on regulated stock exchanges' prices (Barbic and Condic-Jurkic, 2011; Megaravalli & Sampagnaro, 2018; Lee & Wang, 2015).

In testing for the existence of the weak form of capital market efficiency in the selected SEE countries, the selected bi-variate and multi-variate statistical tests on the sample data yield results on statistically significant causal and cointegrating relationships between macroeconomic fundamentals and regulated stock exchanges' prices. Such results prove the respective capital market inefficiency in respect to a priori inclusion of macroeconomic information in regulated stocks' prices. In a closer outlook, a dynamic assessment of the relationships is provided, highlighting time validity and relationship strength and direction.

The results of the statistical study discard the existence of linear relationships. Panel PMG results for the group data confirm inexistence of statistically significant short-run relationship of regulated stock exchanges' prices with macroeconomic indicators. It is in alignment with former and recent empirical research utilizing panel PMG in the case study for three countries in Asia, Japan, China, and India (Megaravalli & Sampagnaro, 2018). The panel PMG results for the group data reveal statistically significant long-run cointegrating relationships that reflects an associating negative impact of an increasing IPI macroeconomic indicators on SMIs, which is in alignment with previous research for the existence of relationship (Fama, 1990; Binswanger, 1999), but contradicts typically interpreted estimating direction (Abu et al., 2016). The statistical study shows the existence of a significant long-run impact versus the inexistence of the short-run significant impact of macroeconomic indicators on regulated stock exchanges' prices. Such findings are in contradiction with the expectations that the control factors such as policy adjustment and the shift in investors' sentiment would curtail the impact from short- to a long-run time horizon. These results therefore attest for markest inefficiency to alleviate the long-run impact of macroeconomic indicators on SMIs. Besides, the inexistence of significant short-run relationships questions the prevalence of presence of portfolio investors as the ones who are more likely to be sensitive to short-run deviations because of delicate strategy on balancing investments' positions. In particular the market environment shapes the results. Vis-à-vis other sectors, in EMEs industrial production holds a relatively more important influence on economic output both in the formative share in GDP and in employment than is the case in advanced economies. More of, if herewith individual country results are considered it becomes more apparent that only for B&H and Serbia long-run relationship between IPI and SMI is stable and the input from these two countries is likely the driving factor on group results. In both markets governments' owned industries are greater formative factors on the economies and on the SMI constituency.

The short-run panel PMG individual country established relationships show positive estimating coefficient by stronger local currency in case of Serbia and of Croatia. In addition, results show positive estimating coefficient by stronger MMIR in case of Slovenia. Descriptive statistics depict Serbian local currency as relatively the most changed during the observed period with higher volatility creating likely greater effect. Yet, in case of Serbia the stable relationship serves as corrective factor in the long run. In the case of Croatia and Slovenia the results prove prior Johansen cointegration findings. However, the research results may be market specific due to lesser prevalence of US$ currency sensitive investors, of representative lesser importance of portfolio investors on the overall capital markets, and of Slovenia implementation of EUR and ECB key rate policies during the observed period.

Panel VAR test results show an altogether a predominant impulse impact by prior values of SMIs on SMI itself. In initial years under research the SMIs decline in value seems to have caused largest negative forecast error variance in consecutive SMIs' value as available from the IRF test outcomes.

Results of the empirical research uncover new information that enables better prospects for understanding and utilizing such information by policy makers, investors, academics, and others in support to the financial intermediation diversity and sustainability. The empirical research results, however, are also a reflection of the surrounding environment that illustrates the underpinning fundamental structure of the selected SEE capital markets' inefficiency, low capitalization, low liquidity, lacking infrastructure, weak intermediation in market-making, and higher inherent costs and risks when compared to benchmarks in advanced countries' capital markets. The identified weaknesses, in particular the subpar investor protection and transparency in the SEE capital markets generate a lack of investors' confidence.

More significant capital market development thus may evolve upon precedent setting up of efficient capital markets' exchanges, ones gathering broader and more diverse set of buyers and sellers. A sufficiently deep base of traders reduces transaction costs and enables position offset capacity versus product delivery capacity. The standardization element encourages a faster learning curve and a stronger client and user relationship that effectively may evolve into trust. Reduced counterparty risk can be achieved through first setting up a central counterparty, and secondly, an efficient margin system that partially counterpoises counterparty default risk. Transparency improvements and set-up of an exchange guarantee funds nevertheless involve high-level legal enhancement, regulatory alignment, and ultimately critical improvements in judicial efficacy and erosion of corruption, which seeks a paramount political support. Therefore, future studies are called upon to incorporate and empirically endogenize into the SEE capital market development nexus additional qualitative factors. These may include event studies and governance indicators including the effectiveness of judicial system and measures of the degree of corruption. Moreover, new studies are called for to test the impact of structural reforms on unexplored SEE countries. New model studies are to be conducted with panel multi-variate tests for reverse direction relationships. Amongst others, new studies are called upon to incorporate a more extensive data set that will then be available under longer time periods, as well as under statistical techniques and methodological innovations.

The relatively short history of the capital markets in the selected SEE countries limits the availability of an extensive data. The available data on the selected markets evidently reveal higher volatility and interrelationship with macroeconomic factors. While these should be observed under the study limitations, the herewith presented statistical test results under the observed time-variant pattern confirm market inefficiency in relation to the efficient capital market theorem.

References

Aizenman, J. (2010). The impossible trinity (aka the policy Trilemma). *The encyclopedia of financial globalization*. UCSC and NBER.

Ajayi, R., & Mougoue, M. (1996). On the dynamic relations between stock prices and exchange rates. *Journal of Financial Research, 19*(2), 193–207.

Alfaro, L., Chanda, A., Kalemli-OZcan, S., & Sayek, S. (2004). FDI and economic growth: The role of local financial markets. *Journal of International Economics*, 89–112.

Alrub, A. A., Tursoy, T., & Rjoub, H. (2016). Exploring the long-run and short-run relationship between macroeconomic variables and stock prices during the restructuring period: Does it matter in Turkish market? *IBIMA Journal of Financial Studies & Research*. Article ID 917071.

Azar, S. A. (2010). Inflation and stock returns. *International Journal of Accounting and Finance, 2*(3/4), 254–274.

Balduzzi, P. (1994). *Stock returns, inflation, and the "proxy hypothesis:" A new look at the data* (NYU Working Paper No. FIN-94-008). New York University, Stern School of Business, Finance Department.

Barbic, T., & Condic-Jurkic, I. (2011). Relationship between macroeconomic fundamentals and stock market indices in select CEE countries. *Ekonomski Pregled, 62*(3–4), 113–133.

Bayraktar, N. (2014). *Measuring relative development level of stock markets: Capacity and effort of countries.* Borsa Istanbul.

Binswanger, M. (1999). Stock market booms and real economic activity: Is this time different? *International Review of Economics and Finance, 9*(4), 387–415.

Binswanger, M. (2001). *Does the stock market still lead real activity? An investigation for the G-7 countries.* University of Saint Gallen, Institute for Economics and the Environment.

Campbell, J., & Vuolteenaho, T. (2004). *Inflation illusion and stock prices* (Working Paper 10263). National Bureau of Economic Research.

Chen, N.-F., Roll, R., & Ross, S. A. (1986). Economic forces and the stock market. *The Journal of Business, 59*(3), 383–403.

Chkili, W., & Nguyen, D. (2014). *Exchange rate movements and stock market returns in regime-switching environment: Evidence for BRICS countries* (Working Paper No. 2014-388). IPAG Business School.

Dickey, D. A., & Fuller, W. A. (1979). Distribution of the estimators for autoregressive time series with a unit root. *Journal of the American Statistical Association, 74*(366), 427–431.

Dodig, A. (2020). Relationship between Macroeconomic Indicators and Capital Markets Performance in Selected Southeastern European Countries. *Zagreb International Review of Economics & Business,* 55-88.

Dodig, A., & Dzidic, A. (2022). Dividend policies in volatile transitioning markets. *Zagreb International Review of Economics & Business.*

Dodig, A., & Bugarcic, M. (2022). Extended relationship between macroeconomic indicators and capital markets performance in selected southeastern European countries. *Economic Thought and Practice, Dubrovnik.*

Domian, D., & Louton, D. (1997). A threshold autoregressive analysis of stock returns and real economic activity. *International Review of Economics and Finance, 6*(2), 167–179.

Engle, R. F., & Granger, C. (1987). Cointegration and error correction: Representation, estimation, and testing. *Econometrica, 55*(2), 251–276.

Erhmann, M., & Fratzscher, M. (2004). *Taking stock: Monetary policy transmission ot equity markets* (ECB Working Paper 354). European Central Bank.

Eurostat. (2018). Eurostat databased. Retrieve November 3, 2019, from https://ec.europa.eu/eurostat/data/database

Fama, E. F. (1990). Stock returns, expected returns, and real activity. *The Journal of Finance, 45*(4), 1089–1108.

Fink, G., Haiss, P., & Vuksic, G. (2005). *Importance of financial sectors for growth in accession countries*. ECBOeNB/CFS—Conference on European Economic Integration, Vienna.

Hall, R. (2001). Struggling to understand the stock market. *American Economic Review, 91*(2), 1–11.

Issahaku, H., Ustarz, Y., & Domanban, P. B. (2013). Macroeconomic variables and stock market returns in Ghana: Any causal link? *Asian Economic and Financial Review, 3*(8), 1044–1062.

Johansen, S. (1991). Estimation and hypothesis testing of cointegration vectors in Gaussian vector autoregressive models. *Econometrica, 59*(6), 1551–1580.

Johnson, R., Jensen, G., & Conover, M. (1999). Monetary environments and international stock returns. *Journal of Banking and Finance, 23*(9), 1357–1381.

Lazarov, D., Miteva-Kacarski, E., & Nikoloski, K. (2016). An empirical analysis of stock market development and economic growth: The case of Macedonia. *South East European Journal of Economics and Business, 11*(2), 71–81.

Lee, C.-C., & Chang, C.-P. (2009). FDI, financial development, and economic growth: International evidence. *Journal of Applied Economics, 12*, 249–271.

Lee, Y.-M., & Wang, K.-M. (2015). Dynamic heterogenous panel analysis of the correlation between stock prices and exchange rates. *Economic Research-Ekonomska Istraživanja, 28*(1), 749–772.

Lin, C.-H. (2012). The comovement between exchange rates and stock prices in the Asian emerging markets. *International Review of Economics and Finance, 22*(1), 161–172.

Megaravalli, A. V., & Sampagnaro, G. (2018). Macroeconomic indicators and their impact on stock markets in ASIAN 3: A pooled mean group approach. *Cogent Economics and Finance, 6*(1), 1–14.

Morck, R., Yeung, B., & Yu, W. (2000). Why do emerging markets have synchronous stock price movements? *Journal of Financial Economics, 58*(1), 215–260.

Mukherjee, T., & Darrat, A. (1986). The behavior of stock market in a developing country. *Economics Letters, 22*(2–3), 273–278.

Olgic, B., & Kusanovic, T. (2016). Determinants of capital market in the new member EU countries. *Economic Research—Ekonomska Istrazivanja, 29*(1), 758–769.

Pesaran, H. M., Shin, Y., & Smith, R. P. (1999). Pooled estimation of long-run relationships in dynamic heterogeneous panels. *Journal of American Statistical Association, 94*(446), 621–634.

Pilinkus, D. (2010). Macroeconomic indicators and their impact on stock market performance in the short and long run: The case of the Baltic states. *Technological and Economic Development of Economy, 16*(2), 291–304.

Shapiro, M. (1988). *The stabilization of the U.S. economy evidence from the stock market* (NBER Working Papers 2645). The National Bureau of Economic Research, Inc.

CHAPTER 5

Summary Closing Considerations and Recommendations.

Global market capitalization of exchange-listed equity market reached record heights at the end of 2016, outpacing the pre-2007/8 crisis peak and recovering from halving in value during 2008. In a similar trend, the value of public debt securities has almost doubled in the preceding ten years (Iwanicz-Drozdowska, Bongini, Smaga, & Witkowski, 2019). In the same period emerging economies account for more than seventy-five percent of the global growth in output and consumption, almost double the share from just two decades ago (International Monetary Fund, 2017). On the backdrop of technological advancements and global economic growth economies are more integrated than ever as foreign investors own more than a quarter of all equities worldwide and more than thirty percent of outstanding debt bonds (Mckinsey & Company, 2017). Nonetheless, global cross-border total flows are still behind the 2007 peak at over US$ twelve trillion. In the environment of an increased systemic risk in 2018 the global economic arena was facing further uncertainty with an economic cycle turning to slowdown. Volatility appeared amidst the turmoil of the global political arena and the instilled trade tariffs. The culmination into economic crisis rapidly spilled over on the back of the COVID-induced health crisis from 2019 to 2020. The increased risk was manifested in at first peaking and then extremely volatile and quickly falling equity valuations, in volatile currencies environment, in

A. Dodig, *Capital Markets in Southeast Europe*,
https://doi.org/10.1007/978-3-031-07210-9_5

capital rush to safety currencies, and in prolonged low interest rates policies. However, in 2021 the situation started to reverse and soon thereafter exchange-listed equity valuations peaked to highest mark ever and for the first time at above US$ one hundred trillion. Akin, the trading volumes boomed to highest ever. The global economic recovery was expected by the end of 2022 at the latest, high inflation was already present, and policy makers have reversed to tapering down of quantitative easing assets purchase program and sporadically increasing interest rates. This time around, versus the 2007/8 crisis, countries globally show more formidable foreign reserves and better budgetary and external balances. However, the transition through the economic cycle, as in the case of 2007/8 crisis, is again very disproportionate between emerging and advanced economies and in aggregate countries show a weaker net worth position. In the ongoing global economic environment, this research focuses on the specific structure of Southeast European economic and capital markets, their performance, and outlook.

The selected Southeast European countries share numerous traits in **(a)** formerly belonging to a common country, **(b)** old and new joint infrastructure, **(c)** common ethnic, cultural, and language similarities, **(d)** commercial brands recognition, and **(e)** being interconnected as the largest mutual trading partners. Regulated stock exchange markets, though sizeable in capitalization at US$ forty-eight billion[1] or roughly thirty-one percent of the gross domestic product value versus estimated eighty percent global average, are concentrated to few players. They exhibit **(a)** large involvement of the government sector, **(b)** low or inexistent involvement of natural persons/retail entities and foreign investors, **(c)** traits of subpar corporate governance, **(d)** poor international visibility with meager or no passive index investments, **(e)** high investor uncertainty, and **(f)** an overall shallow trading liquidity at the estimated turnover ratio of under fifteen percent of capitalization versus forty percent global average. Capital markets initially evolved in the 1990s transition period as one of the strategic by-products in privatization processes of transferring ownership from state-owned to private hands. Simultaneously, local institutional and privatization and pension funds development were subpar for evolving exclusively for the purpose of conducting the privatization processes. It was followed by at first local concentration of

[1] Data shown are aligned to the consistent presentation and are as of year-end 2016.

ownership and then by attracting initial foreign investments in capital markets, which fueled quick growth in capitalization and turnover but only to drop very soon and painfully during the 2007/8 crisis. The crisis resulted in almost half in value fall in turnover and capitalization from which the Southeast European capital markets have largely not recovered to date and continue to sub-perform during the COVID crisis aftermath. In this setting the pace of evolvement of legal, regulatory, institutional, and infrastructure framework was not synchronized with that of the swift but short-lasting growth in the size of the capital markets. Thus, capital markets have not served the full purpose of providing protection of minority ownership rights, instilling best practice corporate governance, and providing sustainable liquidity.

An effective economic system runs a dynamic set of complementary financial market tools wherein the depth of the market provides the capacity for risk diversification and for checks and balances support. Financial system is vital for economic prospects and is characterized by a network of financial players, financial infrastructure, surrounding legislation, and the surrounding regulation and judiciary efficacy that in many ways facilitates bringing together suppliers and users of capital. As they were the first to evolve and are now dominant in many frontiers and emerging financial markets, banks have developed the principal role in managing deposits, which made up the basis for providing loans. Banks are an effective solution to an adverse selection between lenders and borrowers. While after the 2007/8 crisis banks have improved capital and liquidity base, it partially came at the expense of the retreat of global banks' operations from foreign back to domestic markets. To a large extent, causes of the retreat include repricing of foreign countries' risks, own strategic reorganizations due to lack of scale and local expertise in foreign markets, and new legal and regulatory disincentives apparent in increasing complexities and thus operating risks. Similar trend again re-emerged during the COVID crisis and simultaneously an increasing importance shifted to other components of the financial system, primarily to capital markets. In capital markets the trend of integration continues with demutualization of trade exchanges, increased debt public offerings, indexation, and recent mergers of exchanges into more concentrated global entities. Capital markets are a complementary and an alternative industry to the banking industry. They enable sustainable low-cost distribution mechanism of multiple financial products. Their purpose is to mobilize savings into long-term investments, address the non-consensus on how companies are to be managed, and provide critical resolutions through innovation within growing securitizations, technological, and decentralization advances.

The relationship between financial markets and aggregate economic performance has long caught attention of various academics, investors, and policy makers, amongst many others. The initial empirical statistical research focused primarily on the banking sector's sole financial intermediary contribution to the aggregate economic performance. Initial empirical research reached a consensus on the existence of a positive relationship (Goldsmith, 1969; King & Levine, 1993; La Porta et al., 2000). With the evolvement of capital markets attention has turned to assessing the contribution of individual capital markets to economic growth or to the contribution of the joint relationship with the banking sector. Thereto empirical research findings were conflicting, though the opinion of the positive and complementary relationship prevails for the developed markets (Fama E. F., 1981; Chen et al., 1986; Dumas et al., 2003). More unclarity can be observed in the case of frontier and emerging markets, with findings often assigned to the specific constraints of the study sample due to inefficiencies in transition economies (Naceur et al., 2007; Koivu, 2002; Fink et al., 2005; Cojocaru et al., 2015). Studies conducted on the impact of macroeconomic indicators' performance on capital markets normally follow the theorem that economic activity should a priori be reflected in listed stocks' prices and particularly more consistently so in the long run (Fama E. F., 1990; Shapiro, 1988). Other findings show that rational expectations for the relationship are empirically justifiable, but also that bubbles and fads exist in correlation (Binswanger, 1999; Domian & Louton, 1997; Erhmann & Fratzscher, 2004; Issahaku et al., 2013). It was also revealed that listed stocks' prices move more in poor economies than in rich economies due to the larger systemic component versus firm-specific component in price variations (Morck et al., 2000).

Altogether, the studies on the relationship between macroeconomic indicators and listed stocks' prices for frontier markets are relatively scarce, inconclusive, and call upon repeat studies for a more extensive data set, more mature market performance stability, and improvements in statistical techniques and methodologies (Chkili & Nguyen, 2014; Lee & Wang, 2015; Megaravalli & Sampagnaro, 2018). Amongst the relevant studies in the Southeast European markets Lazarov et al. (2016) observe a positive relationship between the listed stocks' capitalization and growth of the gross domestic product for ten Southeast European countries (including countries in this research) and four Central European countries in the study period from 2002 to 2012. They studied a small sample due to only twenty observations in total per variable. Drazenovic and Kusanovic (2016) observed the impact of a set of diverse factors on the level of listed stocks' capitalization in Central European countries including Slovenia and Croatia. The findings showed statistically significant factors in **(a)** the impact of privatization reform, **(b)** the prevalence of investment funds, **(c)** the size of life insurance premiums, and **(d)** inflation. On the other hand, factors that proved non-significant were **(a)** the size of the existing pension funds, **(b)** European Bank for Reconstruction and Development indicator of large-scale privatization level, **c)** European Bank for Reconstruction and Development indicator of banking financial institutions reform level, **(d)** inflation level, **e)** gross savings level, and **(f)** nominal growth rate of the gross domestic product (Drazenovic & Kusanovic, 2016). In the context of Southeast Europe, a single specific previous research discussed the relationship between macroeconomic indicators and capital markets' return using bi-variate cointegrating relationship study for the cases of Croatia and Slovenia. The findings showed statistically significant relationship between stock exchange market indices and key interest rate, and between stock exchange market indices and inflation rate (Barbic & Condic-Jurkic, 2011).

This research presents the top-down assessment of global financial system environment, practices, and trends, and provides an in-depth assessment of individual selected Southeast European capital markets' structure and their environment, practices, and trends. Econometric bi-variate and multi-variate empirical statistical testing is conducted on the time series and the existence of the cross country relationship between the set of selected macroeconomic indicators measured in gross domestic product per capita, local currency value, credit availability, industry growth, and inflation to capital markets' performance, approximated through stock exchange indices. Testing of the transmission role between the economic results and capital markets' performance employs Johansen cointegration, Granger causality, panel pooled mean group estimation, and panel vector autoregressive techniques and methodologies to test the eleven-years relationship and its dynamics. For this purpose, a more holistic econometric analysis on time-series and cross-country meaningful relationship is conducted, on its causality, and on inferring capacity in transition economies with short-lived and low capital market activity to date. Bi-variate and multi-variate models examine the existence of the weak form of capital market efficiency in the selected Southeast European countries. They test for presence of the statistically significant relationships and prove capital market inefficiency in terms of an a priori inclusion of macroeconomic information in stock exchange market indices. In closer outlook the study provides a dynamic assessment of the relationships highlighting time validity and direction of relationship. The panel cross-country testing approach is used to improve reliability under increased data variation and a lower regressors collinearity from the limited availability of the individual country sample data. The pooled mean group estimation technique further allows fixing of long-run coefficients and intercepts. It captures homogenous factors amongst the Southeast European countries while allowing for short-run coefficients and intercepts fluctuations and enabling increased explicit accounting of individual country factors. The pooled mean group estimation technique simultaneously treats stationary and non-stationary data, thus improving results' consistency. In addition, pooled mean group technique allows the dynamic assessments of results, which is not possible in static testing present in fixed effects, random effects, and mean group statistical techniques and methodologies. Initial diagnostics of the data sample have shown simultaneous data series stationarity and non-stationarity in level data series information. Granger and vector autoregression tests validity are pre-conditioned with data stationarity and for those methods data series are therefore transformed with differencing until reaching stationarity in the second-level transformation. Since data information is lost in the transformation processes, the pooled mean group technique is preferred since its results have better reliability and consistency in practice.

Results of the panel pooled mean group statistical test confirm the inexistence of statistically significant linear relationship and of short-run cointegrating relationships. Such test outcome is in alignment with recent research that utilized panel pooled mean group in a case study for Japan, China, and India (Megaravalli & Sampagnaro, 2018). The panel pooled mean group test outcome shows that the existent statistically significant long-run cointegrating relationship forms a negative contributing coefficient by increasing industrial production indices on stock exchange market indices, which is in alignment with previous research for the existence of relationship (Binswanger, 1999; Fama, 1990), but contradicts typically interpreted estimating direction (Abu et al., 2016). In particular the market environment shapes the results. Vis-à-vis other sectors, in emerging markets the industrial production holds a relatively more important influence on economic output both in the formative share in GDP and in employment than is the case in advanced economies. More of, if herewith individual country results are considered it becomes more apparent that only for B&H and Serbia long-run relationship between industrial production indices and stock market indices is stable and the input from these two countries is likely the driving factor on group results. In both markets governments' owned industries are greater formative factors on the economies and on constituting the stock market indices. The significant long-run impact attests to the inefficiency of Southeast European capital markets in a priori including the information in the listed stocks' prices. Where a short-run relationship exists, inefficiency may be alleviated from existence in long-run relationships by implementing control factors such as policy adjustment and a shift in investors' sentiment. Contemporary example of shift in investors' sentiment may appear in case that a prolonged inflation continues and is already built into expectation and decision making for future investment performance. Results of the multi-variate panel pooled mean group model test discard bi-variate statistical tests' results on the existence of long-run relationship between the stock exchange index with the foreign exchange, inflation, key interest rate, balance of payments net financial account, and economic output per capita indicators. The findings contradict former conclusions in similar research comprehensively (Binswanger, 2001; Domian & Louton, 1997) but are aligned with fads and bubbles that are apparent in emerging markets (Chkili & Nguyen, 2014; Lin, 2012; Pilinkus, 2010). However, such results may be market specific due to lesser prevalence of natural persons/retail entities investors, of foreign investors, of US$ sensitive investors, or of structural specification derailing relationship implementation.

Results of the statistical testing and of the comprehensive empirical research uncover new information that enables better understanding and prospects for utilization by policy makers, investors, academics, and others. They can also be used as support to the diversity and sustainability of financial intermediation. Nonetheless, statistical testing techniques and methodologies have limited capacities and the results should be observed with this constraint in mind, while it is critical to also understand the operating market environment which is assessed in detail. In-depth structural and environment assessment shows that in their inherent interconnectedness Southeast European markets also turn to cooperation in harmonizing conditions with standards of the European Union. Access to capital for micro and small enterprises, and later inclusion of natural persons/retail entities seem to be critical constraints in the current participation rate of the domestic market. The benefits for Southeast European enterprises' convergence from private and bank funding to public listings are manifested in better liquidity and better solvency. It also provides a greater opportunity for resilient growth, more sustainable profitability, and an increase of labor force. Securitizations may reduce the cost of funding while contributing to a better diversification of funding base and an improved capital efficiency and risk allocation. Southeast European markets show a large growth of governments' funding via bonds and bills. Yet, trivial additional value is passed on to the development of capital markets since commercial banks are predominant investors, the trade mostly occurs on the over-the-counter markets while altogether secondary trading is immaterial. In a closer comparable outlook to trends in the other frontier and emerging markets it seems that securitizations and particularly the asset-backed products may emerge as an accessible and important channel for further and for longer-term financing. Longer-term financing, in turn, is instrumental for financial institutions to efficiently channel capital to long-term partnerships, in project financing, in renewable projects, in equity partnership, in real estate markets, and inclusively supporting enterprises in supply chain to the construction sector, etc. It seems that in capital markets' legislation bottlenecks include the holistic definition and effectiveness of financial derivatives and structured products, as well as the harmonization with complementary insolvency regimes, taxation, and pension system reform. For regulated exchanges in capital markets, regional integration ponders requests for deeper and more liquid client base. It would enable a greater access and exposure to global markets, greater competitiveness and economies of scale, implementation of higher transparency, and ultimately an avenue to compete globally. Steps in this direction have already been taken in the availability of data on the regulated exchanges on a single place like the Vienna Exchange, and later in the Southeast European link project that links smaller Southeast European markets for data sharing. Closer integration also questions cross-membership on Southeast European regulated exchanges aimed at reaching the intermediating cost efficiency and diversified service. Ultimately it leads to the integration of exchanges to the extent of free trading between the listed counterparts already operating or striving to operate in one single economic zone. For this reason, consideration is given to potential establishment of a regional central counterparty which might fill the capacity to introduce better risk diversification and a potential introduction for exchange-traded derivates. In the future it can be expected that local pension funds and insurance companies as institutional investors will play a more significant role in the capital market due to an increasing scope of business inherent in demographic change of an aging population needing to ensure adequate income in the older age (Drazenovic & Kusanovic, 2016). Thereto, increasing international investors participation may also be more plausible. Nevertheless, the current environment is hindered by the perception of high stage of corruption and inefficient judicial system both being material hurdles to overcome in order to progress.

Liquidity in the selected Southeast European capital markets is meager and information asymmetries overshadow credibility in operations. In general, the capital markets are rather inefficient and play a non-significant role within their respective financial systems and economies. The existing capital markets do not efficiently protect minority ownership rights, do not exhibit best standards in corporate governance, and do not employ sustainable liquidity in cost-effective savings and investments solutions. Much of the current condition is attributable to legacy from historical developments in transitioning from a planned to a free market economy when stock exchanges were installed rapidly as vehicles to process privatizations. An opportunity for improvement may be found in strengthening transparency and corporate governance standards, and in the form of more efficient and better harmonized legal and regulatory environment. Instilling efficient judiciary system is necessary to enable further improvements. Integration of the selected Southeast European markets can provide an opportunity to reach better operating efficiencies and a more scalable exposure for an increase in internationalization and faster growth of the markets. Integration may also be an opportunity to share efforts to create a regional central counterparty for contracts enforcement and to increase the safety net for the market. Building on the trend of the growing debt securities issuances and trading in Southeast Europe may be possible by introducing structural products such as mortgages and other asset-backed securities. The ongoing processes may further increase liquidity by reorganizing non-performing assets to a structure that allows resolution, for example in the process form of closed to open-end privatization funds' transformation. More opportunity for increasing liquidity may lie in successfully completing planned privatizations of systemic players listed on the stock exchanges and in enabling structural reforms that allow greater local institutional investors involvement. It is a paradox that as local institutional business operations are growing a bottleneck arises for their greater involvement in local capital markets due to lack of investment options.

A larger scale growth of the Southeast European financial markets may be reached by further inter-regional integration. It may lead to an efficiently larger market with higher liquidity and deeper investor base. Another upcoming trend may lie ahead in the coherent enhancement and alignment of legislation and regulation at the European Union *acquis* level, which in the future may permit more liberal capital movement and may expand availability for use to a wider public. Precondition, however, is instilling higher public awareness of the value-added components of the capital markets traits and product structure. The initial benefits in capital market improvements are likely to be realizable through greater use by the current capital market players in both regulated and non-regulated markets. This research strives to create and share knowledge of value-adding factors in the use of capital markets. It highlights the dynamics of the operating environment and contributes to leading the path in generating preconditions for the sustainable capital and economic market growth.

Past results are not an exclusive indicator of future performance and should be viewed in the context of the operating environment in these markets. Nevertheless, as one may ignore the financial system environment learnings, at some point one will not be able to ignore the consequences of an ignored reality. This research raises awareness of the diversified financial system environment's characteristics, of opportunities, and of caveats unquestionably seeking adaptation in the selected Southeast European capital markets. Due to increased uncertainty of efforts to foster innovative financial products, claims that a smaller capital market economy cannot be competitive versus market "Goliaths," and that large or advanced market failures are necessarily hereditary to developing markets should be thoroughly questioned. Where deep capital electronic markets exhibit overextended moves in frenzy times (Kleinman, 2013), a nascent, smaller capital market may be naturally hedged and thus serve as a global example of a better-struck balance.

Future research may consider multiple interesting additions including expansion of research countries to grasp more advanced but still similar frontier and emerging continental or intercontinental markets. It could also extend the time of observations and thus capture further economic cycles. It might include additional variables encompassing individual components of the balance of payments and other testing techniques and methodologies. One of such approaches may be utilizing autoregressive integrated moving average and general autoregressive conditional heteroskedasticity models to test the efficient capital market hypothesis by an event study. In long-term studies one ought to consider statistically testing and endogenizing factors for political, social, regulatory, legal, judicial, degree of corruption, and similar determinants on capital markets performance in the Southeast European economies.

References

Alrub, A. A., Tursoy, T., & Rjoub, H. (2016). Exploring the long-run and short-run relationship between macroeconomic variables and stock prices during the restructuring period: Does it matter in Turkish market? *IBIMA Journal of Financial Studies & Research*. Article ID 917071.

Barbic, T., & Condic-Jurkic, I. (2011). Relationship between macroeconomic fundamentals and stock market indices in select CEE countries. *Ekonomski Pregled, 62*(3–4), 113–133.

Binswanger, M. (1999). Stock market booms and real economic activity: Is this time different? *International Review of Economics and Finance, 9*(4), 387–415.

Binswanger, M. (2001). *Does the stock market still lead real activity? An investigation for the G-7 countries*. University of Saint Gallen, Institute for Economics and the Environment.

Chen, N.-F., Roll, R., & Ross, S. A. (1986). Economic forces and the stock market. *The Journal of Business, 59*(3), 383–403.

Chkili, W., & Nguyen, D. (2014). *Exchange rate movements and stock market returns in regime-switching environment: Evidence for BRICS countries* (Working Paper No. 2014-388). IPAG Business School.

Cojocaru, L., Falaris, E. M., Hoffman, S. D., & Miller, J. B. (2016). Financial system development and economic growth in transition economies: New empirical evidence from the CEE and CIS countries. *Emerging Markets Finance and Trade, 52*(1), 223–236.

Domian, D., & Louton, D. (1997). A threshold autoregressive analysis of stock returns and real economic activity. *International Review of Economics and Finance, 6*(2), 167–179.

Dumas, B., Harvey, C., & Ruiz, P. (2003). Are correlations of stock returns justified by subsequent changes in national outputs? *Journal of International Money and Finance*, 777–811.

Erhmann, M., & Fratzscher, M. (2004). *Taking stock: Monetary policy transmission ot equity markets* (ECB Working Paper 354). European Central Bank.

Fama, E. F. (1981). Stock returns, real activity, inflation and money. *The American Economic Review, 71*(4), 545–565.

Fama, E. F. (1990). Stock returns, expected returns, and real activity. *The Journal of Finance, 45*(4), 1089–1108.

Fink, G., Haiss, P., & Vuksic, G. (2005). *Importance of financial sectors for growth in accession countries*. ECBOeNB/CFS—Conference on European Economic Integration, Vienna.

Goldsmith, W. R. (1969). *Financial structure and development*. Yale University Press.

International Monetary Fund. (2017). *Global financial stability report: Is growth at risk?* World Economic and Financials Surveys.

Issahaku, H., Ustarz, Y., & Domanban, P. B. (2013). Macroeconomic variables and stock market returns in Ghana: Any causal link? *Asian Economic and Financial Review, 3*(8), 1044–1062.

Iwanicz-Drozdowska, M., Bongini, P., Smaga, P., & Witkowski, B. (2019). The role of banks in CESEE countries: exploring non-standard determinants of economic growth. *Post-Communist Economies, 31*(3), 349–382.

King, R., & Levine, R. (1993). Finance and growth: Schumpeter might be right. *The Quarterly Journal of Economics, 108*(3), 717–737.

Kleinman, G. (2013). *Trading commodities and financial futures*. Pearson Education, Inc. FT Press.

Koivu, T. (2002). *Do efficient banking sectors accelerate economic growth in transition countries?* (BOFIT Discussion Papers [14]) Bank of Finland, Institute for Economies in Transition.

La Porta, R., Lopez-de-Silanes, F., Shleifer, A., & Vishny, R. (2000). *The economic consequences of legal origins*. Harvard University.

Lazarov, D., Miteva-Kacarski, E., & Nikoloski, K. (2016). An empirical analysis of stock market development and economic growth: The case of Macedonia. *South East European Journal of Economics and Business, 11*(2), 71–81.

Lee, Y.-M., & Wang, K.-M. (2015). Dynamic heterogenous panel analysis of the correlation between stock prices and exchange rates. *Economic Research-Ekonomska Istraživanja, 28*(1), 749–772.

Lin, C.-H. (2012). The comovement between exchange rates and stock prices in the Asian emerging markets. *International Review of Economics and Finance, 22*(1), 161–172.

Mckinsey and Company. (2017). *Mckinsey global institute: "The new dynamics of financial globalization"*.

Megaravalli, A. V., & Sampagnaro, G. (2018). Macroeconomic indicators and their impact on stock markets in ASIAN 3: A pooled mean group approach. *Cogent Economics and Finance, 6*(1), 1–14.

Morck, R., Yeung, B., & Yu, W. (2000). Why do emerging markets have synchronous stock price movements? *Journal of Financial Economics, 58*(1), 215–260.

Naceur, S. B., Ghazouani, S., & Omran, M. (2007). The determinants of stock market development in the Middle-Eastern and North African region. *Managerial Finance, 33*(7), 477–489.

Pilinkus, D. (2010). Macroeconomic indicators and their impact on stock market performance in the short and long run: The case of the Baltic states. *Technological and Economic Development of Economy, 16*(2), 291–304.

Olgic Drazenovic, B., & Kusanovic, T. (2016). Determinants of capital market in the new member EU countries. *Economic Research—Ekonomska Istrazivanja, 29*(1), 758–769.

Shapiro, M. (1988). *The stabilization of the U.S. economy evidence from the stock market* (NBER Working Papers 2645). The National Bureau of Economic Research, Inc.

Appendix A: Data Collection and Descriptive Statistics

A.1. Data Values of Dependent and Independent Variables

See Tables A.1 and A.2; Figs. A.1, A.2, A.3, A.4, A.5, A.6, A.7, and A.8.

A.2. Data Sources and Limitations

A.2.1. Sources

This empirical research assessment captures primary and secondary data sourced from various private and public institutions. Indicative stock exchanges performance is measured through indices sourced directly from inherent exchange. Data on BATX index, in BAM, is sourced directly from Vienna Stock Exchange's historical data. Legislative, regulatory,

Table A.1 SEE countries' per capita income level groups (year-end 2020 data)

Threshold	*GNI/Capita (current US$)*	*SEE country*
Low income	<1045	
Lower middle income	1046–4095	
Upper middle income	4096–12,695	B&H (6080), Serbia (7402), North Macedonia (5750)
High income	>12,696	Croatia (14,530), Slovenia (25,360)

Source World Bank (2022)

A. Dodig, *Capital Markets in Southeast Europe*,
https://doi.org/10.1007/978-3-031-07210-9

Table A.2 SEE countries' currencies preview table of exchange rates with US$

Year-end	*2005*	*2010*	*2016*	*2019*	*2021*
Euro	0.84	0.75	0.96	0.89	0.88
HRK	6.23	5.57	7.17	6.65	6.64
BAM	1.66	1.47	1.86	1.75	1.72
RSD	72.22	79.28	117.14	104.92	103.93
MKD	51.86	46.68	58.33	54.95	54.30

Source Selected SEE countries' central banks' mid-rates

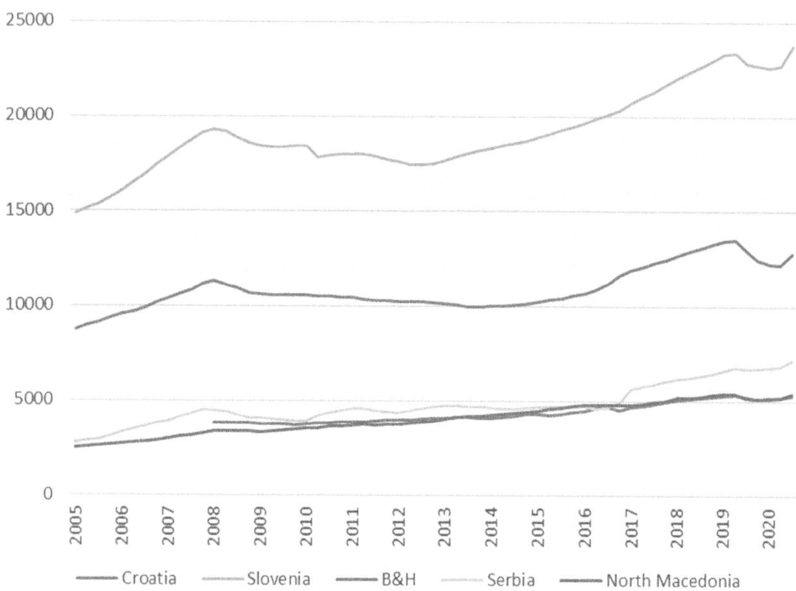

Fig. A.1 SEE countries' GDPPC trailing one-year values (in Euro) (*Source* Eurostat [2022] and the selected SEE countries' central banks and statistics agencies)

and market dynamics data are collected from primary sourcing with law companies, investment brokers, fund managers, and commercial banks operating in the inherent capital markets.

Macroeconomic indicators are collected from a diverse source base in the following order:

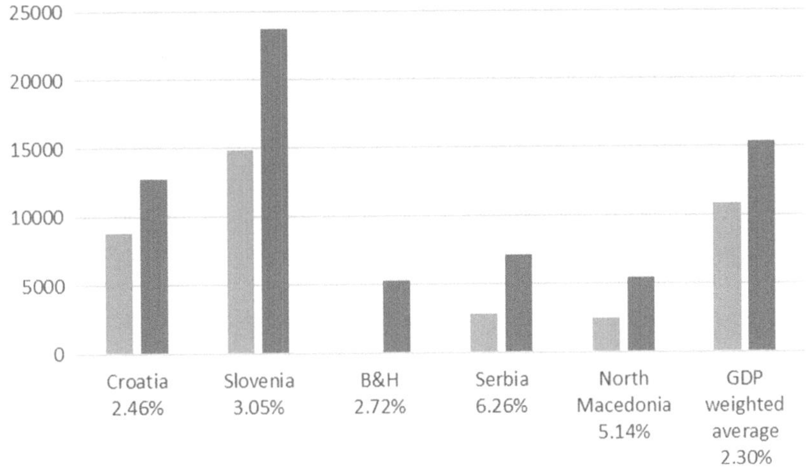

Fig. A.2 SEE countries' GDPPC eleven-years change and compound annual growth rate (CAGR) (in Euro) (*Source* Eurostat [2022] and the selected SEE countries' central banks and statistics agencies)

1. Eurostat (2022) and European Commission Directorate-General is used for harmonized statistical data, for data on:
   i. IPI (utilizing NACE Rev.2 methodology which includes unadjusted data on sections on manufacturing, mining and quarrying, and electricity, gas, steam, and air conditioning supply at prices index of 2015 = 100).
   ii. HICP, with exception of B&H (collected data is on an unadjusted basis with year-end 2015 = 100 base unit). HICP data follows European Classification of Individual Consumption by Purpose methodology.
   iii. GDP data (under expenditure approach and European System of Accounts 2010 methodology).
2. Data from respective SEE countries' central banks are utilized for:
   i. FX, currency exchange rate data (per mid-rate) is sourced from the selected countries' central banks' sources.
   ii. MMIR, key interest rates, with note that ECB (2022) is the source for case of Slovenia and B&H. HNB (2022) provides key

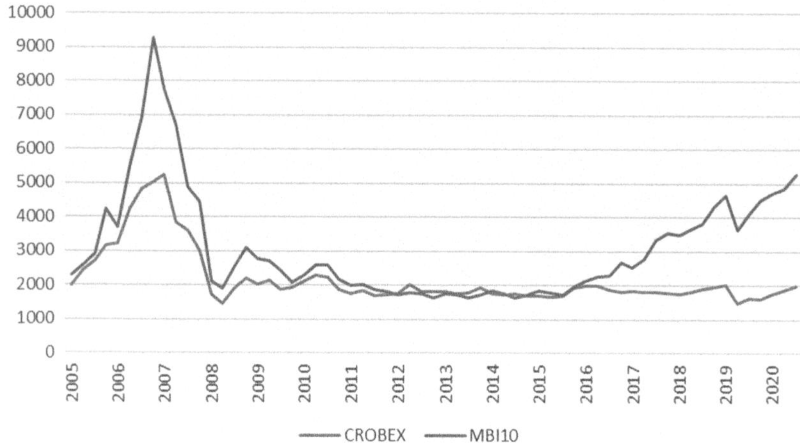

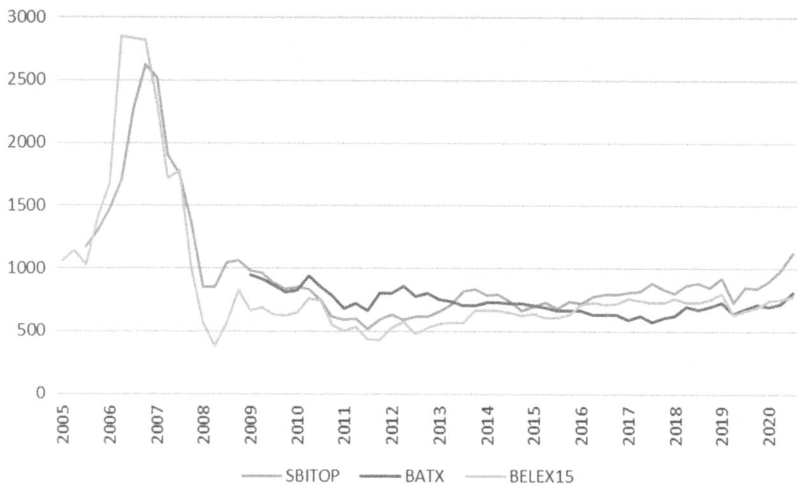

Fig. A.3 SEE countries' stock indices quarterly values (in local currency) (*Source* Eurostat [2022] and the selected SEE countries' central banks and statistics agencies)

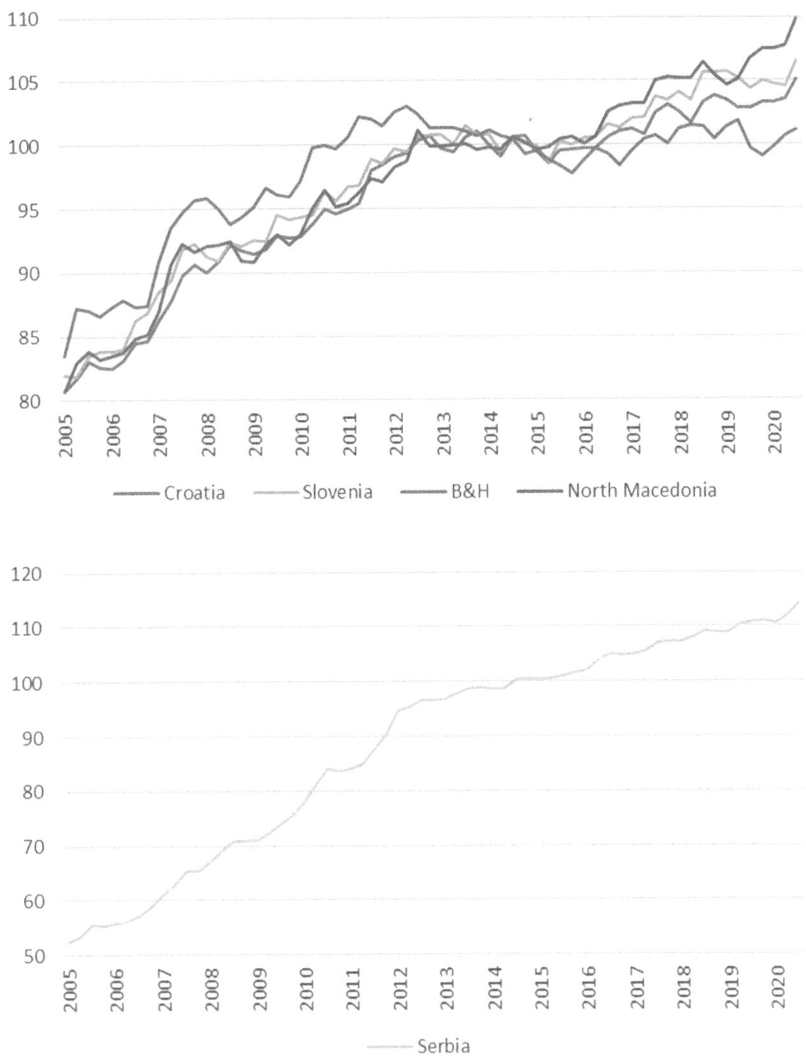

Fig. A.4 SEE countries' HICP quarterly values (*Source* Eurostat [2022] and the selected SEE countries' central banks and statistics agencies)

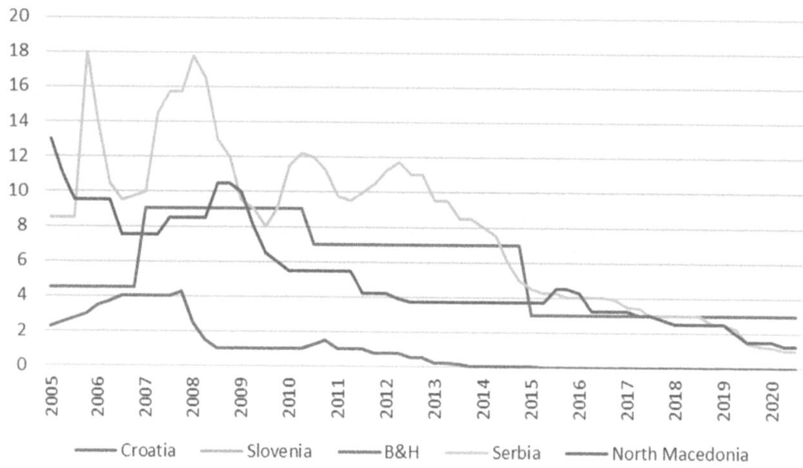

Fig. A.5 SEE countries' MMIR quarterly values (in percent) (*Source* Eurostat [2022], and the selected SEE countries' central banks and statistics agencies)

discount rate, NBS (2022) provides key discount rate in prior to September 2006 and key interest rate thereafter, NBRM (2022) provides key interest rate, and we use key refinancing rate from ECB.

3. National statistics agencies: Croatian Bureau of Statistics (2022), Statistical Office of the Republic of Serbia (2022), Republic of Macedonia State Statistical Office (2022), Statistical Office of the Republic of Slovenia (2022), and Agency for Statistics for Bosnia and Herzegovina (2022) are used for data on:

   i. Population per most recent census. North Macedonia in 2002, Slovenia and Serbia in 2002 and 2011, B&H in 1991 and 2013, and Croatia in 2001 and 2011, respectively.
   ii. Consumer Purchasing Index in case of B&H (referenced for year-end 2010 = 100 base unit and then re-referenced to 2015 = 100). For B&H, Consumer Purchasing Index follows Classification of Individual Consumption by Purpose methodology.

4. Data from IMF is utilized for BOPNFA.

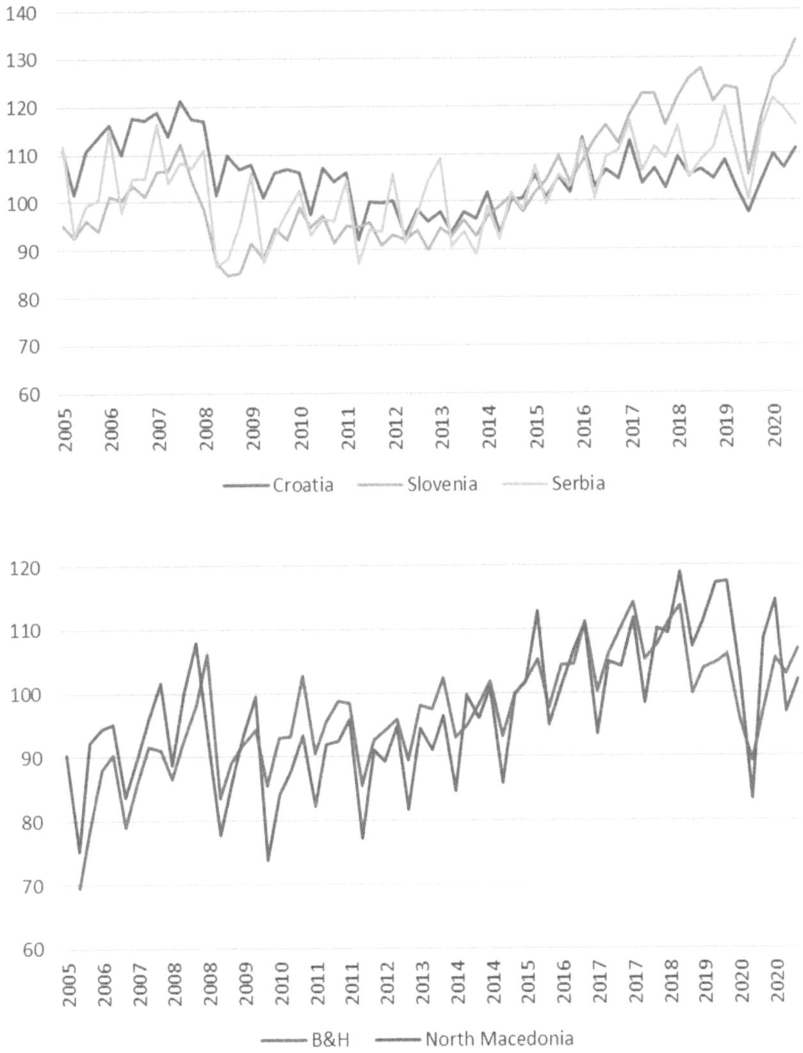

Fig. A.6 SEE countries' IPI quarterly values (*Source* Eurostat [2022] and the selected SEE countries' central banks and statistics agencies)

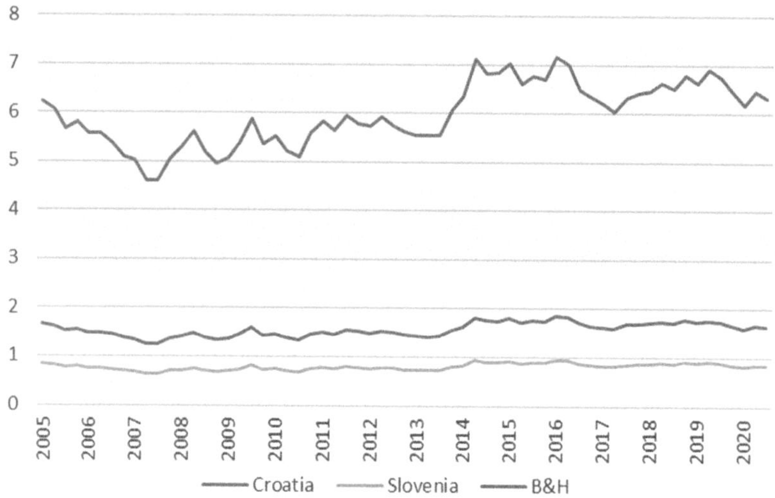

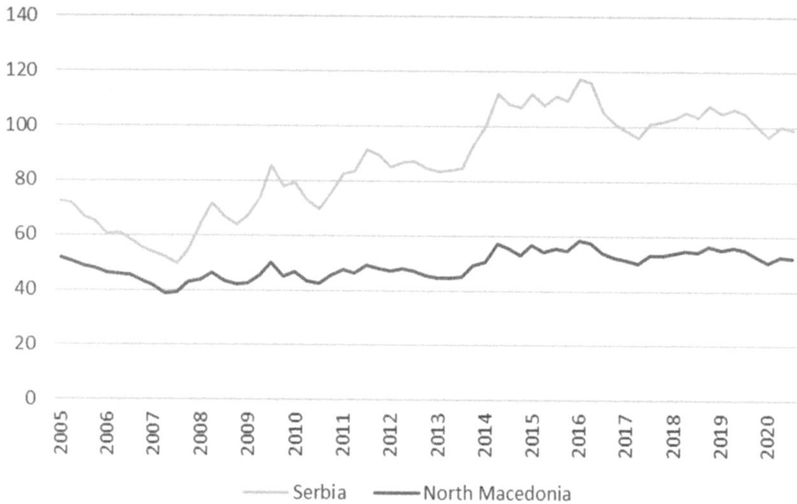

Fig. A.7 SEE countries' FX rate with US$ quarterly values (inverse is shown for better clarity) (*Source* Eurostat [2022] and the selected SEE countries' central banks and statistics agencies)

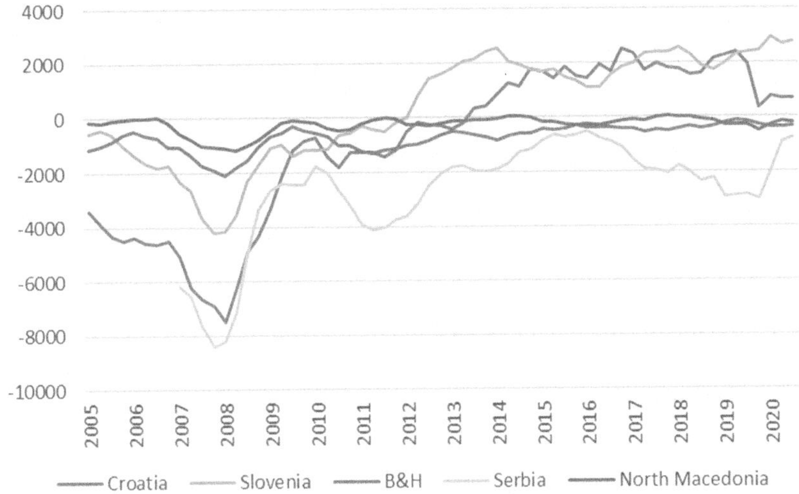

Fig. A.8 SEE countries' BOPNFA one-year trailing values (in Euro million) (*Source* Eurostat [2022] and the selected SEE countries' central banks and statistics agencies)

A.2.2. Limitations

In the case of B&H it was not plausible nor available to use independent variables at the Government Entity level (e.g. BOPNFA indicator was unavailable). In overall, using equivalent independent variables on two different dependent variables (e.g. on the BIRS and SASX-10 indices) would create an endogeneity problem between the set variables. In solution it was decided to use a single country index (e.g. BATX) although it was established in December 2009 and later than other comparable SEE stock exchanges' indices. Such an approach achieved better reliability and consistency with comparable single country indices and the overall empirical data testing techniques and methodologies. As BATX index was introduced in December 2009 index values for B&H for sixteen quarterly periods starting with initial value from the year-end 2005 to end of September 2009 are not available. Original data information was used as converging manually to create and populate the missing entries could distort the business environment structure and the relationship interpretation. For such reason a weighted joint index between BIRS and SASX-10 indices was not considered.

In the case of B&H and Slovenia, this research used Euro area macroeconomic indicators for key interest rate and for FX data. B&H does not run its own monetary policy and the currency is fixed to the Euro. Slovenia, on the other hand, joined the Euro area starting in year 2007. In the case of Slovenia, for year-end 2005 and for all quarterly periods in year 2006 this research again does not use any manually computed data in replacement of the unavailable data to maintain consistency and harmonization with Euro data for the other periods. In case of Slovenia SBITOP index was introduced in April 2006 and thus the index value is unavailable for two time quarterly time periods in the research scope, for year-end 2005 and for end of March in year 2006.

For B&H and Serbia, BOPNFA results are not available for year-end 2005 and for full year 2006 under otherwise an IMF sixth methodology.

For the specific case of B&H, GDP data, calculated in expenditure approach, are not available for periods starting at year-end 2005 until and including year-end 2007. The National Statistics Office had responded to researcher's enquiry but could not indicate if such data would be made available at a later stage.

B&H does not calculate inflation by HICP approach and thus this research used the local Consumer Price Index indicator, which is only available in reference to year-end 2010 = 100 base unit as the most recent. Therefore, to achieve consistency in this research HICP data are manually and comprehensively referenced to year-end 2015 = 100 base unit. For B&H, the Consumer Price Index indicator is not available on quarter-end values, other than for year-end values, for the period from beginning in year 2006 through year-end 2010.

Lastly, for the case of B&H and a single time period for year-end 2005 IPI indicator value is not available.

A.3. Descriptive Statistics

The empirical data contain quarterly indicators for periods starting in year-end 2005 and through mid-year 2021. The total number of observations exceeds two hundred and ninety for each individual variable. SMIs and GDPPC variables data exhibit an increasing trend in the early observation period and then a falling one in the 2007/2008 crisis period before returning to the increasing trend thereafter. SMIs scale of growth and fall is larger than is seen in GDPPC indicator, which is more standardized. In addition, SMIs data exhibits leptokurtic kurtosis exemplifying volatility and positive skewness. On the contrary, HICP data shows high negative skewness though it has slight positive fat tail. IPI values have remained relatively less changed in the whole observation period though a slight increasing trend is apparent in the initial periods while there is a falling trend in the interim. HICP values post a continuing increasing trend in the whole observation period and the most significant nominal change happens in the case of Serbia. While MMIR figures are lower in the end of the observation period for all countries, all countries but North Macedonia show data with an increasing trend in the initial period and then a decreasing trend. HICP, IPI, and MMIR show most apparent bell-shaped data. FX indicator's data is next with such characteristic. BOPNFA indicator data are the most volatile of all due to concentration wherein a single large transaction may shift and impact the results and, due to frequent positive or negative sign transactional impact. Nonetheless, there is an upward overall trend which is apparent by the increasing BOPNFA figures and an overall normalization from larger negative results in the initial period to more positive ones in the later observation period (See Tables A.3, A.4, A.5, A.6, A.7 and A.8).

Table A.3 Group data—descriptive statistics

Variable	*Years*	*Observations*	*Mean*	*Median*	*Max*	*Min*	*St. Dev.*	*Skewness*	*Kurtosis*
SMI	2005Q4–2021Q2	297	1612.54	1041.80	9283.00	380.83	1292.52	2.27	7.08
GDPPC	2005Q4–2021Q2	303	8803.13	5198.95	23,721.29	2488.35	6019.56	0.96	−0.45
FX	2005Q4–2021Q2	315	0.42	0.17	1.58	0.01	0.48	0.89	−0.68
MMIR	2005Q4–2021Q2	310	0.04	0.03	0.18	0.00	0.04	0.97	0.47
HICP	2005Q4–2021Q2	315	95.31	99.39	114.17	52.50	10.88	−1.77	3.68
IPI	2005Q4–2021Q2	314	101.23	100.82	133.60	69.63	10.42	0.13	0.11
BOPNFA	2005Q4–2021Q2	307	−801.02	−504.81	2939.15	−8407.88	2033.12	−1.02	1.94

Table A.4 Croatia—descriptive data statistics

Variable	*Years*	*Observations*	*Mean*	*Median*	*Max*	*Min*	*St. Dev.*	*Skewness*	*Kurtosis*	*CAGR and nominal % change*
SMI	2005Q4–2021Q2	63	2175.40	1855.19	5239.03	1451.30	842.94	2.41	5.27	−0.06% −0.85%
GDPPC	2005Q4–2021Q2	63	10,873.69	10,523.94	13,530.30	8765.44	1159.55	0.76	−0.22	2.46% 45.78%
FX	2005Q4–2021Q2	63	0.17	0.17	0.22	0.14	0.02	0.45	−0.41	−0.10% −1.55%
MMIR	2005Q4–2021Q2	63	0.06	0.07	0.09	0.03	0.02	0.13	−1.61	−2.58% −33.33%
HICP	2005Q4–2021Q2	63	96.14	99.39	105.10	80.72	6.79	−0.84	−0.44	1.72% 30.21%
IPI	2005Q4–2021Q2	63	105.42	105.43	121.20	92.07	6.86	0.22	−0.37	0.01% 0.12%
BOPNFA	2005Q4–2021Q2	63	−922.86	−255.49	2532.05	−7488.39	2834.18	−0.73	−0.67	NA −119.59%

Table A.5 Slovenia—descriptive data statistics

Variable	*Years*	*Observations*	*Mean*	*Median*	*Max*	*Min*	*St. Dev.*	*Skewness*	*Kurtosis*	*CAGR and nominal % change*
SMI	2006Q2–2021Q2	61	957.88	832.37	2623.68	520.23	445.42	2.35	5.48	−0.28% −4.13%
GDPPC	2005Q4–2021Q2	63	19,121.91	18,485.80	23,721.29	14,881.06	2173.19	0.49	−0.34	3.05% 59.41%
FX	2005Q4–2021Q2	63	1.26	1.27	1.58	1.05	0.13	0.35	−0.61	0.00% 0.07%
MMIR	2007Q1–2021Q2	58	0.01	0.00	0.04	0.00	0.01	1.73	1.84	−100% −100%
HICP	2005Q4–2021Q2	63	97.14	99.67	106.50	81.85	6.75	−0.77	−0.35	1.71% 29.98%
IPI	2005Q4–2021Q2	63	103.74	100.37	133.60	84.57	12.60	0.66	−0.69	2.22% 40.48%
BOPNFA	2005Q4–2021Q2	63	387.31	1109.67	2939.15	−4185.75	1955.36	−0.62	−0.65	NA −617.37%

Table A.6 B&H—descriptive data statistics

Variable	*Years*	*Observations*	*Mean*	*Median*	*Max*	*Min*	*St. Dev.*	*Skewness*	*Kurtosis*	*CAGR and nominal % change*
SMI	2009Q4–2021Q2	47	728.67	710.46	944.18	578.78	89.18	0.70	0.03	−1.29% −13.88%
GDPPC	2008Q4–2021Q2	51	4359.75	4163.56	5320.18	3724.26	537.53	0.56	−1.17	2.72% 39.94%
FX	2005Q4–2021Q2	63	0.65	0.65	0.81	0.54	0.07	0.36	−0.65	0.05% 0.75%
MMIR	2005Q4–2021Q2	63	0.01	0.01	0.04	0.00	0.01	1.31	0.42	−100% −100%
HICP	2005Q4–2021Q2	63	97.62	99.70	102.98	83.44	4.89	−1.38	0.90	1.25% 21.20%
IPI	2006Q1–2021Q2	62	97.03	97.55	114.17	69.63	8.90	−0.43	0.42	2.84% 53.37%
BOPNFA	2005Q4–2021Q2	63	−730.46	−594.24	−138.00	−2082.83	438.78	−1.23	1.20	−7.63% −70.80%

Table A.7 Serbia—descriptive data statistics

Variable	*Years*	*Observations*	*Mean*	*Median*	*Max*	*Min*	*St. Dev.*	*Skewness*	*Kurtosis*	*CAGR and nominal % change*
SMI	2005Q4–2021Q2	63	867.57	692.93	2849.35	380.83	558.83	2.58	6.19	−1.97% −26.48%
GDPPC	2005Q4–2021Q2	63	4767.56	4577.98	7158.16	2790.46	1058.17	0.60	−0.13	6.27% 156.52%
FX	2005Q4–2021Q2	63	0.01	0.01	0.02	0.01	0.00	0.91	−0.10	−2.00% −26.88%
MMIR	2005Q4–2021Q2	63	0.08	0.09	0.18	0.01	0.05	0.25	−0.75	−12.90% −88.24%
HICP	2005Q4–2021Q2	63	88.47	96.67	114.17	52.50	19.21	−0.52	−1.17	5.14% 117.46%
IPI	2005Q4–2021Q2	63	103.21	104.43	121.60	86.57	9.04	0.00	−0.83	0.23% 3.66%
BOPNFA	2007Q4–2021Q2	55	−2725.15	−2074.79	−499.02	−8407.88	1924.88	−1.55	2.03	−14.26% −87.47%

Table A.8 North Macedonia—descriptive data statistics

Variable	*Years*	*Observations*	*Mean*	*Median*	*Max*	*Min*	*St. Dev.*	*Skewness*	*Kurtosis*	*CAGR and nominal % change*
SMI	2005Q4–2021Q2	63	3087.91	2538.86	9283.00	1633.20	1625.90	1.71	3.20	5.53% 130.41%
GDPPC	2005Q4–2021Q2	63	4046.37	3947.40	5413.40	2488.35	864.88	−0.02	−1.18	5.14% 117.37%
FX	2005Q4–2021Q2	63	0.02	0.02	0.03	0.02	0.00	0.38	−0.59	−0.03% −0.39%
MMIR	2005Q4–2021Q2	63	0.05	0.04	0.13	0.01	0.03	0.77	−0.33	14.02% −90.38%
HICP	2005Q4–2021Q2	63	97.20	99.62	109.84	80.70	7.35	−0.52	−0.54	2.01% 36.10%
IPI	2005Q4–2021Q2	63	96.67	95.87	118.87	73.80	10.77	0.04	−0.46	0.79% 13.00%
BOPNFA	2005Q4–2021Q2	63	−258.26	−162.73	36.06	−1170.53	294.75	−1.76	2.51	2.50% 46.69%

Appendix B: Presentation of Statistical Methodologies in Use

B.1. Johansen Cointegration

In regression analysis of order ρ, in Formula (2) below, Y_t is a k-vector of non-stationary variables, X_t is a d-vector of deterministic variables, and ε_t is a vector of innovations.

$$Y_t = A_1 Y_{t-1} + \cdots + A_p Y_{t-\rho} + BX_t + \varepsilon_t \tag{2}$$

Johansen and Juselius test the number of cointegrating vectors with two likelihood ratio testing (Johansen & Juselius, 1990). The first for the null of r cointegrating vectors versus alternative $r + 1$ vectors is maximum eigenvalue statistic. The second, trace statistic, runs the hypothesis of at most r cointegrating vectors against the alternative. In both tests the number of lags is based on generalization of SBIC by which critical values are tabulated.

B.2. Granger Causality

In testing causality in bi-variate relationships, Granger test examines with F-test whether all β_i are equal to zero. If null hypothesis is rejected in Formula (3), then X is said to Granger- cause Y. Stationarity is a precondition for Granger test. To transform non-stationary data to stationarity

A. Dodig, *Capital Markets in Southeast Europe*,
https://doi.org/10.1007/978-3-031-07210-9

data we apply differencing per Formula (4).

$$\begin{gathered} Y_t = c_1 + \sum_{i=1}^{p-1} \alpha_i Y_{t-n} + \sum_{i=1}^{p-1} \beta_i X_{t-n} + \mu_t, \\ H_0 : \beta_1 = \beta_2 = \ldots \beta_p = 0, \end{gathered} \tag{3}$$

$$\begin{gathered} \Delta Y_t = c_1 + \sum_{i=1}^{p-1} \alpha_i \Delta Y_{t-n} + \sum_{i=1}^{p-1} \beta_i \Delta X_{t-n} + \mu_t, \\ H_0 : \beta_1 = \beta_2 = \ldots \beta_p = 0. \end{gathered} \tag{4}$$

B.3. Panel Vector Autoregression Algorithm

Per Formula (5) below Z_{it} is a matrix of endogenous variables for all countries, $A(L)$ is a matrix polynomial in the lag operator, L, with the VAR coefficients, and with countries identified per $i = 1,\ldots5$, μ_i is a constant value, n represents number of periods, and ε_{it} represents vector of normally, identically distributed disturbances. Given that the data in levels series are largely non-stationary, we transform the sample data to differences form until reaching stationarity that is found in entirety under the second difference transformed data series as apparent per process in Formula (4).

$$\Delta Z_{it} = \mu_i + A_i(L)\Delta Z_{it-n} + \varepsilon_{it} \tag{5}$$

Appendix C: Discussion of Statistical Tests' Results

C.1. Tests' Results

C.1.1. Data Stationarity

Table A.9 shows results of unit roots tests for nominal data series, in first differences level form data series, and in second differences nominal data series. The results illustrate that data sample series exhibit non-stationary characteristic in large majority for the nominal data. The opposite is true for the first differences level data, which are predominantly stationarity. Lastly, the second differences level data series are entirely stationary.

Data series differencing is conducted through transformations processes (e.g. as presented in Formulas 4 and 5). Data level transformation process comes with ex-post lesser information capacity due to removal of identifying variance from precedent data series level dimension.

Data non-stationarity is the necessary precondition for Johansen cointegration testing. Inversely, data stationarity is the necessary precondition for the Granger causality method and for panel VAR method testing. Panel PMG estimation technique however has the capacity to treat both stationary and non-stationary data and as such permits use of nominal level data series in the panel PMG model.

In Table A.9, variables with p-value lower than five percent are considered stationary for the relevant level data series; otherwise, the same variable data series is considered non-stationary in the relevant level data series.

A. Dodig, *Capital Markets in Southeast Europe*,
https://doi.org/10.1007/978-3-031-07210-9

Table A.9 Results of ADF unit root tests

Country	*Variable*	*Data choice per data series levels*	*ADF in nominal level*		*ADF in first differences*		*ADF in second differences*	
			Z(t)	*p-value for Z(t)*	*Z (t)*	*p-value for Z(t)*	*Z(t)*	*p-value for Z(t)*
Croatia	CROBEX	Level → 2006Q4–2021Q2; First diff. → 2007Q1–2021Q2; Second diff. → 2007Q2–2021Q2	−2.598 (2)	0.0934	−4.183 (1)	0.0007	−5.297 (2)	0.0000
	GDPPC	Level → 2006Q4–2021Q2; First diff. → 2007Q1–2021Q2; Second diff. → 2007Q2–2021Q2	0.004 (3)	0.9589	−3.908 (2)	0.0020	−4.218 (4)	0.0006
	FX	Level → 2006Q4–2021Q2; First diff. → 2007Q1–2021Q2; Second diff. → 2007Q2–2021Q2	−1.747 (1)	0.4069	−7.590 (0)	0.0000	−7.059 (4)	0.0000
	MMIR	Level → 2006Q4–2021Q2; First diff. → 2007Q1–2021Q2; Second diff. → 2007Q2–2021Q2	−1.128 (1)	0.7037	−7.688 (0)	0.0000	−7.348 (2)	0.0000

Country	*Variable*	*Data choice per data series levels*	*ADF in nominal level*		*ADF in first differences*		*ADF in second differences*	
			Z(t)	*p-value for Z(t)*	*Z (t)*	*p-value for Z(t)*	*Z(t)*	*p-value for Z(t)*
	HICP	Level → 2006Q4–2021Q2; First diff. → 2007Q1–2021Q2; Second diff. → 2007Q2–2021Q2	−2.851 (3)	0.0514	−2.429 (4)	0.1337	−5.401 (3)	0.0000
	IPI	Level → 2006Q4–2021Q2; First diff. → 2007Q1–2021Q2; Second diff. → 2007Q2–2021Q2	−1.894 (4)	0.3347	−2.415 (4)	0.1376	−7.857 (3)	0.0000
	BOPNFA	Level → 2006Q4–2021Q2; First diff. → 2007Q1–2021Q2; Second diff. → 2007Q2–2021Q2	−1.416 (2)	0.5748	−3.209 (2)	0.0195	−4.188 (4)	0.0007

(continued)

Table A.9 (continued)

Country	*Variable*	*Data choice per data series levels*	*ADF in nominal level*		*ADF in first differences*		*ADF in second differences*	
			Z(t)	*p-value for Z(t)*	*Z (t)*	*p-value for Z(t)*	*Z(t)*	*p-value for Z(t)*
Slovenia	SBITOP	Level → 2007Q2–2021Q2; First diff. → 2007Q3–2016Q1; Second diff. → 2007Q4–2016Q1	−2.377 (2)	0.1484	−3.820 (2)	0.0027	−8.683 (0)	0.0000
	GDPPC	Level → 2006Q4–2021Q2; First diff. → 2007Q1–2021Q2; Second diff. → 2007Q2–2021Q2	0.083 (2)	0.9649	−2.527 (1)	0.1090	−7.638 (0)	0.0000
	FX	Level → 2006Q4–2021Q2; First diff. → 2007Q1–2021Q 2; Second diff. → 2007Q2–2021Q2	−1.853 (1)	0.3545	−7.623 (0)	0.0000	−7.117 (4)	0.0000

Country	*Variable*	*Data choice per data series levels*	*ADF in nominal level*		*ADF in first differences*		*ADF in second differences*	
			Z(t)	*p-value for Z(t)*	*Z (t)*	*p-value for Z(t)*	*Z(t)*	*p-value for Z(t)*
	MMIR	Level → 2006Q4–2021Q2; First diff. → 2007Q1–2021Q2; Second diff. → 2007Q2–2021Q2	−1.626 (2)	0.4694	−4.229 (1)	0.0006	−7.558 (1)	0.0000
	HICP	Level → 2006Q4–2021Q2; First diff. → 2007Q1–2021Q2; Second diff. → 2007Q2–2021Q2	−2.321 (2)	0.1653	−2.698 (4)	0.0744	−4.995 (3)	0.0000
	IPI	Level → 2006Q4–2021Q2; First diff. → 2007Q1–2021Q2; Second diff. → 2007Q2–2021Q2	−0.413 (1)	0.9078	−9.453 (0)	0.0000	−4.323 (3)	0.0004

(continued)

Table A.9 (continued)

Country	*Variable*	*Data choice per data series levels*	*ADF in nominal level*		*ADF in first differences*		*ADF in second differences*	
			Z(t)	*p-value for Z(t)*	*Z (t)*	*p-value for Z(t)*	*Z(t)*	*p-value for Z(t)*
	BOPNFA	Level → 2006Q4–2021Q2; First diff. → 2007Q1–2021Q2; Second diff. → 2007Q2–2021Q2	−1.139 (2)	0.6992	−3.665 (1)	0.0046	−5.379 (4)	0.0000
B&H	BATX	Level → 2010Q4–2021Q2; First diff. → 2011Q1–2021Q2; Second diff. → 2011Q2–2021Q2	−2.535 (1)	0.1072	−7.376 (0)	0.0000	−6.132 (1)	0.0000
	GDPPC	Level → 2009Q4–2021Q2; First diff. → 2010Q1–2021Q2; Second diff. → 2010Q2–2021Q2	0.714 (1)	0.9901	−5.280 (0)	0.0000	−5.454 (4)	0.0000

Country	*Variable*	*Data choice per data series levels*	*ADF in nominal level*		*ADF in first differences*		*ADF in second differences*	
			Z(t)	*p-value for Z(t)*	*Z (t)*	*p-value for Z(t)*	*Z(t)*	*p-value for Z(t)*
	FX	Level → 2006Q4–2021Q2; First diff. → 2007Q1–2021Q2; Second diff. → 2007Q2–2021Q2	−1.880 (1)	0.3415	−7.327 (0)	0.0000	−7.364 (4)	0.0000
	MMIR	Level → 2006Q4–2021Q2; First diff. → 2007Q1–2021Q2; Second diff. → 2007Q2–2021Q2	−1.626 (2)	0.4694	−4.229 (1)	0.0006	−7.558 (1)	0.0000
	HICP	Level → 2006Q4–2021Q2; First diff. → 2007Q1–2021Q2; Second diff. → 2007Q2–2021Q2	−2.763 (3)	0.0637	−4.076 (2)	0.0011	−4.486 (3)	0.0002

(continued)

Table A.9 (continued)

Country	*Variable*	*Data choice per data series levels*	*ADF in nominal level*		*ADF in first differences*		*ADF in second differences*	
			Z(t)	*p-value for Z(t)*	*Z (t)*	*p-value for Z(t)*	*Z(t)*	*p-value for Z(t)*
	IPI	Level → 2007Q1–2021Q2; First diff. → 2007Q2–2021Q2; Second diff. → 2007Q3–2021Q2	−1.755 (4)	0.4031	−3.064 (4)	0.0293	−7.858 (3)	0.0000
	BOPNFA	Level → 2006Q4–2021Q2; First diff. → 2007Q1–2021Q2; Second diff. → 2007Q2–2021Q2	−2.858 (3)	0.0505	−3.792 (4)	0.0030	−3.846 (4)	0.0025
Serbia	BELEX15	Level → 2006Q4–2021Q2; First diff. → 2007Q1–2021Q2; Second diff. → 2007Q2–2021Q2	−2.485 (3)	0.1191	−3.797 (1)	0.0029	−3.286 (4)	0.0155

Country	*Variable*	*Data choice per data series levels*	*ADF in nominal level*		*ADF in first differences*		*ADF in second differences*	
			Z(t)	*p-value for Z(t)*	*Z (t)*	*p-value for Z(t)*	*Z(t)*	*p-value for Z(t)*
	GDPPC	Level → 2006Q4–2021Q2; First diff. → 2007Q1–2021Q2; Second diff. → 2007Q2–2021Q2	−0.119 (2)	0.9476	−3.343 (1)	0.0131	−5.607 (1)	0.0000
	FX	Level → 2006Q4–2021Q2; First diff. → 2007Q1–2021Q2; Second diff. → 2007Q2–2021Q2	−1.317 (2)	0.6211	−5.445 (1)	0.0000	−6.398 (4)	0.0000
	MMIR	Level → 2006Q4–2021Q2; First diff. → 2007Q1–2021Q2; Second diff. → 2007Q2–2021Q2	−1.198 (1)	0.6744	−5.855 (1)	0.0000	−6.474 (2)	0.0000

(continued)

Table A.9 (continued)

Country	*Variable*	*Data choice per data series levels*	*ADF in nominal level*		*ADF in first differences*		*ADF in second differences*	
			Z(t)	*p-value for Z(t)*	*Z (t)*	*p-value for Z(t)*	*Z(t)*	*p-value for Z(t)*
	HICP	Level → 2006Q4–2021Q2; First diff. → 2007Q1–2021Q2; Second diff. → 2007Q2–2021Q2	−1.634 (2)	0.4656	−4.550 (1)	0.0002	−5.583 (3)	0.0000
	IPI	Level → 2006Q4–2021Q2; First diff. → 2007Q1–2021Q2; Second diff. → 2007Q2–2021Q2	−0.959 (4)	0.7679	−3.525 (4)	0.0074	−6.887 (3)	0.0000
	BOPNFA	Level → 2008Q4–2021Q2; First diff. → 2009Q1–2021Q2; Second diff. → 2009Q2–2021Q2	−3.763 (2)	0.0033	−2.464 (4)	0.1244	−5.534 (4)	0.0000

Country	*Variable*	*Data choice per data series levels*	*ADF in nominal level*		*ADF in first differences*		*ADF in second differences*	
			Z(t)	*p-value for Z(t)*	*Z (t)*	*p-value for Z(t)*	*Z(t)*	*p-value for Z(t)*
North Macedonia	MBI10	Level → 2006Q4–2021Q2; First diff. → 2007Q1–2021Q2; Second diff. → 2007Q2–2021Q2	−1.870 (3)	0.3465	−3.901 (1)	0.0020	−4.266 (3)	0.0005
	GDPPC	Level → 2006Q4–2021Q2; First diff. → 2007Q1–2021Q2; Second diff. → 2007Q2–2021Q2	−0.474 (2)	0.8971	−3.573 (4)	0.0063	−4.238 (4)	0.0006
	FX	Level → 2006Q4–2021Q2; First diff. → 2007Q1–2021Q2; Second diff. → 2007Q2–2021Q2	−1.772 (1)	0.3944	−8.021 (0)	0.0000	−7.073 (4)	0.0000

(continued)

Table A.9 (continued)

Country	*Variable*	*Data choice per data series levels*	*ADF in nominal level*		*ADF in first differences*		*ADF in second differences*	
			Z(t)	*p-value for Z(t)*	*Z (t)*	*p-value for Z(t)*	*Z(t)*	*p-value for Z(t)*
	MMIR	Level → 2006Q4–2021Q2; First diff. → 2007Q1–2021Q2; Second diff. → 2007Q2–2021Q2	−1.551 (1)	0.5082	−6.245 (0)	0.0000	−6.745 (3)	0.0000
	HICP	Level → 2006Q4–2021Q2; First diff. → 2007Q1–2021Q2; Second diff. → 2007Q2–2021Q2	−1.004 (1)	0.7518	−6.896 (0)	0.0000	−5.148 (3)	0.0000
	IPI	Level → 2006Q4–2021Q2; First diff. → 2007Q1–2021Q2; Second diff. → 2007Q2–2021Q2	−1.115 (4)	0.7092	−3.902 (4)	0.0020	−5.883 (4)	0.0000

Country	*Variable*	*Data choice per data series levels*	*ADF in nominal level*		*ADF in first differences*		*ADF in second differences*	
			Z(t)	*p-value for Z(t)*	*Z (t)*	*p-value for Z(t)*	*Z(t)*	*p-value for Z(t)*
	BOPNFA	Level → 2006Q4–2021Q2; First diff. → 2007Q1–2021Q2; Second diff. → 2007Q2–2021Q2	−3.366 (2)	0.0122	−3.830 (1)	0.0026	−4.692 (4)	0.0001

Note Optimal selection order criteria is shown per quarter and is determined using SBIC, choice of lags is presented in parentheses () and relevant data time period is shown in the adequate column

The required precondition for panel VAR testing validity is the mandatory use of stationary data. Thereto, panel unit root tests are conducted first. By using panel unit root tests, the Levin, Lin, and Chu (LLC) test (Levin et al., 2002), the Fisher ADF *chi* square test (Maddala & Wu, 1999), and the Fisher Phillips Perron (PP) *chi* square test (Choi, 2001) the null hypothesis was tested about the presence of unit roots for the panel model data. Based on the empirical *p*-value, the null hypothesis is refuted regarding the presence of unit roots for HICP and IPI variables meaning that these variables are stationary in the nominal value; else, all variables are stationary in the first difference values. Testing by newer generation unit root test was not available because of data limitations reducing balance. In addition, due to the test determined stationarity of data in nominal level panel series precondition is not meet to conduct panel multi-variate cointegration testing. Subsequently, precondition is not met in determining plausibility of panel multi-variate causality testing without prior awareness on cointegration existence. Ultimately, precondition is met to conduct panel multi-variate VAR testing.

In Table A.10, variables with *p*-value lower than five percent are considered stationary for the relevant level data series; otherwise, the same variable data series is considered non-stationary in the relevant level data series.

C.1.2. Johansen Cointegration

Table A.11 summarizes results of Johansen cointegration tests for bivariate long-run research model relationships. The number of cointegration vectors is tested using maximum likelihood based Δ_{MAX} and Δ_{TRACE} statistics per introduced by Johansen (1991) and Johansen and Juselius (1990).

Presence of long-run cointegration in a variables' relationship pair illustrates dependence in relationship and the inexistence of a "random price walk" for the counterparty pair indicator. Therefore, within research inherent market environment and sample data the test results by existence of a cointegrating relationship depict examples of a capital market inefficiency. Inefficient markets provide an opportunity for arbitration impact through intermediary utilization of market anomalies under inefficiencies which are at display. Table A.12 shows the statistical test results for the null hypothesis that the number of CEs wherein the λ_{trace} is less than equal to the specified and with the $\lambda_{\max}$ that the number of cointegrating vectors is the specified against an alternative of an additional cointegrating

Table A.10 Results of panel unit root tests

Variable	*LLC Z(t) (p-value for Z(t))*	*Fisher ADF Z(t) (p-value for Z(t))*	*Fisher PP Z(t) (p-value for Z(t))*
Nominal level data			
SMI	−1.06 (0.1454)	18.24 (0.0510)	15.12 (0.1277)
GDPPC	1.15 (0.8746)	1.00 (0.9998)	1.77 (0.9978)
FX	−0.58 (0.2850)	9.12 (0.5206)	9.06 (0.5265)
MMIR	0.15 (0.0727)	9.52 (0.4837)	9.99 (0.4414)
HICP	−3.61 (0.0002)	14.23 (0.1626)	41.44 (0.0000)
IPI	−1.29 (0.0988)	24.45 (0.0065)	58.19 (0.0000)
BOPNFA	−1.22 (0.1118)	19.77 (0.0315)	10.53 (0.3953)
First differences level data			
SMI	−4.88 (0.0000)	61.55 (0.0000)	121.12 (0.0000)
GDPPC	−1.96 (0.6396)	73.32 (0.0000)	63.44 (0.0000)
FX	−9.46 (0.000)	106.84 (0.000)	169.19 (0.000)
MMIR	−9.14 (0.0000)	95.85 (0.0000)	144.76 (0.0000)
HICP	−9.34 (0.0000)	125.81 (0.0000)	163.50 (0.0000)
IPI	−13.44 (0.0000)	176.67 (0.0000)	142.98 (0.0000)
BOPNFA	−0.82 (0.2039)	56.16 (0.0000)	76.46 (0.0000)

vector. If the λ test statistic is greater than the five percent critical value, then the null hypothesis is rejected in favor of the alternative. In Table A.12 the interpretation examples are shown. The first row in the case of Croatia shows CROBEX to MMIR cointegrating relationship with one cointegrating vector. None of the significant results revealed two or more cointegrating vectors.

Table A.11 Summary results of Johansen cointegration for pairs of research variables

Country	*SMI*	*GDPPC*	*FX*	*MMIR*	*HICP*	*IPI*	*BOPNFA*
Croatia	*CROBEX*	No	No	Yes	Yes	Yes	Yes
Slovenia	*SBITOP*	No	No	Yes	Yes	No	Yes
B&H	*BATX*	No	No	No	Yes	Yes	No
Serbia	*BELEX15*	No	Yes	No	Yes	No	NA*
North Macedonia	*MBI10*	No	No	No	No	No	NA*

Note Null hypothesis is rejected at five percent level ($p < 0.05$)
*Data for the macroeconomic indicator variable is stationary in nominal level data series and thus the cointegration test for the variables' relationship pair is miss-specified and is unstable due to differences in stationarity, which is apparent with simultaneous non-stationarity in SMI nominal level data value

C.1.3. Granger Causality

The results of statistically significant Granger causality existence are summarized in Table A.13 for both the causal direction impact from macroeconomic indicators on SMI and for the causal direction impact from SMI on macroeconomic indicators individually for each of the studied SEE countries. Table A.14 illustrates Granger statistical test results that show relationship pair relevant *chi*-squared values, relevant *p*-values, and the relevant data series lag selection per SBIC. Granger method statistical test identifies spurious short-run bilateral lead-lag relationships. However, Granger test is miss-specified for relationship pairs where cointegration exists. Results for such cointegrating indicator pairs are unreliable. **The obtained Granger test results imply limited support for the argument of macroeconomic variables variations predictive causing of variations in inherent SMI, and vice versa.** Bi-variate relationships ignore model behavior presumption and/ or unobserved bias impact and as such may be spurious in nature. Moreover, Granger test requires full data series stationarity, which is in this research only reached in the second-level differences data series. Two data transformation processes are conducted to reach second-level differences dana and inherently valuable data information is lost in the process. Therefore, the transformation process deducts further from Granger test results' robustness and from reliability in practical interpretations.

At five percent level of significance threshold, the only macroeconomic indicator to Granger cause impact SMI proves to be MMIR in

Table A.12 Results of ΔMAX and ΔTRACE statistics for pairs of SMI and selected macroeconomic variables with present cointegration

Country	*Pair of indicators*	*Hypothesized no. of CE(s)*	λ_{trace}	*5% critical value*	λ_{max}	*5% critical value*
Croatia	CROBEX to MMIR	None*	15.5944	15.41	13.1591	14.07
	2006Q2–2021Q2 (2)	At most 1	2.4353	3.76	2.4353	3.76
	CROBEX to HICP	None*	29.7508	15.41	21.6551	14.07
	2006Q3–2021Q2 (3)	At most 1	8.0957	3.76	8.0957	3.76
	CROBEX to IPI	None*	16.0486	15.41	14.4369	14.07
	2006Q3–2021Q2 (4)	At most 1	1.6117	3.76	1.6117	3.76
	CROBEX to BOPNFA	None*	20.1763	15.41	18.8575	14.07
	2006Q1–2021Q2 (1)	At most 1	1.3188	3.76	1.3188	3.76
Slovenia	SBITOP to MMIR	None*	76.5901	15.41	74.5257	14.07
	2008Q1–2021Q2 (4)	At most 1	2.0644	3.76	2.0644	3.76
	SBITOP to HICP	None*	19.7491	15.41	14.7349	14.07
	2006Q4–2021Q2 (2)	At most 1	5.0143	3.76	5.0143	3.76
	SBITOP to BOPNFA	None*	23.8367	15.41	21.7932	14.07
	2006Q4–2021Q2 (2)	At most 1	2.0435	3.76	2.0435	3.76

(continued)

Table A.12 (continued)

Country	*Pair of indicators*	*Hypothesized no. of CE(s)*	λ_{trace}	*5% critical value*	λ_{max}	*5% critical value*
B&H	BATX to HICP	None*	16.8104	15.41	12.5973	14.07
	2010Q1–2021Q4 (1)	At most 1	4.2132	3.76	4.2132	3.76
	BATX to IPI	None*	25.3417	15.41	18.3015	14.07
	2010Q1–2021Q4 (1)	At most 1	7.0402	3.76	7.0402	3.76
Serbia	BELEX15 to FX	None*	16.8647	15.41	13.6876	14.07
	2006Q1–2021Q2 (1)	At most 1	3.1771	3.76	3.1771	3.76
	BELEX15 to HICP	None*	16.6718	15.41	15.2434	14.07
	2006Q3–2021Q2 (3)	At most 1	1.4284	3.76	1.4284	3.76

Note Optimal selection order criteria is shown per quarter and is determined by SBIC. Choice of lags is presented in parentheses (). * Null hypothesis is rejected at five percent level ($p < 0.05$)

Table A.13 Summary results of Granger causality for pairs of variables

Country	*SMI*	*GDPPC*	*FX*	*MMIR*	*HICP*	*IPI*	*BOPNFA*
Direction of selected macroeconomic indicator causality on stock exchange index							
Croatia	CROBEX	No	No	NA***	NA***	NA***	NA***
Slovenia	SBITOP	No	No	NA***	NA***	No	NA***
B&H	BATX	No	No	No	NA***	NA***	No
Serbia	BELEX15	No	NA***	Yes**	NA***	No	No
North Macedonia	MBI10	No	No	No	No	No	No
Direction of stock exchange index causality on selected macroeconomic indicator							
Croatia	CROBEX	No	No	NA***	NA***	NA***	NA***
Slovenia	SBITOP	No	No	NA***	NA***	Yes*	NA***
B&H	BATX	No	No	No	NA***	NA***	No
Serbia	BELEX15	No	NA***	Yes**	NA***	No	Yes**
North Macedonia	MBI10	No	Yes*	No	No	Yes*	No

Note Optimal selection order criteria is determined by SBIC

* $p < 0.05$, ** $p < 0.01$

***Due to determined existence of statistically significant indicators pair cointegration relationship or due to unavailable Johansen test results for the given pair of indicators, Granger test and results as such are miss-specified. In such cases reparameterization into an error correction model is necessary and is completed in this research with panel PMG results

the case of Serbia. In the contrary directional relationship impact, SMI significantly impacts MMIR and BOPNFA in Serbia. SMI Granger causes IPI indicators in two cases, in Slovenia and in North Macedonia. Lastly SMI also Granger causes FX in the case of North Macedonia. In case of the existence of statistically significant Granger predictive causality in the direction of macroeconomic indicator on SMI, then such capital market may be inefficient. In the absence of capital market asymmetries, a causal impact from macroeconomic indicators otherwise should be a priori included in SMI in an effective market. Nonetheless, such an interpretation is limited to spurious bi-variate causality relationship interpretation under Granger testing methodology.

In practice, capital market asymmetries may exist in transactions costs, settlement delays, and market uncertainties amongst others. In cases where SMI variation Granger causes variation in an economic aggregate output, SMI takes the role of a leading indicator of future macroeconomic developments and of real economic activities. In the existence of

Table A.14 Results of Granger causality test

Country	*SMI*	*GDPPC*	*FX*	*MMIR*	*HICP*	*IPI*	*BOPNFA*
Direction of selected macroeconomic indicator causality on stock exchange index							
Croatia	CROBEX	1.982 (0.371)	1.418 (0.234)	NA***	NA***	NA***	NA***
Slovenia	SBITOP	0.250 (0.882)	0.474 (0.789)	NA***	NA***	0.133 (0.936)	NA***
B&H	BATX	0.381 (0.537)	0.170 (0.680)	2.987 (0.084)	NA***	NA***	0.252 (0.616)
Serbia	BELEX15	1.130 (0.568)	NA***	14.106** (0.003)	NA***	2.524 (0.640)	4.366 (0.113)
North Macedonia	MBI10	1.791 (0.181)	0.268 (0.605)	2.404 (0.121)	0.007 (0.933)	9.130 (0.058)	4.103 (0.129)
Direction of stock exchange index causality on selected macroeconomic indicator							
Croatia	CROBEX	5.911 (0.052)	3.763 (0.052)	NA***	NA***	NA***	NA***
Slovenia	SBITOP	3.432 (0.180)	5.931 (0.052)	NA***	NA***	7.310* (0.026)	NA***
B&H	BATX	0.640 (0.424)	0.274 (0.601)	1.062 (0.303)	NA***	NA***	0.167 (0.683)
Serbia	BELEX15	1.992 (0.369)	NA***	19.855** (0.000)	NA***	9.120 (0.058)	20.197** (0.000)
North Macedonia	MBI10	1.788 (0.181)	4.371* (0.037)	1.409 (0.235)	0.046 (0.830)	10.983* (0.027)	2.032 (0.362)

Note chi^2-value shown on top, and p-value shown in brackets (). Optimal selection order criteria is shown per quarter and is determined by SBIC

* $p < 0.05$, ** $p < 0.01$

***Due to determined existence of statistically significant indicators pair cointegration relationship or due to unavailable Johansen test results for the given pair of indicators, Granger test and results as such are miss-specified. In such cases reparameterization into an error correction model is necessary and is completed in this research with panel PMG results

such causal relationship some research claim no violation of informational efficiency (Bhattacharya & Mukherjee, 2006) though others claim the contrary (Plihal, 2016); even so, in case of SEE the capital markets are an immaterial constituent of the aggregate economic output as is pragmatically apparent in marginal turnover, which is an unlikely cause of an aggregate economic performance (Table A.15).

Table A.15 Summary of existent Johansen and Granger pair relationship

Country	*SMI*	*Bi-variate Johansen test on long-run cointegrating relationship between SMI with selected macroeconomic indicator*	*Bi-variate Granger test on causal relationship between SMI with selected macroeconomic indicator:* → indicates causality direction
Croatia	*CROBEX*	MMIR, HICP, IPI, BOPNFA	
Slovenia	*SBITOP*	MMIR, HICP, BOPNFA	SBITOP → IPI
B&H	*BATX*	HICP, IPI	
Serbia	*BELEX15*	FX, HICP	MMIR → BELEX15 BELEX15 → MMIR BELEX15 → BOPNFA
North Macedonia	*MBI10*		MBI10→ FX MBI10→ IPI

C.1.4. Panel VAR—Impulse-Response Functions and Forecast Error Variance Decomposition

Panel vector autoregression model estimates are seldom interpreted on a standalone basis. In using IRF and FEVD this research analyzes inter-relationships amongst the model variables. Prior to utilizing the statistical tests it is necessary to check the stability condition of the estimated panel VAR through eigenvalues. The resulting Table A.16 of eigenvalues confirms that the matrix estimate is stable as values are smaller than one.

Table A.16 Eigenvalue stability condition

Eigenvalue Real	*Imaginary*	*Modulus*
0.6728677	0	0.6728677
−0.4421397	0	−0.4421397
0.4193741	0	0.4193741
0.3343388	0	0.3343388
0.1565845	0	0.1565845
0.0473831	0	0.0473831
0.0072478	0	0.0072478

Note All the eigenvalues lie inside the unit circle and panel VAR does satisfy stability condition

Thereafter we predict through FEVD measures the proportion of movement in a sequence that is attributable to own shock versus movement to shocks of another variable. In other words, FEVD tells how much of the forecast error variance of each of the variables can be explained by exogenous shocks to the other variables and to itself. FEVD test results point out that the own SMI value impulse predominates SMI response at not less than ninety-four percent at any forecast period. Through ten quarters and onwards forecast, the accountability of other variables increases from under aggregate of 2.8 to 5.2% that altogether is immaterial.

The IRF plots reveal visually an indicative preview information on response of one variable to a single unit impulse in another variable. This assumption is solely indicative due to statistical methodological deficiencies. The illustrations show a broad scope reaction in group SMI for one unit structural shock in each individual macroeconomic variable. In graphs in Fig. A.9 IRFs are plotted on the Y-axis and studied periods on the X-axis. In an exemplary interpretation, SMI lagged impulse shock impact on itself follows unique response trend in initial large decrease in SMI until eventually balancing out to little effect in the medium to long run. In practical observation the initial period is that of the 2007/2008 crisis that indeed caused a very significant slump in value in the initial period and one that the studies markets have largely not recovered from (Table A.17).

C.1.5. A Panel Pooled Mean Group
See Tables A.18 and A.19.

C.2. Research Hypotheses and Findings

This research aims to examine the relationship between the selected macroeconomic indicators and capital markets' indices. Therefore, it is important to probe long-run and short-run relationships and the direction of their impact. The relationship testing includes panel data from five SEE emerging markets, including two EU member and high-income countries and three non-EU member countries, using data for the period from year-end 2005 to year-end 2016.

The main question that this research aims to answer is: "Are the selected SEE macroeconomic indicators - GDPPC, FX, MMIR, IPI,

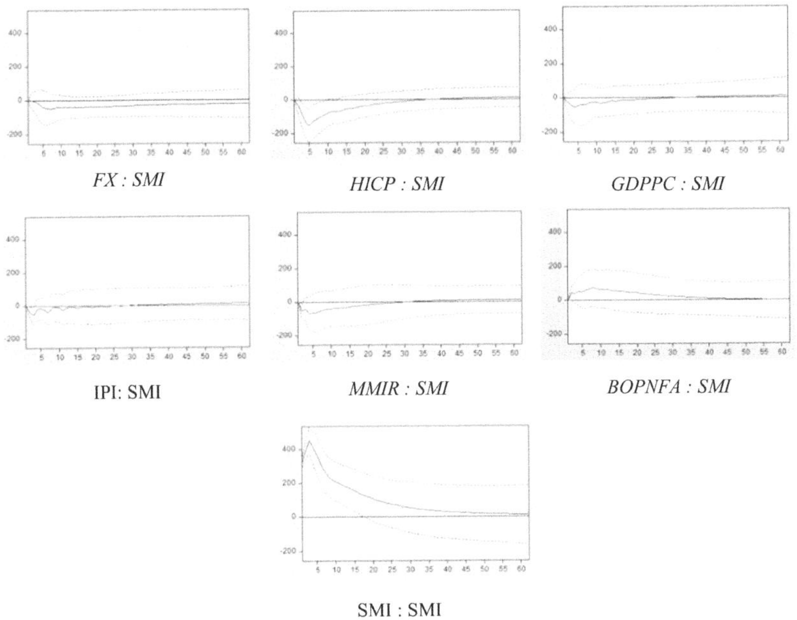

Fig. A.9 Panel VAR—Impulse response to variables' shock (*Note* "impulse variable: response variable" order; ninety-five percent confidence interval results)

Table A.17 Forecast error variance decomposition (in percent)

Forecast horizon (in quarters) on response variable SMI	*Impulse variable*						
	SMI	*GDPPC*	*FX*	*MMIR*	*HICP*	*IPI*	*BOPNFA*
1	100	0	0	0	0	0	0
2	97.16	0.28	0.00	1.88	0.01	0.02	0.65
3	95.73	0.57	0.05	2.47	0.01	0.02	1.15
4	95.15	0.78	0.08	2.61	0.01	0.02	1.35
5	94.92	0.90	0.09	2.64	0.01	0.02	1.41
6	94.83	0.96	0.09	2.65	0.01	0.02	1.43
7	94.79	0.99	0.10	2.65	0.01	0.02	1.44
8	94.77	1.00	0.10	2.65	0.01	0.02	1.44
9	94.77	1.01	0.10	2.65	0.01	0.02	1.44
10 to 62	94.76	1.01	0.10	2.65	0.01	0.02	1.44

Note Optimal selection order criteria is shown per quarter and is determined by SBIC at one lag

Table A.18 Panel PMG test results—SEE countries' group score

Variable	*Coefficient*	
	Long run	*Short run*
GDPPC	0.0156831	−0.0386697
	(0.0412202)	(0.0785686)
FX	540.8298	54,181.85
	(447.1179)	(34,109.62)
MMIR	−3420.001	1571.529
	(1903.436)	(6148.275)
HICP	−7.363017	−10.28606
	(5.064314)	(28.05417)
IPI	−8.043966*	2.114272
	(3.875923)	(1.448386)
BOPNFA	0.0144359	0.1961086
	(0.0338866)	(0.127)
ECT***	−0.1954243**	
	(0.066773)	
Constant		470.5857**
		(123.9867)
Log likelihood	−1849.527	
Hausman test	8.67 [0.0698]	

Author's calculations were made using ("xtpmg") per routine in Stata Thirteen. The left column panel shows long-run effects. The right column panel reports short-run effects and the speed of adjustment Hausman test indicates PMG consistency with *p*-value > five percent thus illustrating non-significance to reject null hypothesis of systemic difference in coefficients; thereon PMG long-run coefficients fixing prevails in the choice of technique
Log-likelihood value determines plausibility function of the model under the observed data

Note [] is *p*-value. Standard errors in parentheses. * $p < 0.05$, ** $p < 0.01$
*** Error correction term

BOPNFA, HICP - related to capital markets' performance in the selected SEE countries - Croatia, Serbia, B&H, North Macedonia and Slovenia?"

More specifically, the aims of this research are to:

1. Determine the causality between macroeconomic indicators and capital markets' indices.
2. Estimate macroeconomic indicators' association, in the long run and in the short run, with capital markets' indices.

Table A.19 PMG test results—SEE individual countries' score

Country	*Croatia*	*Slovenia*	*B&H*	*Serbia*	*North Macedonia*
Long run					
GDPPC	0.0156831	0.0156831	0.0156831	0.0156831	0.0156831
	(0.0412202)	(0.0412202)	(0.0412202)	(0.0412202)	(0.0412202)
FX	540.8298	540.8298	540.8298	540.8298	540.8298
	(447.1179)	(447.1179)	(447.1179)	(447.1179)	(447.1179)
MMIR	−3420.001	−3420.001	−3420.001	−3420.001	−3420.001
	(1903.436)	(1903.436)	(1903.436)	(1903.436)	(1903.436)
HICP	−7.363017	−7.363017	−7.363017	−7.363017	−7.363017
	(5.064314)	(5.064314)	(5.064314)	(5.064314)	(5.064314)
IPI	−8.043966*	−8.043966*	−8.043966*	−8.043966*	−8.043966*
	(3.875923)	(3.875923)	(3.875923)	(3.875923)	(3.875923)
BOPNFA	0.0144359	0.0144359	0.0144359	0.0144359	0.0144359
	(0.0338866)	(0.0338866)	(0.0338866)	(0.0338866)	(0.0338866)
ECT***	−0.1152737	−0.1010417	−0.3865435**	−0.3234697**	−0.0507928
	(0.0549461)	(0.0561914)	(0.1198133)	(0.0621111)	(0.0572258)
Short run					
GDPPC	0.0232696	0.1141208	−0.0035507	0.0150588	−0.3422467
	(0.2269075)	(0.0928183)	(0.1262061)	(0.1085914)	(1.580937)
FX	10,169.31*	296.5474	253.3876	85,403.31**	174,786.7
	(5069.456)	(344.5294)	(238.4165)	(16,828.78)	(89,966.36)
MMIR	6243.024	17,092.69*	4323.33	646.8131	−20,448.21
	(5528.953)	(6963.053)	(5686.263)	(1470.102)	(14,371.79)
HICP	29.33738	28.63758	13.58735	−3.012367	−119.9802
	(54.47709)	(23.06338)	(8.446722)	(13.77124)	(94.62072)
IPI	2.667525	−1.472417	0.3855123	1.806676	7.184062
	(7.094242)	(4.240075)	(1.418615)	(1.448717)	(7.50687)
BOPNFA	0.0976903	0.0994451	0.0810201	0.0031981	0.6991895
	(0.0817248)	(0.0661962)	(0.0611335)	(0.0261976)	(0.7689466)
Constant	406.3372	124.466	723.7213*	780.5986**	317.8054
	(219.1174)	(136.9538)	(339.2799)	(272.8626)	(278.1859)
Log likelihood		−1849.527			
Hausman test		8.67 [0.0698]			

Note [] is p-value. Standard errors in parentheses. * $p < 0.05$, ** $p < 0.01$
*** Error correction term, coefficient, and standard error

3. Analyze the relationship between macroeconomic indicators and capital markets' indices not tested in prior research. For the first time, new variables are introduced. The test uses BOPNFA indicator for all the selected markets. For the first time the comprehensive overall relationship in North Macedonia, B&H, and Serbia is

analyzed. For the first time in SEE, the research utilizes simultaneous comprehensive multiple statistical estimation techniques and approaches of statistical testing with Johansen, Granger, panel PMG, and panel VAR methodologies.

The empirical analysis uses panel testing with Stata thirteen program.

Considering the theoretical framework and empirical analysis, the following hypotheses have been established and the statistical test results yielded the respective findings:

Hypothesis 1: There is a statistically significant impact relationship between the selected macroeconomic indicators and the capital markets' indices.

Research findings: Bi-variate Granger test results have yielded statistically significant causal relationships between the selected macroeconomic indicators and the capital markets indices in all the individual SEE countries except in Croatia. Besides, multi-variate panel PMG results have shown the statistically significant estimating short-run relationship direction of macroeconomic indicators on listed stocks' indices in all the observed SEE countries with the exception of North Macedonia. Panel PMG cross-country results have also shown statistically significant long-run cointegration with the associating contribution of three macroeconomic indicators to SMI.

Hypothesis 2: There is a statistically significant long-run relationship between the selected macroeconomic indicators and the capital markets' indices.

Research findings: Bi-variate Johansen test results have yielded statistically significant cointegrating relationships between the selected macroeconomic indicators and the SMIs in all the observed SEE countries but North Macedonia. The multi-variate panel PMG cross-country results have shown the statistically significant long-run cointegrating relationship with the associating contribution of three macroeconomic indicators to SMI. Statistically significant PMG pair relationships are summarized in Table 5.1 in the main text, while a summary of the significant Johansen pair relationship is provided in Table A.11.

Hypothesis 3: There is a statistically significant short-run relationship between the selected macroeconomic indicators and the capital markets' indices.

Research findings: Multi-variate panel PMG results have shown statistically significant short-run cointegrating relationships between macroeconomic indicators and SMI in all the observed SEE countries with the exception of North Macedonia. Statistically significant PMG pair relationships are summarized in Table 5.1 in the main text, while a summary of the significant Granger pair relationship is provided in Table A.13.

Bibliography

Books and Chapters in Books

Aghion, P., Howitt, P., Brant-Collett, M., Garcia-Penalosa, C., & Waggoner, R. (1998). *Endogenous growth theory*. MIT Press.

Alajbeg, D., & Bubas, Z. (2001). *Vodic kroz hrvatsko trziste kapitala za gradjane*. Institut za javne financije.

Eric, D., & Stosic, I. (2012). Development of the European financial system: Challenges for Balkan countries integration process. In *European integration process in Western Balkan countries*, 114–143.

Flotynski, M. J. (2015). *The impact of macroeconomic variables on the capital market*. Poznan University of Economics.

Goldsmith, W. R. (1969). *Financial structure and development*. Yale University Press.

Kleinman, G. (2013). *Trading commodities and financial futures*. Pearson Education, Inc. FT Press.

La Porta, R., Lopez-de-Silanes, F., Shleifer, A., & Vishny, R. (2000). *The economic consequences of legal origins*. Harvard University.

Levine, R. (2005). Finance and growth: Theory and evidence. In P. Aglu & S. Durlauf (Ed.), *Handbook of economic growth* (1st ed., Vol. 1, Chapter 12, pp. 865–934). Elsevier.

Mehl, P. A., Vespro, C., & Winkler, A. (2006). Financial sector development in south-eastern Europe: Quality matters. In *Financial development, integration and stability: Evidence from Central, Eastern and South-Eastern Europe* (Chapter 12, pp. 186–203).

A. Dodig, *Capital Markets in Southeast Europe*,
https://doi.org/10.1007/978-3-031-07210-9

Ramaswamy , S., & Scott, R. (2005). Managing a multi-currency bond portfolio. In F. Fabozzi, *Indexing, structured and active bond portfolio management: State-of-the-art* (Chapter 19). Wiley.

Academic Articles, Working Papers and Studies

Ahmed, S. (2008). Aggregate economic variables and stock markets in India. *International Research Journal of Finance and Economics*, 141–164.

Aizenman, J. (2010). The impossible trinity (aka the policy Trilemma). *The encyclopedia of financial globalization.* UCSC and NBER.

Ajayi, R., & Mougoue, M. (1996). On the dynamic relations between stock prices and exchange rates. *Journal of Financial Research, 19*(2), 193–207.

Alberola, E., Erce, A., & Serena, J. M. (2014). International reserves and gross capital flows. Documentos de Discusion 01148 FLAR. *Fondo Lationamericano de Reservas - FLAR.*

Alfaro, L., Chanda, A., Kalemli-OZcan, S., & Sayek, S. (2004). FDI and economic growth: The role of local financial markets. *Journal of International Economics*, 89–112.

Alrub, A. A., Tursoy, T., & Rjoub, H. (2016). Exploring the long-run and short-run relationship between macroeconomic variables and stock prices during the restructuring period: Does it matter in Turkish market? *IBIMA Journal of Financial Studies & Research.* Article ID 917071.

Ariel, R. (1990). High stock returns before holidays: Existence and evidence on possible causes. *The Journal of Finance, 45*(5), 1611–1626.

Arrow, K. J. (1962). The economic implications of learning-by-doing. *Review of Economic Studies, 29*, 155–173.

Arsov, S. (2005). *Post-privatization retrospective of Macedonia—Could we have done it better?* Ss. Cyril and Methodius University—Faculty of Economics.

Azar, S. A. (2010). Inflation and stock returns. *International Journal of Accounting and Finance, 2*(3/4), 254–274.

Balduzzi, P. (1994). *Stock returns, inflation, and the "proxy hypothesis:" A new look at the data* (NYU Working Paper No. FIN-94-008). New York University, Stern School of Business, Finance Department.

Barbic, T., & Condic-Jurkic, I. (2011). Relationship between macroeconomic fundamentals and stock market indices in select CEE countries. *Ekonomski Pregled, 62*(3–4), 113–133.

Bayraktar, N. (2014). *Measuring relative development level of stock markets: Capacity and effort of countries.* Borsa Istanbul.

Bhattacharya, B., & Mukherjee, J. (2006). Indian stock price movements and the macroeconomic context—A time-series analysis. *Journal of International Business and Economics, 5*(1), 167–181.

Beck, T., & Levine, R. (2002). *Stock markets, banks, and growth: Panel evidence* (Working Paper 9082). National Bureau of Economic Research.

Beck, T., Levine, R., & Loayza, N. (2000). Financial intermediation and growth: Causality and causes. *Journal of Monetary Economics, Elsevier, 46*(1), 31–77.

Billet, M. T., Flannery, M. J., & Garfinkel, J. A. (1995). The effect of lender identity on a borrowing firm's equity returns. *The Journal of Finance, 50*(2), 699–718.

Binswanger, M. (1999). Stock market booms and real economic activity: Is this time different? *International Review of Economics and Finance, 9*(4), 387–415.

Binswanger, M. (2001). *Does the stock market still lead real activity? An investigation for the G-7 countries*. University of Saint Gallen, Institute for Economics and the Environment.

Bossone, B., Mahajan, S., & Zahir, F. (2003). *Financial infrastructure, group interests, and capital accumulation* (IMF Working Paper). International Monetary Fund 2003 (024).

Bossone, B., & Lee, J.-K. (2004). *In finance, size matters: The "systemic scale economies" hypothesis* (IMF Staff Papers, Vol. 51, No. 1). International Monetary Fund 2004 (001).

Bossone, B., & Promisel, L. (2012). *Strengthening financial systems in developing countries*. The World Bank.

Campbell, J., & Vuolteenaho, T. (2004). *Inflation illusion and stock prices* (Working Paper 10263). National Bureau of Economic Research.

Canales-Kriljenko, J. I. (2004). *Foreign exchange market organisation in selected developing and transition economies: Evidence from a survey* (IMF Working Paper No. 04/4). International Monetary Fund 2004 (004).

Cetorelli, N., & Goldberg, L. S. (2011). Global banks and international shock transmission. Evidence from the crisis. *IMF Economic Review, 59*(1), 41–76.

Chen, N.-F., Roll, R., & Ross, S. A. (1986). Economic forces and the stock market. *The Journal of Business, 59*(3), 383–403.

Chkili, W., & Nguyen, D. (2014). *Exchange rate movements and stock market returns in regime-switching environment: Evidence for BRICS countries* (Working Paper No. 2014-388). IPAG Business School.

Choi, I. (2001). Unit root tests for panel data. *Journal of International Money and Finance, 20*(2), 249–272.

Claessens, S., & Varangis, P. (1991). *Hedging crude oil imports in developing countries* (Policy Research Working Paper Series 755). The World Bank.

Cojocaru, L., Falaris, E. M., Hoffman, S. D., & Miller, J. B. (2015). Financial system development and economic growth in transition economies: New empirical evidence from the CEE and CIS countries. Bankable Frontier Associates, University of Delaware, Gallaudet University.

Cojocaru, L., Falaris, E. M., Hoffman, S. D., & Miller, J. B. (2016). Financial system development and economic growth in transition economies: New empirical evidence from the CEE and CIS countries. *Emerging Markets Finance and Trade, 52*(1), 223–236.

Crane, D. B., Froot, K. A., Scott, P., Mason, André Perold, R. C., Merton, Z., Bodie, Sirri, E. R., & Tufano, P. (1995). *The global financial system: A functional perspective*. Harvard Business School Press.

Curkovic, M., & Kristo, J. (2017). Performance measurement of UCITS investment funds in Croatia. *UTMS Journal of Economics, 8*(1), 11–18.

Dahiya, S., Puri, M., & Saunders, A. (2003). Bank borrowers and loan sales: New evidence on the uniqueness of bank loans. *The Journal of Business, 76*(4), 563–582.

Dickey, D. A., & Fuller, W. A. (1979). Distribution of the estimators for autoregressive time series with a unit root. *Journal of the American Statistical Association, 74*(366), 427–431.

Dinniah, N., & Mahmood, W. (2007). Stock returns and macroeconomic influences: Evidence from 6 Asian-Pacific countries. *Financial Economics, and Futures Market Research Group.*

Domian, D., & Louton, D. (1997). A threshold autoregressive analysis of stock returns and real economic activity. *International Review of Economics and Finance, 6*(2), 167–179.

Dodig, A. (2020). Relationship between macroeconomic indicators and capital markets performance in selected southeastern European countries. *Zagreb International Review of Economics & Business*, 55–88.

Dodig, A., & Dzidic, A. (2022). Dividend policies in volatile transitioning markets. *Zagreb International Review of Economics & Business*, 133–153.

Dodig, A., & Bugarcic, M. (2022). Extended relationship between macroeconomic indicators and capital markets performance in selected southeastern European countries. *Ekonomski Vjesnik, Osijek*, 36.

Drucker, S., & Puri , M. (2005). On the benefits of concurrent lending and underwriting. *The Journal of Finance*, 2763–2799.

Dumas, B., Harvey, C., & Ruiz, P. (2003). Are correlations of stock returns justified by subsequent changes in national outputs? *Journal of International Money and Finance*, 777–811.

Engle, R. F., & Granger, C. (1987). Cointegration and error correction: Representation, estimation, and testing. *Econometrica, 55*(2), 251–276.

Erhmann, M., & Fratzscher, M. (2004). *Taking stock: Monetary policy transmission ot equity markets* (ECB Working Paper 354). European Central Bank.

Errunza, V., & Hogan, K. (1998). Macroeconomic determinants of European stock market volatility. *European Financial Management, 4*(3), 361–377.

Fama, E., & Malkiel, B. (1970). Efficient capital markets: A review of theory and empirical work. *The American Finance Association—The Journal of Finance, 25*(2), 383–417.

Fama, E. F. (1981). Stock returns, real activity, inflation and money. *The American Economic Review, 71*(4), 545–565.

Fama, E. F. (1990). Stock returns, expected returns, and real activity. *The Journal of Finance, 45*(4), 1089–1108.

Ferrucci, G. (2003). *Empirical determinants of emerging market economies' sovereign bond spreads* (Working Paper No. 205). Bank of England.

Fink, G., Haiss, P., & Vuksic, G. (2005). *Importance of financial sectors for growth in accession countries*. ECBOeNB/CFS—Conference on European Economic Integration, Vienna.

Flannery, M. J., & Protopapadakis, A. (2002). Macroeconomic factors do influence aggregate stock returns. *The Review of Financial Studies, 15*(3), 751–782.

Fungacova, Z., & Hanousek, J. (2011). Determinants of firm delisting on the Prague stock exchange. *Prague Economic Papers, 2011*(4), 348–365.

Gerber, A. (2008). Direct versus intermediated finance: An old question and a new answer. *European Economic Review, 52*(1), 28–54.

Granger, C. (1988). Some recent development in a concept of causality. *Journal of Econometrics, 39*(1–2), 199–211.

Griffin, J., & Baltagi, B. (1997). Pooled estimators vs. their heterogenous counterparts in the context of dynamic demand for gasoline. *Journal of Econometrics, 77*(2), 303–327.

Halilbegovic, S., & Mekic, A. (2017). Usage of derivatives in emerging markets: The case of Bosnia and Herzegovina. *Asian Economic and Financial Review, 7*(3), 248–257.

Hall, R. (2001). Struggling to understand the stock market. *American Economic Review, 91*(2), 1–11.

Hasseeb, M. K. (2015). *Impact of the real economy on stock market performance: Evidence from Arab countries* (Master's Thesis). The American University in Cairo, AUC Knowledge Fountain.

Hernandez-Trillo, F. (1999). Financial derivatives introduction and stock return volatility in an emerging market without clearinghouse: The Mexican experience. *Journal of Empirical Finance, 6*(2), 153–176.

Issahaku, H., Ustarz, Y., & Domanban, P. B. (2013). Macroeconomic variables and stock market returns in Ghana: Any causal link? *Asian Economic and Financial Review, 3*(8), 1044–1062.

Im, K. S., Pesaran, M. H., & Shin, Y. (2003). Testing for unit roots in heterogeneous panels. *Journal of Econometrics, 115*, 53–74.

Iwanicz-Drozdowska, M., Bongini, P., Smaga, P., & Witkowski, B. (2019). The role of banks in CESEE countries: exploring non-standard determinants of economic growth. *Post-Communist Economies, 31*(3), 349–382.

Jaksic, M., & Puric, J. (2014). Uporedna analiza poslovanja Beogradske, Zagrebačke i Varšavske Berze. *Bankarstvo, 43*(6), 86–111.

James, C. (1987). Some evidence on the uniqueness of bank loans. *Journal of Financial Economics, 19*(2), 217–235.

Jazairi, N. (2009). *Stock market price indexes.* York University.

Johansen, S. (1991). Estimation and hypothesis testing of cointegration vectors in Gaussian vector autoregressive models. *Econometrica, 59*(6), 1551–1580.

Johansen, S., & Juselius, K. (1990). Maximum likelihood estimation and inference on cointegration—With applications to the demand for money. *Oxford Bulletin of Economics and Statistics, 52*(2), 169–210.

Johnson, R., Jensen, G., & Conover, M. (1999). Monetary environments and international stock returns. *Journal of Banking and Finance, 23*(9), 1357–1381.

Karamustafa, O., & Kucukalle, Y. (2003). *Long run relationships between stock market returns and macroeconomic performance.* Finance, University Library of Munich.

King, R., & Levine, R. (1993). Finance and growth: Schumpeter might be right. *The Quarterly Journal of Economics, 108*(3), 717–737.

Koivu, T. (2002). *Do efficient banking sectors accelerate economic growth in transition countries?* (BOFIT Discussion Papers [14]) Bank of Finland, Institute for Economies in Transition.

Kozarevic, E., Kokorovic, M., & Civic, B. (2014). The use of financial derivatives in emerging market economies: An empirical evidence from Bosnia and Herzegovina's non-financial firms. *Research in World Economy, 5*(1).

Lazarov, D., Miteva-Kacarski, E., & Nikoloski, K. (2016). An empirical analysis of stock market development and economic growth: The case of Macedonia. *South East European Journal of Economics and Business, 11*(2), 71–81.

Lee, C.-C., & Chang, C.-P. (2009). FDI, financial development, and economic growth: International evidence. *Journal of Applied Economics, 12*, 249–271.

Lee, Y.-M., & Wang, K.-M. (2015). Dynamic heterogenous panel analysis of the correlation between stock prices and exchange rates. *Economic Research-Ekonomska Istraživanja, 28*(1), 749–772.

Levin, A., Lin, F., & Chu, C. J. (2002). Unit root tests in panel data: Asymptotic and finite- sample properties. *Journal of Econometrics, 108*(1), 1–24.

Levine, R. (1997). Financial development and economic growth; views and agenda. *Journal of Economic Literature, 35*(2), 688–726.

Levine, R., & Zervos, S. (1998). Stock markets, banks, and growth. *American Economic Review, 88*(3), 537–558.

Lien, D., & Zhang, M. (2008). A survey of emerging derivatives markets. *Emerging Markets Finance and Trade, 44*(2), 39–69.

Lin, C.-H. (2012). The comovement between exchange rates and stock prices in the Asian emerging markets. *International Review of Economics and Finance, 22*(1), 161–172.

Maddala, G. S., & Wu, S. (1999). A comparative study of unit root tests with panel data and a new simple test. *Oxford Bulletin of Economics and Statistics, 61*(S1), 631–652.

Marinkovic, S., & Skakavac, A. (2010). Derivatives market in Serbia—current developments and perspectives. *Economics and Organization, 7*(1), 47–59.

Megaravalli, A. V., & Sampagnaro, G. (2018). Macroeconomic indicators and their impact on stock markets in ASIAN 3: A pooled mean group approach. *Cogent Economics and Finance, 6*(1), 1–14.

Mencinger, J. (2006). Privatization in Slovenia. *EIPF and University of Ljubljana—Slovenian Literature Review*, 3–65.

Morck, R., Yeung, B., & Yu, W. (2000). Why do emerging markets have synchronous stock price movements? *Journal of Financial Economics, 58*(1), 215–260.

Mukherjee, T., & Darrat, A. (1986). The behavior of stock market in a developing country. *Economics Letters, 22*(2–3), 273–278.

Naceur, S. B., Ghazouani, S., & Omran, M. (2007). The determinants of stock market development in the Middle-Eastern and North African region. *Managerial Finance, 33*(7), 477–489.

Nasseh, A., & Strauss, J. (2000). Stock prices and domestic and international macroeconomic activity: A cointegration approach. *The Quarterly Review of Economics and Finance, 40*(2), 229–249.

Nijam, H. M., Ismail, S., & Musthafa, A. (2015). The impact of macroeconomic variables on stock market performance; evidence from Sri Lanka. *Journal of Emerging Trends in Economics and Management Sciences, 6*(2), 151–157.

Olgic Drazenovic, B., & Kusanovic, T. (2016). Determinants of capital market in the new member EU countries. *Economic Research—Ekonomska Istrazivanja, 29*(1), 758–769.

Philips, S., & Clifford, S. (1980). Trading costs for listed options: The implications for market efficiency. *Journal of Financial Economics, 8*(2), 179–201.

Pesaran, H. M., Shin, Y., & Smith, R. P. (1999). Pooled estimation of long-run relationships in dynamic heterogeneous panels. *Journal of American Statistical Association, 94*(446), 621–634.

Pilinkus, D. (2010). Macroeconomic indicators and their impact on stock market performance in the short and long run: The case of the Baltic states. *Technological and Economic Development of Economy, 16*(2), 291–304.

Plihal, T. (2016). Stock market informational efficiency in Germany: Granger causality between DAX and selected macroeconomic indicators. *Procedia—Social and Behavioral Sciences, 220*, 321–329.

Roll, R., Chordia, T., & Subrahmanyam, A. (2008). Liquidity and market efficiency. *Journal of Financial Economics, 87*(2), 249–268.

Samargandi, N., Fidrmuc, J., & Ghosh, S. (2014). Is the relationship between financial development and economic growth monotonic? Evidence from a sample of middle income countries. *World Development 68 (C)*, 66–81.

Seba, M. G. (2017). 20 years of the Croatian capital market. *Zagreb International Review of Economics and Business 20 (SCI)*, 41–58.

Shapiro, M. (1988). *The stabilization of the U.S. economy evidence from the stock market* (NBER Working Papers 2645). The National Bureau of Economic Research, Inc.

Solow, R. M. (1956). A contribution to the theory of economic growth. *The Quarterly Journal of Economics, 70*(1), 65–94.

Spaseska, T., Vitanova, G., Sotiroski, K., Odzaklieska, D., Risteska-Jankuloska, A., & Risteska, F. (2017). The impact of Macedonian stock exchange performance on economic growth in republic of Macedonia. *Balkan and Near Eastern Journal of Social Sciences, 3*(3), 131–143.

Tobias, A., & Song, H. (2009). *Money, liquidity, and monetary policy* (Staff Report No. 360). Federal Reserve Bank of New York.

Tsuyuguchi, Y., & Wooldridge, P. (2008). The evolution of trading activity in Asian foreign exchange markets. *Emerging Markets Review, 9*(4), 231–246.

Reports and Other Sources

Agency for Statistics for Bosnia and Herzegovina. (2022). Retrieved January 2, 2022, from http://www.bhas.ba/index.php?lang=en

Banja Luka Stock Exchange. (2018). Retrieved May 18, 2019, from https://www.blberza.com/Pages/docview.aspx?page=sp4

Banja Luka Stock Exchange. (2022). Retrieved January 18, 2022, from https://www.blberza.com/periodicalstatreports.aspx

Bank for International Settlements. (2014). *Basel Committee on Banking Supervision - Consultative Document - Basel 3*. The Net Stable Funding Ration.

Belgrade Stock Exchange. (2022). Retrieved January 19, 2022, from https://www.belex.rs/eng/trgovanje/izvestaj/godisnji

Buffet, W. (2012). *2012 Berkshire Hathaway annual report*. Annual Report.

Central Bank of Bosnia and Herzegovina. (2016). Retrieved May 15, 2022, from https://www.cbbh.ba/?lang=en

Central Depository and Clearing Company Inc. (2018). *Quarterly report: I quarter 2018*. Zagreb.

Central Securities Depository of the Republic of Macedonia. (2017). *2016 annual report.*

Croatian Bureau of Statistics. (2022). Retrieved January 1, 2022, from https://www.dzs.hr/Eng/system/starte.htm

Desjardins, J. (2017). *Visual capitalist.* Retrieved July 5, 2017, from http://www.visualcapitalist.com/all-of-the-worlds-stockexchanges-by-size/

DIRECTIVE 2004/39/EC. (2004). Retrieved April 10, 2016, from http://eur-lex.europa.eu/legalcontent/

The Economic Times. (2016, February 08). Retrieved February 8, 2016, from https://economictimes.indiatimes.com/p/put-call-ratio/articleshow/50901067.cms

European Bank for Reconstruction and Development. (2017). *Corporate governance in transition economies—FYR Macedonia country report.*

European Central Bank. (2022). Retrieved January 1, 2022, from https://sdw.ecb.europa.eu/

European Investment Bank. (2016). *Bosnia and Herzegovina—Assessment of financing needs of SMEs in the Western Balkans countries.*

Eurostat. (2018). Eurostat databased. Retrieved November 3, 2018, from https://ec.europa.eu/eurostat/data/database.

Eurostat. (2022). Eurostat database. Retrieved January 3, 2022, from https://ec.europa.eu/eurostat/data/database

The International Country Risk Guide (ICRG). (2018). PSR Group. Retrieved October 12, 2018, from https://www.prsgroup.com/explore-our-products/international-country-risk-guide/

International Monetary Fund. (2017). *Global financial stability report: Is growth at risk?* World Economic and Financials Surveys.

International Monetary Fund. (2017). *World economic outlook—Gaining momentum?* World Economic and Financial Surveys.

International Monetary Fund. (2022). *Database.* Retrieved January 9, 2022, from https://data.imf.org

KDD Centralna Klirinsko Depotna Druzba d.d. Ljubljana. (2022). *Main figures 2021.*

Kelley, D., Singer, S., & Herrington, M. (2015). *Global entrepreneurship monitor: 2015/16 global report.* Global Entrepreneurship Research Association.

Ljubljana Stock Exchange. (2018). Ljubljana stock exchange statistics. Retrieved April 28, 2019, from https://www.ljse.si/cgi-bin/jve.cgi?doc=2330

Ljubljana Stock Exchange. (2022). *Ljubljana stock exchange statistics.* Retrieved January 17, 2022, from www.ljse.si/en/ammia;/66.

Macedonian Privatization Agency. (not-disclosed). *Privatization in the Republic of Macedonia.* Jewish Community Bitola.

Macedonian Stock Exchange. (2018). Retrieved May 18, 2022, from https://www.mse.mk/en

Macedonian Stock Exchange. (2022). *Annual statistical report*. Retrieved January 19, 2022, from http://www.mse.mk/en/stats

Maverick, J. (2016). *Investopedia*. Retrieved January 1, 2016, from http://www.investopedia.com/ask/answers/052715/how-big-derivatives-market.asp

Mckinsey and Company. (2005). *US$ 118 trillion and counting: Taking stock of the world's capital market*. Mckinsey Global Institute.

Mckinsey and Company. (2017). *Mckinsey global institute: "The new dynamics of financial globalization"*.

McLannahan, B. (2018, March 16). US bank derivatives books larger since rescue of Bear Stearns. *Financial Times*.

Munchau, W. (2018, August 28). Tinkering will not deliver a stronger role for the Euro. *Financial Times*.

National Bank of Bosnia and Herzegovina. (2022). Retrieved January 22, 2022, from http://statistics.cbbh.ba/Panorama/novaview/SimpleLogin_en_html.aspx

National Bank of Croatia. (2022). Retrieved January 22, 2022, from https://www.hnb.hr/en/statistics/statistical-data

National Bank of Finland. (2018). Retrieved February 22, 2018, from https://www.suomenpankki.fi/en/financial-stability/the-financial-system-in-brief/

National Bank of Serbia. (2016). Retrieved May 18, 2022, from https://nbs.rs/en/indeks/index.html

National Bank of Serbia. (2022). Retrieved January 22, 2022, from https://www.nbs.rs/internet/english/80/index.html

National Bank of the Republic of Macedonia. (2016). *Financial Stability Report for the Republic of Macedonia in 2016*.

National Bank of the Republic of Macedonia. (2022). Retrieved January 22, 2022, from http://www.nbrm.mk/statistika-en.nspx

National Bank of Slovenia. (2022). Retrieved January 22, 2022, from https://www.bsi.si/en/statistics

O'Harrow, R. (2010, April 21). A primer on financial derivatives. *Washington Post*.

Rakocevic, R. (2016). *The impact of global capital markets on capital market in Serbia*. University of Belgrade—Faculty of Political Sciences.

Republic of Macedonia State Statistical Office. (2018). Retrieved May 1, 2018, from http://makstat.stat.gov.mk/PXWeb/pxweb/en/MakStat/?rxid=46ee0f64-2992-4b45-a2d9-cb4e5f7ec5ef

Republic of Serbia Securities Commission. (2017). *2016 Annual report*. Belgrade.

Registry of Securities of Federation of Bosnia and Herzegovina. (2018). Retrieved March 2, 2018, from http://www.rvp.ba/english/

Rovčanin, A., & Hanić, A. (2014). The use of financial derivatives in risk management purposes of non-financial firms in Bosnia and Herzegovina.

Samitas, A. G., & Kenourgios, D. F. (2004, May 28th–30th). Market efficiency and signaling: An event study analysis for Athens stock exchange. In *Proceedings of the1st Applied Financial Economics (AFE) International Conference on Advances in Applied Financial Economics*, (pp. 163–175).

Sarajevo Stock Exchange. (2018). Retrieved May 15, 2019, from http://www.sase.ba/v1/en-us/SASE/About-SASE/SASE-History

Sarajevo Stock Exchange. (2022). Retrieved January 15, 2022, from http://www.sase.ba/v1/en-us/Reports/Other-reports/Annual-Reports

Securities Commission Banja Luka Stock Exchange. (2022). Retrieved January 1, 2022, from https://www.crhovrs.org/index.php/en/

Statistical Office of the Republic of Serbia. (2022). Retrieved January 1, 2022, from http://www.stat.gov.rs/en-us/o-nama/statisticki-sistem-srbije-1/

Statistical Office of the Republic of Slovenia. (2022). Retrieved January 1, 2022, from https://www.stat.si/statweb/en?AspxAutoDetectCookieSupport=1

Vienna Stock Exchange. (2018). Retrieved May 5, 2018, from https://www.wienerborse.at/en/indices/index-values/historical-data/?ISIN=AT0000A0FSC7&ID_NOTATION=32133504

The Wall Street Journal. (2009, December 8). Retrieved December 8, 2017, from http://blogs.wsj.com/marketbeat/2009/12/08/volcker-praises-the-atm-blasts-finance-execs-experts/

World Bank. (2015). *Financial sector assessment program—Bosnia and Herzegovina—Capital markets.* Washington, DC.

World Bank. (2016). *Doing business 2016—Measuring regulatory quality and efficiency.* Washington DC: Creative Commons Attribution CC. https://doi.org/10.1596/978-1-4648-0667-4

World Bank. (2022). Retrieved November 10, 2018, and January 8, 2022 from https://datahelpdesk.worldbank.org/knowledgebase/

Zagreb Stock Exchange. (2017). Retrieved April 21, 2018, from http://zse.hr/default.aspx?id=32877

Zagreb Stock Exchange. (2022). Retrieved January 14, 2022, from http://zse.hr/

Index

A. Dodig, *Capital Markets in Southeast Europe*,
https://doi.org/10.1007/978-3-031-07210-9

The manufacturer's authorised representative in the EU is Springer Nature Customer Service Centre GmbH, Europaplatz 3, 69115 Heidelberg, Germany. If you have any concerns regarding our products, please contact ProductSafety@springernature.com

Printed and bound by CPI Group (UK) Ltd, Croydon, CR0 4YY
22/09/2026
02221054-0011